SLOVAKIA ON THE ROAD TO INDEPENDENCE

ADST-DACOR
Diplomats and Diplomacy Series

Since 1776, extraordinary men and women have represented the United States abroad under all sorts of circumstances. What they did and how and why they did it remain little known to their compatriots. In 1995 the Association for Diplomatic Studies and Training (ADST) and Diplomatic and Consular Officers, Retired, Inc. (DACOR) created the Diplomats and Diplomacy book series to increase public knowledge and appreciation of the involvement of American diplomats in world history. *Slovakia on the Road to Independence* by Paul Hacker is the thirty-ninth volume in the series.

OTHER TITLES IN THE SERIES

Brown, Gordon, *Toussaint's Clause: The Founding Fathers and the Haitian Revolution*

Cohen, Herman J., *Intervening in Africa: Superpower Peacemaking in a Troubled Continent*

Goodby, James E., Dmitri Trenin, and Petrus Buwalda, with Yves Pagniez, *A Strategy for Stable Peace: Towards a Euroatlantic Security Community*

Grove, Brandon, *Behind Embassy Walls: The Life and Times of an American Diplomat*

Hart, Parker T., *Saudi Arabia and the United States: Birth of a Security Partnership*

Hume, Cameron R., *Mission to Algiers: Diplomacy by Engagement*

Kux, Dennis, *The United States and Pakistan, 1947–2000: Disenchanted Allies*

Lidegaard, Bo, *Defiant Diplomacy: Henrik Kauffmann, Denmark, and the United States in World War II and the Cold War, 1939–1958*

Loeffler, Jane C., *Architecture of Diplomacy: Building America's Embassies*

Milam, William B., *Bangladesh and Pakistan: Flirting with Failure in Muslim South Asia*

Miller, Robert H., *Vietnam and Beyond: A Diplomat's Cold War Education*

Neumann, Ronald E., *The Other War: Winning and Losing in Afghanistan*

Newsom, David D., *Witness to a Changing World*

Parker, Richard B., *Uncle Sam in Barbary: A Diplomatic History*

Pezzullo, Ralph, *Plunging into Haiti: Clinton, Aristide, and the Defeat of Diplomacy*

Platt, Nicholas, *China Boys: How U.S. Relations with the PRC Began and Grew*

Richmond, Yale, *Practicing Public Diplomacy: A Cold War Odyssey*

Schaffer, Howard B., *Ellsworth Bunker: Global Troubleshooter, Vietnam Hawk*

Wilkowski, Jean, *Abroad for Her Country: Tales of a Pioneer U.S. Woman Ambassador*

AN AMERICAN DIPLOMAT'S EYEWITNESS ACCOUNT

SLOVAKIA

ON THE ROAD TO INDEPENDENCE

★ ★ ★ ★ ★ ★ ★

PAUL HACKER

THE PENNSYLVANIA STATE UNIVERSITY PRESS
UNIVERSITY PARK, PENNSYLVANIA

An ADST-DACOR Diplomats and Diplomacy Book

Library of Congress Cataloging-in-Publication Data

Hacker, Paul, 1946–
Slovakia on the road to independence :
an American diplomat's eyewitness account / Paul Hacker.
p.   cm.
Includes bibliographical references and index.
Summary: "An eyewitness account by an American diplomat
of the events that led up to Slovakia's independence in 1993.
Includes an examination of Slovakia's post-independence
development"—Provided by publisher.
ISBN 978-0-271-03623-6 (cloth : alk. paper)
ISBN 978-0-271-03624-3 (pbk. : alk. paper)
1. Slovakia—Politics and government—1945–1992.
2. Slovakia—Politics and government—1993- .

I. Title.
DB2838.7.H33 2010
943.73'043—dc22
2009036347

To my wife, Eeva,
the best companion one could have on life's journey,
and son Alex,
the hope of the future

In loving memory of my father, Samuel M. Hacker
(February 5, 1911–August 23, 1976),
who put me on the road that would
one day lead to Slovakia

and of my mother, Annie R. Hacker
(May 7, 1916–November 1, 2009),
who in her 90th year was the first
editor of this work, and who experienced
the joy of seeing the first proof pages
of this book in the last week of her life.

CONTENTS

FOREWORD

Claiborne de Borda Pell
November 22, 1918–January 1, 2009

U.S. Senator, 1961–1997
Chairman, Senate Foreign Relations Committee, 1987–1995

I have always had a special feeling for the people of Slovakia. They are warm-hearted, welcoming, and have a wonderful *joie de vivre*. At the same time, history has not always been kind to the Slovaks. Living for a millennium under Hungarian rule, they voluntarily joined with the Czechs in a common state after signing the Pittsburgh Agreement in the United States on May 18, 1918, in Pittsburgh, Pennsylvania. The United States was heavily involved in the formation of the Czecho-Slovak state. The country's first president, Tomáš Garrigue Masaryk, whose wife Alice was American, himself proclaimed the independence of Czechoslovakia from the steps of Independence Hall in Philadelphia on October 28, 1918.

Slovakia's position in the independent state of Czechoslovakia was often a matter of controversy, as some Slovaks regarded their position as inferior to that of the Czechs or felt the promises of autonomy received in 1918 were not adequately implemented. In 1938, in the wake of the Munich Crisis, Slovakia received autonomous status and in March 1939, under pressure of Adolf Hitler, proclaimed its independence. Large chunks of its territory were ceded to Hungary and Poland. While for some Slovaks the wartime era was one of prosperity and relative peace (until 1944), the fact remains that the administration of Msgr. Jozef Tiso actively collaborated in the deportation of most of Slovakia's Jewish population, which led to their immediate murder in Auschwitz, and that it allied itself with the criminal regime of Nazi Germany.

When I first came to Slovakia in November 1947 to open the U.S. Consulate General, Slovakia was in the midst of a major political crisis. The Communists were flexing their muscles and their Secretary General told me they would not "rule out" a resort to force. While the Slovak Democrats won the 1946 elections in Slovakia (the Communists had a plurality in the Czech part of the country), the Slovak Communists did everything possible to undermine their adversaries through various forms of provocation and contrived plots. The Communist putsch in Prague, which was successfully completed on February 25, 1948, was immediately followed by the forced removal of non-Communists from political and economic positions they had held. The Slovak Communists faithfully followed the model used in Prague to force their rivals from power.

The formal opening of our consulate general in Bratislava followed the coup only by a matter of days. Much of my work in Slovakia in the remaining months of my tenure in 1948 was to chronicle the deteriorating situation. The Communist secret police wasted little time in using their mania about "Western spies" to ferret out the people who had loyally served our consulate general. Several were arrested, and some never came back. John Hvasta, whom I hired as a translator and assistant, escaped from Leopoldov Prison, where he was serving a sentence on trumped-up charges of "espionage," and for two years roamed around the country under the nose of the secret police, until he found refuge in our Prague embassy. Eventually he returned safely to the United States. I was able to smuggle another employee out of the country by allowing him to hide in the trunk of my official car when I was making a trip over the border to Austria. In 1968, at the height of the Prague Spring, I returned to Slovakia with one of our embassy officers and got as far as Užhorod, which was part of the eastern province of Ruthenia in the prewar republic, and today is the capital of the sub-Carpathian region of Ukraine.

I first had the occasion to meet Paul Hacker when Bill Luers, then our incoming ambassador to Czechoslovakia, brought him along to my Senate Foreign Relations Committee office in 1986 just before assuming his post. I met Paul on his own when he was about to follow in my footsteps in reopening our Consulate after a hiatus of forty-two years caused by the Cold War. Our paths crossed again in 1991, when Ambassador Shirley Temple Black led a ceremony rededicating our Consulate and honoring several of the employees from my time, several of whom did not survive. In 1992, accompanied by my wife, Nuala, I returned with a Senate delegation headed by Majority Leader George Mitchell of Maine. In the wake of the 1992 elections in Czechoslovakia, the country was on a firm course to split, and our delegation had the chance of exchanging views with Slovaks from various parts of the political spectrum. Mr. and Mrs. Hacker were kind enough to share their residence with us and a number of Slovak parliamentarians, and he kept as many fans as he could find going full blast as he offered a luncheon in heat that was over 100 degrees.

When it was my time to deliver some remarks during the ceremony rededicating our Consulate, I admitted that I was a bit envious of Paul, since he would be responsible for helping guide our relations with Slovakia under much more favorable circumstances than I faced in 1948. Of course, in 1991, our official policy was to try to preserve Czechoslovakia as a unified country—a policy which soon gave way to the "realities on the ground." But even in the early 1990s, the situation of an American consul general could have its downsides. Paul had to face expectations from many quarters. As he mentions in this book, Slovaks expected him to take a "pro-Slovak" attitude when he was charged with carrying out a unified U.S. policy for the entire country. As he also explains, there were many remnants of past thinking in Slovakia, epitomized by his exchange with Minister of Communications Roman Hofbauer, whose attitude toward Radio Free Europe didn't seem to differ much from that of his Communist predecessors.

He also had to deal with the expectations of a non-career ambassador whose views about how to present our policy were forged by decades in the public limelight, and who felt the autonomy of a consulate should be strictly limited.

Although I may be prejudiced because of my status as the only U.S. senator who served in our Foreign Service, I believe that the role played by members of our Foreign Service in contributing to our national goals can never be overemphasized. The lobby of the Department of State is covered with the names of those colleagues who gave their lives for our country in both heroic and tragic circumstances. While service in Slovakia may not have been quite so dramatic either in the 1940s or 1990s, it often has been a balancing act. One of the curious episodes that Paul describes is on the evening of the Consulate's rededication, when he and his staff were invited to a reception in the Carlton Hotel next door, sponsored by the Slovak League of America. They were forced to decline because the League at the time was pressing for Slovak independence, which went against our policy. Although Ambassador Black tried to convince me to stay away, I attended the reception in the end, joking that I was probably the only "Slovak nationalist" in the U.S. Senate.

Paul's description of the dilemmas posed by the opening of Trnava University in late 1992 also illustrates the factors pulling on U.S. representatives. One of the first rules of diplomacy is not to make unnecessary enemies. Certainly, a diplomat's effectiveness is also dependent to some degree on his or her ability to maintain a smooth working relationship with the host government. But what happens when that government starts to take measures that threaten basic freedoms, including academic freedom? There are many ways of expressing disapproval, and Paul chose to do so with a certain subtlety that made the point without engaging in a head-on collision. The price of standing up for principles can be sacrificing good relations with the government to which one is accredited, but it is a price we sometimes have to pay.

Although advancing age has prevented me from returning to Slovakia, I know that the country has been developing at an enviable pace and that it is firmly grounded in Western and European institutions. In 1992, when other parts of Europe were erupting in murderous fratricide, the Czechs and Slovaks found a peaceful and dignified way in which to realize their national aspirations. After independence, Slovakia indeed had some ups and downs in its economic and political development. This book, which chronicles the rocky road that Slovakia has traveled, also ends on a note of hope that Slovakia and its people have gained the maturity to be useful contributing members of the international community. This is a view that, six decades after I came to a very different place, I am proud to share.

Newport, Rhode Island
August 2008

POLITICAL PARTY AND ORGANIZATIONAL ACRONYMS

ANO (Aliancia Nového Občana): Alliance of the New Citizen

ČZM (Československý Zväz Mládeže) (Czech: ČSM or Československý Svaz Mládeže): Czechoslovak Youth League

DS (Demokratická strana): Democratic Party

DÚ (Demokratická únia): Democratic Union

Egyutelles (Coexistence)

FBIS (Federálná bezpečnostná informačná služba): Federal Security Information Service

HZD (Hnutie za demokraciu): Movement for Democracy

HZDS (Hnutie za demokratické Slovensko): Movement for a Democratic Slovakia

KDH (Kresťanskodemokratické hnutie): Christian Democratic Movement

KSČ (Komunistická strana Československa; Slovak initials KSČS): Communist Party of Czechoslovakia

KSS (Komunistická strana Slovenska): Communist Party of Slovakia

MS (Matica Slovenská): Slovak Heritage Society

MKDH (Maďarské Kresťanskodemokratické hnutie): Hungarian Christian Democratic Movement

MNI (Maďarská nezavislá iniciativa): Hungarian Independent Initiative

NRSR (Národná rada Slovenskej republiky): National Council of the Slovak Republic; also known as NR (Národná rada) or National Council

ODS (Czech) (Občanská demokratická strana): Civic Democratic Party

ODÚ (Občianska demokratická únia): Civic Democratic Union

SDA (Sociálnodemokratická alternativa): Social Democratic Alternative

SDK (Slovenská demokratická koalicia): Slovak Democratic Coalition

SDKÚ (Slovenská demokratická a kresťanská únia): Slovak Democratic and Christian Union

SDĽ (Strana demokratickej ľavice): Party of the Democratic Left

SDSS (Sociálnodemokratická strana Slovenska): Social Democratic Party of Slovakia

SF (Slobodné Fórum): Free Forum

SIS (Slovenská informačná služba): Slovak Information Service

SKDH (Slovenské Kresťanskodemokratické hnutie): Slovak Christian Democratic Movement

SMER—Sociálná Demokracia (Direction—Social Democracy)

SMK (Strana Maďarskej Koalicie; Magyar Koalíció Pártja [MKP]): Party of
the Hungarian Coalition

SNR (Slovenská národná rada): Slovak National Council

SNS (Slovenská národná strana): Slovak National Party

SOP (Strana občianskeho porozumenia): Party of Civic Understanding

SWC Slovak World Congress

SZ (Strana zelených): Green Party (Slovakia)

SZM (Socialistický zväz mladých): Socialist Youth Union

SZS (Strana zelených na Slovensku): Slovak Green Party

VPN (Verejnosť proti násiliu): Public Against Violence

ZRS (Združenie Robotnikov Slovenska): Association of Slovak Workers

ZSM (Zväz Socialistickej Mládeže) (Czech: SSM, Svaz Socialistické Mládeže):
Union of Socialist Youth

* * * * * * *

INTRODUCTION

On January 1, 1993, Czechoslovakia ceased to exist as a country and split into two independent states, the Czech and Slovak republics. I had been privileged to observe the processes that culminated that day from my vantage point in Bratislava, the capital of the Slovak Republic, where I had the responsibility in October 1990 of reopening the U.S. Consulate, which had been closed for more than forty years.

As did thousands of Slovaks, I began that day braving the freezing temperatures on the Square of the Slovak Uprising, the Times Square of Bratislava, where the New Year's celebration this time had an extra ring to it. While many Slovaks celebrated the birth of a new nation that early morning, there were others who regarded the breakup of their country as a tragedy and felt much the same as Californians would if they were separated from the rest of the United States in a new country with borders at the Rocky Mountains. But their voices had been drowned out by the unstoppable course of events that climaxed that day.

Later that afternoon, I finished what had been a full day's work, despite the holiday. As a way of "closing the loop" on these events, I sent a farewell message to Ambassador Adrian Basora in Prague, to whom I had reported up to the stroke of midnight, when the two successor states came into being. The feeling was indeed strange. When one says farewell to a colleague in our Foreign Service, it is usually because one of us is leaving his post. In this case, neither of us was leaving, but the country to which we had both been accredited was now a part of history. I informed the ambassador that I had just carried out my last duty as consul general—the head of what until then had been the U.S. Consulate General in Slovakia. An hour earlier, I had exchanged notes with Slovakia's foreign minister, Milan Kňažko, whereby the United States formally granted recognition to the now independent Slovak Republic. I had typed out the note myself from a text I received the previous afternoon at our embassy in Vienna—we had no communication facilities of our own. The original note, which would arrive six weeks later, was signed by President George Bush and was addressed to Slovakia's prime minister, Vladimír Mečiar, who would be acting head of state until the new country's first president was elected a month later.

Feeling a bit nostalgic that day, and still unaccustomed to my new role in charge of what was now the U.S. Embassy, I thanked the ambassador for his guidance and support and expressed regret that the breakup of the country would mean the end of our professional relationship. Quickly correcting myself, I borrowed the term that Kňažko had marketed to soften the split's impact on Western opinion: our relations would be "transformed," rather than ended. While the Slovaks would be responsible for their own fate, our embassy in Slovakia would now look directly to Washington, not Prague, for direction and guidance. The Department of State had decided several months earlier that for political reasons, our Prague embassy should end all responsibility for Slovakia at the moment of independence. I also wrote to John Evans, the deputy chief of mission in Prague, to thank him for being my "light in the darkness." I had reported to him for the previous eighteen months. John faxed back an encouraging reply, predicting that independence would work out well for both countries in the end, and that our new status as an embassy would not cause major headaches. As I read his message, I noticed an unexpected change: it was now headlined "Česko," the still unofficial name for the new Czech-only entity. The "Slovensko" that signified the Slovak part of the state was gone.

From this day on, we would need to rely on our colleagues in Vienna, forty-five miles away, for administrative support, until we could get on our feet. Just as would be true for Slovakia itself, the embassy's growing pains would be seen in the sweating of a thousand small details. After the country split, and until an ambassador was named, I would be his place-holder, with the title of "chargé d'affaires *ad interim*." When I departed that July, my place was taken by Eleanor Sutter, who by coincidence was a fellow graduate of the Bronx High School of Science, class of 1962. That fall, Ted Russell, John's predecessor as deputy chief of mission in Prague, arrived to become the first U.S. ambassador to Slovakia.

Our transformation into an embassy was taking place with several anomalies. Our only communications were by phone or fax, which meant considerable frustration in trying to move messages. The act of establishing diplomatic relations itself epitomized the Catch-22 situation in which I found myself: the note I was to deliver had a confidential classification, yet it was to be handed over to a foreign government. Our building was not cleared to hold or even draft classified communications, but I had no choice except to bend the rules. Classified messages had to be drafted at our Vienna embassy, and any incoming classified traffic had to be read and stored there as well. Thus, I was a frequent commuter to the Austrian capital—a situation which an outsider might regard with considerable envy, but one which was in reality tense and trying due to the extreme congestion that often barred our way to the Austrian border (in both directions), and the need to travel country roads until we reached the highway just outside the city.[1] When I arrived in Bratislava late on the afternoon of New Year's Eve, there was no one at the Slovak Foreign Ministry around to answer the phone and thus arrange my meeting with Kňažko. The duty officer who was supposed to be present was nowhere to be found.

Thus, I needed to wait until the following day to make the necessary arrangements. I caught up with the foreign minister that morning at the Slovak National Council building, where Slovakia's deputies were meeting to formally proclaim their country's independence (Slovak National Council was Parliament, or SNR in its Slovak initials; since October 1992, its official name has been the National Council of the Slovak Republic, or NRSR in its Slovak initials). Due to a ruling by our lawyers, we could not formally recognize a government before it declared its own independence. I had been instructed to ask Kňažko to confirm that the Slovak government consented to my appointment as chargé d'affaires. He never answered the question, obviously surprised that I had even brought up the issue. He agreed to meet that afternoon in the French-built Hotel Forum, following his first press conference there as foreign minister of independent Slovakia.

The journalists present seemed to be more interested in Kňažko's account of his festering dispute with Mečiar than in the less colorful details of Slovak foreign policy (Kňažko would be ousted two months later). But Kňažko— an actor by profession—had a well-honed sense of how to dodge such questions. Afterwards, we retired to the appropriately named Consul Room next door, where at 3:23 P.M. we formally exchanged documents of recognition while the cameras were rolling. I wondered how my colleagues in Washington would react to the photographers pointing at their confidential note, but no one took notice. I subsequently learned that shortly after midnight that day, when Mečiar began receiving chiefs of mission soon after he had addressed the crowd from the podium at the Square of the Slovak Uprising, he growled the question "Where are the Americans? Late as usual." However, we had never received an invitation to come to the event, and when I explained this later to Mečiar, his immediate reaction was that the slip-up was another example of Kňažko's incompetence.

The next day, at a reception for chiefs of mission it was obvious how radically things had begun to change. Before January 1, we were a tight-knit group of about fifteen consuls general. The core of this group was the old Soviet bloc, plus Cuba, but minus Vietnam, which pulled out just before I arrived. The Germans took over from their East German colleagues; the day I arrived in Slovakia, coincidentally, Germany was reunited. The Italians, French, British, Chinese, and South Africans set up their offices after our own consulate was reestablished. Now, the rear of the government building at 1 Freedom Square—until 1989 named for Klement Gottwald, Czechoslovakia's first Communist president, whose statue across the street was dynamited in the heady days of 1989—was filled with the Mercedes and other luxury vehicles belonging mostly to the Prague diplomatic community. Mečiar and Kňažko had sagaciously postponed their reception for one day, knowing that the Prague diplomatic corps would be celebrating the independence of the Czech Republic on New Year's Day. This was one of several pragmatic moves. The Slovak government had offered to accredit all Prague-based ambassadors automatically. We declined to accept this proposal, and the jurisdiction of the Prague embassy now ended at the Czech-Slovak border, which overnight became an international boundary. Until January 1, my Bulgarian colleague had acted as the dean of the local consular corps. He was now dethroned in favor of the Prague-based Papal Nuncio. The Nuncio himself, however, did not make many trips to Bratislava, and the "job" of dean of the local corps was then handed to Jaroslav Šedivý, the new Czech ambassador, who in any case continued to operate out of his own home capital for several months.

I had good reason to feel part of the larger historical processes engulfing not only Czechoslovakia but all of former Eastern Europe. Our consulate general was originally established in November 1947 by Claiborne Pell, then a young Foreign Service officer. But when I arrived in Bratislava, Senator Pell was the chairman of the Senate Foreign Relations Committee. During its first period of life, the consulate had a short but dramatic history. Our building housed the German Commercial Bank during World War II, and when it opened in March 1948, the Communist coup that would plunge Czechoslovakia into a totalitarian nightmare was just a week old. Pell remained about six months to set up a "listening post."

Operations became increasingly difficult as the Communist regime launched a deliberate campaign to isolate its citizens from the West, and from Western institutions. Consulate personnel were harassed, and Slovaks who ventured into our consulate building were interrogated and warned off. Some of them developed the technique of timing their exit from our ground floor library precisely with the arrival of the next streetcar. At that time, streetcars were of the open variety, so a passenger could run out of our building with the plausible excuse that he was "just trying to get on the tram." But in May 1950, the full force of Stalinism came down hard on the country. At that time, five-sixths of our embassy personnel were declared "personae non gratae," our consulate library was closed, and on May 27 we had to stop all operations in Slovakia. Several of our Slovak employees were arrested, and some never returned from prison.

For the next forty years, the building remained virtually empty, except for an upstairs apartment used to house visiting embassy personnel who were conducting official business in Slovakia. During the period of Communist rule, the empty building remained a symbol for many Slovaks who hoped that a U.S. presence would one day be reestablished. While we had hoped to reopen the consulate in 1974 as part of a deal that would give Czechoslovakia "Most Favored Nation" status, when the arrangement fell through, the Bratislava opening was canceled, and our colleagues who had been designated to restart operations had to be reassigned. When I served as Czechoslovak desk officer from 1983 to 1985, the reopening of the consulate was regarded as a long-term objective, to follow the signing of a claims agreement and a consular agreement. Both of these events actually were accomplished just before the end of Communist rule in the country.

I had arrived in Slovakia on October 3, 1990, to reopen our consulate. When our embassy car crossed the Morava River into Slovakia that evening, I imagined how De Soto must have felt centuries earlier when crossing the Mississippi. In those days, there was no border between the Czech and Slovak republics, but just a small sign noting "West Slovak Region." However, one could still see remnants of the barbed wire fences that had prevented movement to the nearby border with Austria for more than forty years. When we got closer to the city, we saw long lines of people waiting by the side of the road. I joked to my wife that they must be awaiting the arrival of the American consul. Actually, they were on a more practical mission: the price of gasoline would go up 50 percent that midnight, and motorists were filling up at the lower price as long as supplies lasted. When we arrived at our building on Hviezdoslav Square (named for one of Slovakia's outstanding nineteenth-century poets), it was deserted as usual.[2] However, we would have to vacate it within two months when an Austrian firm began a six-month renovation project that would gut the structure in order to construct needed safety and security improvements, including a fire stairway that our inspectors insisted was essential. As we were the "new guys on the block," we initially had to fight with everyone else for parking space in front of our building. After a while, the Bratislava government reserved a section of the street for consulate vehicles. In time, with the increasing threat of terrorism, the building was isolated by barriers designed to prevent car bombs.

On May 27, 1991, forty-one years to the day after it was closed, we held a rededication ceremony in a cramped "multipurpose room" on the consulate building's third floor. The ceremony was presided over by Ambassador Shirley Temple Black, and included Senator Pell as guest of honor, as well as Czechoslovak Foreign Minister Jiří Dienstbier and Slovak Prime Minister Ján Čarnogurský. There was also a handful of invitees who had a direct personal connection with our former consulate general. Like Dienstbier and Čarnogurský themselves, most had suffered harassment or imprisonment; one artist was invited to commemorate the memory of his father, who had been murdered in prison after serving for just one month on the consulate staff.

The ceremony had a certain Potemkin Village quality to it. The rest of the building would not be ready for occupancy for several more months, and we would not begin full operations before October. Actually, the festivities were arranged to suit Pell's convenience, as well as our mission to "relaunch in Slovakia." Joined by his wife, Pell insisted on staying overnight at the decaying Carlton Hotel next door. He had first set up shop there on arriving in Bratislava in 1947, and the pull of nostalgia overcame any qualms about the quality of accommodations.

Our position at the time was somewhat anomalous. No better illustration could be found than the fact that we had to decline an invitation from the Slovak League of America to join them for a reception in the Carlton Hotel celebrating our reopening. At that time, our policy was still firmly in favor of "preserving Czechoslovakia's territorial integrity," which meant that the country should remain one whole. This policy (see chapter 18) was rooted in the belief that further divisions in Europe would be detrimental to the successor states' viability, not to mention the possibility of fueling further instability.[3] But most Slovak-American organizations, starting with the Slovak League, traditionally favored an independent Slovakia. Because of this sharp policy difference, we found ourselves in the strange position of having to boycott a reception that had been planned in our honor. Relations were not helped when the League's secretary general, quite at odds with the truth, bragged to the Slovak youth daily *Smena* that the reopening would never have taken place without pressure from his organization.

He came closer to the facts, however, when he mentioned that Ambassador Black had tried to dissuade Pell from participating in the reception. Pell felt, however, that he could not refuse an invitation from people to whom he felt a kinship (the senator liked to remark that he was the "only Slovak nationalist" in the U.S. Senate). Among his closest protégés was John Hvasta, a Slovak-born American citizen who had worked for Pell when the original consulate was in operation, and was arrested as an American spy. Sentenced in 1949 to three years' (later increased to ten) imprisonment in the infamous Leopoldov prison, Hvasta escaped in 1952. After a harrowing journey that lasted nearly two years, he made his way to our embassy in Prague, where he was granted refuge until the Communist authorities finally allowed him to return home in 1954.[4] When I first met Hvasta in 1985, I was Czechoslovak desk officer at the Department of State. In one of the more remarkable cases of politics making strange bedfellows, Hvasta arrived at our office with Evžen Loebl, then a professor of economics at Sarah Lawrence College. Loebl, of Jewish background, was one of the three survivors of the infamous 1952 Slánský purge trial, in which ten other defendants were hanged on trumped-up charges. After Loebl fled Slovakia during the 1968 Soviet-led invasion, he at first gravitated to academia (Sarah Lawrence College), and then later found a niche with the Slovak World Congress—a Toronto-based organization noted for its pro-independence stand for Slovakia, as well as its favorable attitude toward the wartime Slovak state that sent tens of thousands of Loebl's brethren to the Auschwitz extermination camp.

On the day of his arrival at our office, Hvasta launched such an emotional attack on the Department of State and our policy of "discrimination" against Slovakia that our office director, Richard Combs, warned him to calm down or be thrown out. While the Department's relations with the American Slovak community were not generally as dramatic as during that incident, they were the relations of organizations with two very different political agendas. Hvasta was a frequent visitor to Slovakia after the Velvet Revolution that overthrew Communism at the end of 1989.

During my tenure as desk officer, Deputy Assistant Secretary in charge of the USSR and Eastern Europe Mark Palmer (later U.S. ambassador to Hungary) presided over a moving ceremony where we welcomed "democratic" Slovak exiles[5] to our offices, and where Palmer received a sheaf of documentary materials to be housed in the U.S. Holocaust Museum, which opened in 1993. The ceremony had a clearly political message: one of the documents showed the picture of Jozef Kirschbaum, then the vice president of the Slovak World Congress. Kirschbaum was dressed in the Nazi uniform of the Academic Hlinka Guard, a Slovak offshoot of the SS for university students, and he was shown making a speech extolling the "Führer's great victory" just achieved in defeating France in 1940. In 1945, Kirschbaum made his way to Canada, where he became a professor of history and a prolific writer giving the nationalist viewpoint on Slovak history.[6] The point was to make clear that the Department of State would have nothing to do with an organization that was so closely associated with people who were apologists for the wartime fascist regime.

Only in the months following the rededication of our building, with the Yugoslav experience of disintegration and inter-republic war in mind, as well as the impending breakup of the USSR, did we back off from the "territorial integrity" phrase. Our more equivocal formula stated the future of the country was one for the Czechs and Slovaks themselves to peacefully decide.

Independence and Diplomatic Ritual

It was against this background that, when Slovakia finally became independent, I was determined to ensure that the opening of our diplomatic relations with that country not be marred by the falsehood that the United States opposed an independent Slovak state. For bureaucratic reasons, it was not until the evening of December 31, a few hours before independence, that I was given clearance to reopen our operations as an embassy on January 4, the first working day after the country split. On short notice, I arranged a simple but symbolic ceremony that day, in the same room where the consulate had been rededicated eighteen months earlier. In addition to our staff, and some resident Americans involved in aid projects, I invited Kňažko, his predecessor Dr. Pavol Demeš, and Ivan Laluha, chairman of the Foreign Relations Committee of the Slovak Parliament. Through this choice of guests, we had one representative each from the present government, past government, and legislative branch. This symbolic configuration also obviated the need to invite scores of guests, who could not have been contacted over the long holiday weekend in any case. I later learned that Mečiar did not take kindly to our invitation to Demeš, a close friend of the United States who was persona non grata to the prime minister due to the fact that he had served in the Čarnogurský government, which ended Mečiar's first period as prime minister in 1991.

Addressing our guests and invited media, I gave a short speech welcoming Slovakia as an independent state, and praising the Slovak contribution to the development of our own country. Kňažko also spoke for a few minutes. Afterwards, I invited all those present to help me raise a new, larger American flag over the building, to mark the opening of full diplomatic relations. Curiously, a statement I had drafted welcoming Slovakia into the community of nations never made it to the media. The only item considered noteworthy was our announcement that henceforth all varieties of non-immigrant visas would now be issued in Bratislava. To make the point, I invited our guests downstairs to our consular section, where I issued Kňažko the first A-1 (diplomatic) visa in Bratislava, and also the first visa with the legend "U.S. Embassy, Bratislava." When the working day was over, I made a fast dash to Vienna to send two cables to mark the historic occasion: the first was a report on the embassy's opening, and the second was a dispatch on Slovakia's becoming an independent state (see appendix F).

In October 1991, when we first began issuing visas, we were allowed to deliver only tourist and short-term business visas. At that time, I had invited Čarnogurský and František Mikloško (then speaker of the Slovak National Council) to receive the first visas issued in Bratislava. With some pride, Čarnogurský answered "yes" to the question of whether he had ever been convicted of a crime, noting that he was one of the last prisoners of conscience of the Communist regime in 1989.

My principal responsibility was to report on events in Slovakia. The Slovak perspective on what was happening in the country was different from that of the Czechs. While our embassy had done what was possible to cover the Slovak scene mainly from Prague, there was no substitute for being "on the ground." I was reminded of a remark once made by Stephen Rosenfeld of the *Washington Post*. Speaking in 1966 to a group of summer interns who had invited him to address them at the Department of State, Rosenfeld noted that as the paper's Moscow correspondent in the mid-1960s, his job was essentially the same as that of our embassy's political counselor. There was one exception: while Rosenfeld could be sure that the Soviet Foreign Ministry was reading his dispatches, the political counselor could never be sure if the Soviets were doing the same to his.

But there is another side to the picture. Barring leaks or breaches of security, a diplomat can be fairly confident that he is writing for only a limited audience within his own government. It may be several decades before his reports are declassified and made available to the general public. The journalist, however, always writes in the public spotlight, and can be called to task at any time regarding the veracity of his facts and interpretations. I was keenly aware of this when I first put my impressions down on paper. Slovakia was very much a blank spot on the political map of our readership back home. What I was not prepared for, though, was the hypersensitivity of our hosts over what was being reported back home on Slovakia. They were not only concerned over what the foreign media wrote about them (fearing a pro-Czech bias), but also worried loudly and publicly over what reports diplomats were sending home, since supposedly their governments took those reports more seriously. This concern existed even though, presumably, no copies of these reports were circulating outside those diplomats' home countries.

This, then, is the story of our sojourn in Slovakia as the republic made the journey from appendage of a Communist dictatorship to a fully sovereign state. We were front-row observers to many of the events that took place—especially since Hviezdoslav Square, where we were located, was a favorite venue for demonstrations. But we also experienced the vexations of getting started in a country still lacking basic infrastructural support, with our umbilical cord to Prague stretching two hundred miles to the northwest. When we held our first Thanksgiving celebration in the consulate building for several score young American volunteers from the Education for Democracy (EFD) project, who had come to Slovakia to teach English, I told our guests that we all could understand what it meant to be pilgrims in a strange new land.

1

BY WAY OF PRELUDE

Although the Foreign Service is filled with stories about mismatches between an officer's background and his or her place of assignment, in my case, I had some twenty-five years of preparation for the task I was now about to undertake. While in college, I decided to put my academic eggs in the East European basket, after settling on political science as my major, and subsequently, life's work, and Russian as the first of a dozen foreign languages I would tackle after my high school French. I felt that Eastern Europe was a case of "so near, and yet so far," and that if I couldn't do anything about Communism at that time, at least I could study its phenomena. I first visited Prague in 1965 as a stop on the way to the USSR with a student group organized by the U.S. National Student Association and conducted by the remarkable Jean-Paul Neuman. Neuman, a Polish-born, French-educated Jew, operated an educational travel service in New York, and his facility with languages was a constant inspiration. One lesson he gave me that I shall never forget took place at a Soviet youth camp in Yalta that summer. The leaders of each of a half dozen student groups were invited to address the gathering. When it came his time, Neuman addressed each group separately in their own language, with a message especially attuned to their history and mentality. While the several hundred students had listened listlessly to each speech, when Neuman came on the stage, they were electrified. Each group applauded, and the Poles even sang "may he live a hundred years." He finished his speech by reading remarks prepared in phonetic Japanese; the Japanese group leader was so moved that he ran up to the stage and embraced Neuman. The message was clear: if you wish to communicate with people from other countries, there is no substitute for doing so in their own languages. For that reason, when I was assigned to Bratislava, I found my own Slovak teacher (our Foreign Service Institute at that time did not offer instruction in Slovak, as we had no representation in Slovakia), determined that I would deal with Slovaks in their language, and not in Czech (about 90 percent of the words are similar).[1] This was a good investment, as many Slovaks whom I met, even if they resented the cool attitude the United States initially had toward the idea of separation, were pleased that an American official thought enough of them to learn their own language, and not just Czech.

But back to Prague. In 1965, the city was in a kind of time warp. Not only were the buildings ancient, but most of the cars were from before 1939 and were equipped with the right-hand drive used before Hitler took over the country that year. Coming from New York, I marveled at the fact that parked cars did not even fill half the available spaces at the curb (which is no longer the case.) A ride on the World War I-vintage trams cost less than four cents. When we had a meeting with representatives of the official Revolutionary Trade Unions (ROH), Neuman riled them by asking why he couldn't pick up a local American newspaper "to check the baseball scores." Of course, he knew full well that one of the first acts the Communists took after seizing power in 1948 was to prohibit the circulation of all non-Communist Western periodicals. After they got nowhere with the usual explanation that there was not enough foreign currency for such luxuries ("oh, we would be willing to pay hard currency"), the ROH representatives gave up and admitted they had a problem that they hoped could be resolved.

I came back for a longer stay with the Experiment in International Living in 1967. The Experiment, founded in 1932, sends young Americans all over the world to live with foreign families, and vice-versa. The program I participated in was arranged by a local engineer informally through his network of friends, and was the first time the Experiment tried to operate in Communist Czechoslovakia. When I arrived in Prague, another American graduate student and I were placed in the home of Quido Partl, who lived with his elderly parents in a multifamily home that the family had solely occupied before 1948. I was especially touched when Quido's father, Otto, produced a copy of *Time* magazine from November 1947. At that time, the periodical could still be openly purchased on the newsstand. He held on to it as a precious relic of a bygone era that he hoped would someday return to his country. Characteristically, the headline story was about the Communist threat to democracy in Czechoslovakia. While the Experiment

offered its participants a survival level course in the language of the country to which they were going, I decided that its depth was insufficient for
my needs, and I wound up teaching myself Czech, using a textbook I had
borrowed from my university library. While three weeks is hardly enough
time to acquire fluency, in that time I was able to learn the rudiments of the
language and to conduct conversations in Czech with people whom I met,
including one Communist worker with whom I struck up an acquaintance
outside a local restaurant, and who then invited me to his weekend cottage.

In fact, by mid-1967, some measured progress toward liberalization had
been made in the country. Although the reports of its proceedings were
censored, the Fourth Writers' Congress was held in Prague that June. Many
participants roundly denounced the Party's restrictions on freedom of
expression. Included was Václav Havel, who had suffered because of his own
"bourgeois" class origin, but had become a celebrated playwright. Havel
would later take the path of open dissidence that would land him in prison,
but eventually to the presidential palace, after he became the conscience
of his nation. Neuman's words were finally getting through in other ways:
the *Times* of London and *Le Monde* were now sold at selected newsstands.
For 20 cents, one could go to hotels catering to foreigners and purchase the
International Herald Tribune. For 10 cents more, *Life* magazine was also available. During our stay, there was a minor sensation when Josef Smrkovský,
a Communist official purged in the 1950s who would become one of the
leading representatives of the 1968 Prague Spring, admitted publicly in a
student newspaper that the reason the Americans had not liberated Prague
in 1945 was not, as Communist propaganda always said, because the United
States wanted to sacrifice the Czechs, but actually because underground
leaders such as he himself told the Americans to stay away.

After three weeks in Prague, our group went to Slovakia. The heart of old
Bratislava had not yet been torn up for a new bridge over the Danube that
opened a few years later. On a train trip to eastern Slovakia, while speaking with a Slovak student, I offered the view (not wishing to be provocative) that Radio Free Europe (RFE) was probably not of much interest to his
generation. On the contrary, he assured me, when they could hear it over
the constant jamming, "Slobodná Europa" was quite popular, especially its
music programs. Some twenty-five years later, the question of RFE would
come back to haunt us despite the fact that the country had undergone a
political transformation.

The following year I had my own experience as a summer intern in the
Research Department of RFE in Munich in that fateful summer before and
after the August 21 invasion. Before I arrived there, I took the opportunity

to visit old friends in Prague at the height of the liberalization of the 1968 Prague Spring. One was exultant, proclaiming that everything was now possible. Another was much more worried about the Russian reaction. Despite my protests, he argued that if the Russians were to invade his country, the United States would do nothing. In the end, he proved quite right.

I followed the peak of the liberalization period, the Soviet-led invasion, and its aftermath from Munich, working sixteen-hour days in the month following the "fraternal assistance." I worked in the Czechoslovak Research Department, headed by Hanuš Hajek, a Czech Jew whose parents had been murdered by the Nazis, but who escaped deportation because his father sent him away in time to Bulgaria. His deputy, Ladislav Nižňanský, had a much more sordid past, although I was only dimly aware of the details at the time. Nižňanský was the commander of a Slovak pro-German unit called Edelweiss, which fought anti-Nazi partisans and committed war crimes. He worked for U.S. intelligence after the war and wound up at RFE about 1954. In 1962, he was sentenced to death in absentia as a war criminal by a Slovak court, but he stayed on at RFE because the motivation of the Slovak court was suspect at the height of the Cold War, and because, as Hajek pointed out, he was "doing a good job" at RFE. Only in 2004, at the age of 86, was he arrested by the Germans and tried for war crimes. Although he admitted involvement in the Edelweiss brigade, he claimed he did so under duress with threats to his life; more than a year later he was freed by the German court. What makes the story even more astounding is that he was present during the operation that captured members of a mission sent by the Office of Strategic Services (OSS) in 1944 to aid the Slovak uprising against the Nazis. The Americans, who were all captured, were murdered by the Nazis; the most ironic fact of all is that, forty-seven years after the deed, and twenty-three years after my encounter with him, I would represent the United States in commemorating the sacrifice of the Americans he helped capture and deliver to their deaths (see chapter 6 for more details).

In October 1969, I returned to what was now an occupied country. Things were quickly going downhill. As I had planned to do my Ph.D. dissertation on Czechoslovakia before the invasion, I tried to latch on to some institutional contacts, such as the Institute of Sociology at the Academy of Sciences. Its director, Miloš Kálab, had been at Columbia University while I was studying there. While he promised to help as much as he could, he was soon dismissed, and his deputy emigrated to the West. I had the same luck when I called on Jiří Hájek, who was the country's foreign minister until he made the fatal error of calling on the UN to condemn the 1968 invasion. When I met him a year later, he was still teaching at Charles University in Prague and headed an embryonic institute of political science that was soon to be abolished in the "normalization" that followed. He would later resurface as one of the leading personalities of the Charter 77 movement for human rights.

When I returned in 1970 and 1973, some colleagues suggested that I might have better luck carrying out research in Slovakia. Since Slovakia had not been affected by the liberal wave that swept through in 1968 (reformers did not play such a prominent role as they did in the Czech Republic), there were fewer Slovaks to purge after that time. I called on Ondrej Pavlik, who headed the Educational Research Institute and had done a study of the political attitudes of working youth. Some portions of the study had made their way into the professional press. I asked him about the possibility of getting my hands on the entire work. He took down from the shelves a thick volume with the word *dôverné* (confidential) emblazoned on the front cover. Given the nature of the work, he did not have permission to let me see it. Would I please go to a "higher instance" (the Ministry of Education) to get permission? Deciding that requesting access to confidential information would give the security police even more reason to be interested in me than they already had, I decided to give up the struggle at that point.

In 1973, I returned to Czechoslovakia on a tourist visa to carry out whatever research was possible under the increasingly dismal circumstances. At that time, the International Research and Exchanges Board (IREX), which was the only U.S organization to have an official exchange relationship with Czechoslovakia that would fit my status, decided not to sponsor me. Lacking such sponsorship, it was exceedingly difficult to make any kind of contacts whatsoever. What finally did me in were the reactions of two American professors who questioned me about my intentions; when one of them turned to the other with the words "your witness, counselor," I knew I could cross IREX off my list.

I decided to focus on political education, in the belief that research focused more directly on education would be easier to handle. My journey started off at the State Pedagogical Library, where my path had been smoothed by Pavel Jambor, a Czech mathematician whom I had befriended while he was studying in New York. Jambor had the misfortune to have discovered the hard way that his brother was in fact a KGB agent, a person who had become a well-known fixture of "normalized" television after 1968 through his biting commentaries. While in New York, Pavel had been told by his brother that their mother was gravely ill and he should come home at once to see her. When he arrived at the airport in Prague, his passport was taken and he was told he would not be needing it any longer. He had been lured home because family members of persons in his brother's position were not supposed to be living in the West. His mother, of course, was in perfect health.

While Bohuslav Gawrecki, the library director, greeted me in a business-like fashion the first day, when I returned, the next day, he did an about-face, informing me that I could not use his facilities unless I "regularized" my stay. Since the library was under the Czech Ministry of Education, I had to address my request to that body. With some trepidation, I visited the Ministry, only to find that Gawrecki had gotten there ahead of me. When I was admitted, I was dressed down for not "reporting myself" earlier and told that the only way I could gain access to anyone was to address a request to the Ministry. I phrased my situation in as general terms as possible, and was somewhat bemused when, a month later, it was the janitor of the building where I was staying who informed me that I was to go to the Ministry for an answer to my request. When I arrived, I was told curtly that my request had been approved, but only because "with the Brezhnev visit to the United States, our relations are improving."

When I returned a few days later, I received a letter that captured the spirit of the times. It started off "to Paul Hacker, citizen of the USA is permitted," and then proceeded to enumerate a number of items that included permission to use professional libraries and carry on conversations with educators and sociologists. Some of my Czech friends were amazed that I had been able to do even that much. But my luck at the State Pedagogical Library did not last long. I made the mistake of talking too openly to one of the assistant librarians, unaware that the janitress cleaning the study where we were talking was an informer. Despite the permit, I was hauled into Gawrecki's office the next morning. He had just finished a meeting with the staff, warning them not to talk to me. He informed me that henceforth, my sole contact would be a certain *soudružka* (female comrade) who just happened to be his deputy.

Months later, I would take revenge at the library. I returned because I had lost my original dissertation and had to reassemble my notes. While I no longer needed the facilities of the library, I decided to see how far I could press my luck. Going into the periodical section, I demanded a certain article from 1968 from an innocuous journal, *Czech Language in the Schools*. Without blinking an eye, the soudružka in charge of periodicals told me to find the volume on the shelves. I told her I had looked again and again, but "you seem to have 1967, but 1968 and 1969 are missing, while you pick up again in 1970." She tried to dismiss me by saying "we didn't receive that issue." In response to my incredulous query as to whether the mails had stopped working for two years, she finally admitted that "you can read it, but you need to have a letter from your employer stating that you need it for official business." Taking out a copy of the Ministry's letter from the previous year, I remarked that I had not made the trip from the United States simply for personal entertainment. I was sat down in one room, then another. After a long wait, I was finally told that the magazine was "in another building" and I could have it the following week. I replied that there was no need to bother; I would get the periodical when I returned to Washington the next week.

I did somewhat better at the University Library, and used the magic letter as an admission ticket to the *služební katalog*, the service catalogue where all the library's holdings, not just the censored version available to the public, were recorded. Books could land on the "Index" not only because of ideologically intolerable content, but also to punish their authors for their transgressions.[2] Thus, a 1967 history textbook by Karel Kaplan was as ideologically correct as anything available in the bookstores. But because its author had been purged for his pro-reform activities after 1968, all his works were closed off. One librarian, himself a purged historian, in a conspiratorial vein showed me a list of his colleagues who had been removed for ideological reasons.

One of my more memorable experiences in the search for "sponsorship" came in Slovakia, where I had gone in search of Jindřich Filipec, then deputy chief of the Institute of Sociology. Filipec had gone to Smolenica, a castle about two hours north of Bratislava, known as the "House of Scientific Workers" and used as a retreat for employees of the Academy of Sciences. Walking up the hill in the darkness from the stop where the bus had let me off, I heard boisterous sounds of a party where Czechs and Slovaks were enjoying themselves with their Soviet comrades. I knocked on the door and told the doorman who I was. He went to fetch Filipec, who seemed to be thoroughly dismayed when he saw me and heard my tale. His first reaction was undoubtedly that this was some kind of CIA (if not KGB) provocation. He told me I would have to send something in writing to him, but he never answered my queries. However, despite these hassles, as well as a year's delay caused by the loss of my draft, I completed my dissertation on "Political Education Under Socialism: The Case of Czechoslovakia," and was awarded the Ph.D. degree in January 1976. Zbigniew Brzezinski, one of my two dissertation advisors, would later become the National Security Advisor to President Jimmy Carter and I would next meet up with him at the July 4 reception I hosted in 1993, a few days before leaving Slovakia. As I liked to tell audiences in Slovakia, I was not just the U.S. consul, but also a certified "doctor of Communism." They appreciated the irony.

2

GETTING ORGANIZED IN SLOVAKIA

The first stage of life in Slovakia involved getting organized for the essentials that would serve us later on. The embassy had arranged for our temporary offices to be housed in the Hotel Devin, two blocks away from the consulate building, with our windows facing the Danube. Despite the fact that the Devin was completed in 1954, it did not have the dumpy feeling of some of its counterparts built around that time. The hotel had an Asian restaurant, with a reasonable facsimile of Chinese and Japanese food (a half dozen Asian restaurants would open before we left Bratislava). Our lifeline with the outside world initially went through one phone line that doubled for fax messages. One of the most frustrating parts of the job was the fact that fax messages we sent and those we received were often so garbled that they had to be resent three times. Phone calls to Prague usually required a dozen tries to work, with another dozen to get from the embassy to the person with whom we wished to speak.

All our telegraphic communications went from Vienna but via Prague. Because Ambassador Black did not want me to send reports about Slovakia without having them vetted by the embassy, everything I sent went to Prague for clearance. As things turned out, this usually meant a 24-hour delay in getting reports to the outside world. Because events were so fast moving, I would often get a call from the embassy's political section asking for input on some report they were sending out that day. When my normal working day was finished, if there was reporting to send out, I had to make a fast trip to Vienna.

When plans were made to reestablish our consulate in 1990, the initial idea was for a small installation to show the flag and do some reporting, but little else. The notion that a single officer could handle these responsibilities soon gave way to a plan for a branch public affairs officer from the U.S. Information Agency (USIA) to handle our educational and cultural diplomacy in Slovakia. These tasks included educational exchanges, exhibits, and informational programs. In the fall of 1990, a Fulbright Commission was established for Czechoslovakia to supervise postgraduate educational exchanges. As the U.S. consul, I was named as one of the ex-officio "Slovak" representatives.

During his May 1990 visit to Washington, Ján Čarnogurský, then deputy federal prime minister, lobbied hard to include the issuance of visas as one of our functions in Slovakia. Without the issuance of visas, he argued, we would not have a consulate worthy of the name. So, the bureaucracy bent, and in deference to Čarnogurský, a consular position was added. However, because it was felt to be beyond our capacity to handle specialty visas, we were initially limited to B-2 (tourist) visas, and later B-1 (business) visas which in any case, both in Czechoslovakia and elsewhere, made up the bulk of our visa issuance. Before we started visa services, Slovaks had to make a personal visit to our Prague embassy to be interviewed for a visa. When we reopened the consulate, Slovaks would sometimes come to us to protest what they saw as "unfair treatment" during the visa process in Prague. They usually based this view on the stereotyped notion that Prague was the hotbed of anti-Slovak bias and they were being refused visas because they were Slovaks. Since our mission was located there, some Slovaks believed that our personnel must have had the same prejudices. However, the real problem was that Slovaks often had difficulty convincing the consular officer that they were bona fide visitors to the United States who did not intend to work or stay. Given the hundreds of thousands of aunts and uncles as well as brothers and sisters in the United States, there was a built-in network that could sometimes be abused. The law stipulates that any doubts on this score must be resolved against the applicant.

When we started issuing visas in late September 1991, some Slovaks were shocked to find that our vice consul followed the same rules that his colleagues did in Prague. Surely, we were told, now that the consulate was issuing visas on its own, we would be more "understanding" of the Slovaks! I tried to avoid second-guessing visa decisions, except when I had personal knowledge of a case. But trusting people's personal integrity did not get one very far. A Slovak-American travel agent from Yonkers, New York, at one time pleaded with me to override a refusal for a visa for his niece to come to the United States. Her husband had applied for political asylum and was debating his future. Despite my better judgment, I gave in, but insisted that the woman's daughter remain behind until she returned. A few weeks later, we received the inevitable blue form informing us that the applicant had applied for change of status to permanent residency in the United States to join her husband. The child's "uncle" then called up to tell us that the child had become "gravely ill" and needed to be treated "at once" in the United States. The next time the travel agent came to visit, I was most undiplomatic with him. We suggested to the "uncle" that Austrian hospitals are a lot closer than American ones for any emergency.

One of the stranger cases came from a respected contact in the local Jewish community. One of his compatriots had married a Czech immigrant to the United States and became a permanent resident. She subsequently divorced and moved back to Slovakia. She now wanted to visit the gentleman in the United States to care for his sick mother. I explained that, due to these circumstances, I could not regard the woman as a bona fide visitor for pleasure, and suggested she apply for a fiancée visa, which would allow her to remain in the United States up to ninety days before remarrying. There were many other attempts to use *protekcia* (pull) to gain visas. Once, Archbishop Ján Sokol himself came to visit to plead the case of a priest who wished to visit his colleagues in the United States. While we were surprised to see such high-level intervention on a visa case, we did not deem it appropriate to challenge the archbishop's veracity.

My wife Eeva was originally from Finland and we were married in Stockholm in 1978 before departing for the United States, where she would take the fast track to U.S. citizenship, so that when we went out to Communist Bulgaria later that summer, she would have a U.S. diplomatic passport and the protection it offered. Swedish was our lingua franca for the first four years, until we learned to communicate in each other's native language. We were already accustomed to what diplomatic life had been under the watchful eyes (and ears) of the Communist secret police. I had mistakenly thought that, when we returned from leave in the United States in January 1991, we would have a ready home to move into. We had settled on a house that was three-quarters completed when we first inspected it. It was located just beneath the Bôrik Hotel, the state guest house, on a steep hill overlooking the Danube, with the proverbial "million dollar view." While the access street was only wide enough for one lane of traffic, the location was a real estate agent's dream.

The story of that house was the story of the Slovak economy in microcosm. The land was owned by the in-laws of an engineer, who lived next door. While Mr. Klas the engineer planned to build the home for his family, costs outstripped his ability to pay them. By the time he saw the embassy's advertisement looking for a home for me, he thought he had found a solution to his problems. But we were all caught in a Catch-22 situation: Klas could not complete the house without an extra injection of cash, and we could not give him anything until the house was completed. He wound up begging and borrowing to bridge the funding gap. Some of the design features would have caused heart failure to an American architect: the downstairs bathroom had two sinks so close together that two persons could not use them simultaneously. The dining room roof had so much glass that we immediately needed to order shades, lest the place become an oven in the summer time. The dining room itself was curious; it had originally been meant as an indoor swimming pool. Since the U.S. government will not pay for swimming pools at its accommodations, Klas wound up boarding up the whole thing and transforming it (at the behest of my wife) into a slightly elevated dining room. Had the boards collapsed, we would have had a nasty fall into the pool excavation.

Winter was a special experience. Several times a week, the furnace stopped operating, and with it the heat and hot water. While one enterprising politician convinced the city fathers of Bratislava to widen the street to our house to improve access, she could not do anything about the winter snow that made it impossible to move anything on the steep hilly street. One of my more memorable occasions occurred while trying to come home one evening. A winter ice storm had left everything super slick. I left my car at the top of the hill, knowing I could never get it up again in the ice and snow. I slowly walked down the hill clinging to a nearby fence for balance. A sympathetic neighbor lent me a helping hand. At first he did not recognize me. When he did, he bowed, and expressed his pleasure at being able to help such a "high personage" as myself. I thanked him and suggested he forget the high personage bit, since he was keeping me from sliding down the hill by guiding my every step.

As the new man in town, I naturally became the subject of curiosity. The first problem was how to politely decline a number of interview requests from local media. Ambassador Black had already decided that, as chief of mission, she would have the sole responsibility to give interviews, which she felt are an ambassador's function. Besides, as she liked to joke, "I have sixty years' experience in public relations." I was also instructed to keep a low profile. When I had visited a Slovak newspaper in Pennsylvania before leaving for Czechoslovakia, the paper recorded the event in a front-page, sympathetic article. That article was noted in our embassy in Prague, and not very happily. While I could not control the newspaper's decision as to what to print, and had not granted a formal interview, the fact that my conversation had been reported was enough to upset the ambassador.

Another reason for shying away from interviews was to avoid replying to the inevitable questions about Czech-Slovak relations. Had I answered such a question by referring to our ambassador, I would have simply reinforced the impression that I was nothing other than a "Prague errand boy," sent down to do the bidding of my masters. Of course, while U.S. policy cannot be different between an embassy and a constituent post, this fact was difficult for some Slovaks to register. They truly expected the consulate to be more "pro-Slovak" than the embassy.

My instructions were to spend my time learning about the country and to tell Slovakia's story back home. As mentioned above, during Ambassador Black's tenure, this story was routed via Prague. After she departed, the embassy arranged that reporting which was not of a highly sensitive nature could go out directly via Vienna. A number of Slovaks seemed overly concerned that my reporting was being distorted in Prague so that it reflected the "Czech" viewpoint. This was part of a general Slovak tendency to falsely generalize that anything at all coming out of Prague, whether from Czech or non-Czech sources, must reflect a pro-Czech, anti-Slovak bias. Only on rare occasions did this fear actually have some basis, and then it was due more to a lack of sensitivity than to a deliberate attempt at censorship. In one case, a long report I had sent out on Slovak anti-Semitism (covered in more detail in chapter 13) was trashed in Prague. In its place, the embassy sent out a report on anti-Semitism in the whole country, as well as the Czech take on Slovak anti-Semitism. The issue was and remains a sensitive one, but the real question was not how the Czechs viewed a phenomenon that was largely confined to Slovakia in any case, but how the issue was seen and experienced from Slovakia itself. When I informed my colleagues in Washington what had happened, they asked me to forward reports directly to them if such incidents were repeated.

Finding competent local staff was essential to getting our operations organized. After interviewing a number of candidates for secretary (the only position I was then allowed to fill), I found Viera Cengelova, a competent young candidate who was working at the Ministry of Forestry as an interpreter. When I returned from leave, I found to my surprise that the embassy had rejected my nomination because her typing skills were not up to standard. This was the first of many incidents where I gradually experienced my own version of what the Slovaks unhappily referred to as "Pragocentralism"—the tendency of their masters in Prague to disregard their feelings and needs.

Of course, while a consulate is a creature of the embassy that it supports, it does need a certain amount of autonomy if it is to operate properly. This was especially the case given the circumstances in Slovakia at the time. Thus, the embassy sent back a list of its own preferred candidates using a "point" system that was irrelevant to my needs, since their top candidates were mediocre in English—a prime requirement for the job. I finally was able to hire Viera, but as a consular assistant, and picked up Eva Salnerová, a Ph.D. from the Academy of Sciences, as my secretary. Renáta Bilevská, who had been educated in the United States and spoke English with an American accent, also joined our team as consular assistant.

Only a few days after my temporary office opened, another job hunter paid a visit. He happened to be a former secret policeman, and was offering his services to help our security. Somewhat taken aback, I looked over the papers he had brought to authenticate his qualifications. He had graduated from the school of the Ministry of Interior, and had received an "A" in, among other things, "agent activities." I complimented him on his background and used a convenient excuse to extricate myself: "Prague has to decide this" was a response that any Slovak could understand.

Our staff gradually multiplied, especially after we moved back into our building in July 1991. Beth Ritchie Poissant joined us that May as our USIA branch public affairs officer; Richard Polka came in August to set up consular operations, and Pat Lerner arrived in January 1992 to set up the first United States Agency for International Development (USAID) operation outside any nation's capital. USAID's prescience proved fortunate when the country split a year after her arrival. By that time, not unlike some other USAID operations, the USAID staff soon exceeded the rest of our Bratislava personnel combined. Late in my tenure, Pat became the first employee to benefit from that newfangled invention called "e-mail," but the rest of us had to lumber along in what seemed to be the Stone Age of communications. We were hamstrung by the lack of a permanent administrative officer—a shortcoming that was not addressed until a few weeks before my departure.

As privatization progressed, I found it noteworthy that Slovak businessmen were able to sell imported products, such as Austrian fruit juices, for as much as 30 percent below the price in their country of origin. One of the more memorable businessmen was Otto Burian, who founded the Slovak Society for Foreign Trade (SLOVEX) in late 1989, and gradually began to branch out to eastern and western capitals. In early 1991, after reading an article about SLOVEX, I called him up, and he showed up in my office ten minutes later, driving a new white Hyundai. This was the only such car in all of Slovakia; he had received it as a gift from his partners in New York.

Burian had already been to New York on an exploratory trip he financed out of his own meager private funds. He later tried going east, opening an office in Kiev, while noting that 90 percent of the Ukraine economy was "black market." Otto was also the next best thing to a local administrative section. When I needed to find another temporary place to live before our house was finally completed, he found me the top floor of a private home on short notice. When we needed to rent tables and chairs for our first July 4 reception, Otto made the arrangements.

But sometimes he was like a conglomerate that expanded too quickly and sacrificed quality along the way. I discovered this fact in a brutally clear fashion the day we moved back to our consulate building in July 1991. While an Austrian firm had done the basic reconstruction, the embassy had hired one of Burian's clients to do the finishing touches inside. At the close of business that day, I needed to pay a visit to the men's room. The toilet stall was a small self-contained space inside a larger bathroom. It could be locked from the inside, but, unlike American toilets, the door completely covered the space from floor to ceiling. Since my previous life's experience never prepared me for what was about to happen, I closed the door and flicked the lock. It offered no resistance, and I knew immediately that something was wrong. I had locked myself in! Given the construction of the door, I had also entombed myself. As everyone had gone home for the day, and the room was inside a larger bathroom, there was no chance anyone would hear, or know how to respond to, cries for help.

Never in my life did I have such an anxious moment, or realize what being locked up in a small space without the possibility of escape could do to a person. I quickly decided that, if I had any hope at all, it would be through my own efforts. I started kicking at the door with all my strength from the cramped space I had available. After much effort, the layer of wood holding the door together started to cave in. I was finally able to punch a hole in the second, outer layer of wood so that light and air from the outer bathroom could come through. While I punched as hard as I could, I found I had another obstacle: the door was held together by several crossbars that were quite thick and not susceptible to kicking. By that time, I had made a hole about three inches wide and a foot long.

In the meantime, the toilet seat had broken and an idea came to me. Using the broken fragment as a knife, I laboriously started to cut through the first wooden crossbar. When the cut went through, I was able to kick the crossbar out and had a hole wide enough to stick my head out but not to free myself from my confinement. But in such a situation, a person finds a way to marshal his resources, and after more cutting with the broken toilet seat, as well as one of my keys, the second bar finally fell through. About two hours after making this biggest mistake of my life, I crawled through, immediately seeing the door handles that the contractor had neglected to install. When I saw the contractor the following morning, I would have liked to assassinate, not just fire him, but as with everything else, I was beholden to arrangements the embassy had already made. His one bit of gallantry in the whole episode was to offer to replace the door at no cost! A few months later, I learned that Mečiar had found himself in a similar predicament, and boasted about how he, too, had fought his way out of a locked bathroom door.

With Otto Burian's help, I also began to visit outlying areas in Slovakia, starting with Poprad, Levoča, and Javorina in May. This trip was especially timely because Vice President Dan Quayle would touch down in Poprad a month later as he made his way from there by helicopter to eastern Slovakia to address the tenth anniversary meeting of the Institute for EastWest Studies. In Poprad, I got my first experience with Slovak showmanship. Our Saturday morning meeting with some sixty assembled local officials was begun with a walk on stage accompanied by a musical fanfare and preprinted stage directions that included instruction as to when to applaud. When I expressed my astonishment at the completeness of the preparations, my hosts, including Poprad mayor Ján Madáč and district *prednosta* Štefan Kubik explained with some embarrassment that they were leftovers from the Communist period, when official welcomes were formalized into a rigid procedure.

The scene then shifted to the local cultural center, where a public forum was held. Most of the questions I received concerned the possibility of joint ventures between U.S. and local firms. No one responded, though, when I asked the audience their own views about local politics. Some other questions I received were indicative of the local temperament: one concerned the separation of church and state in the United States; another, from a nationalist politician, asked whether the United States would prohibit Americans from investing in an independent Slovakia.

We had dinner that night with František Tondra, the bishop of Spiš. I found his views on the role of the Catholic Church in Slovakia to be much more flexible than those voiced earlier by Archbishop Sokol. Tondra denied that believers occupying public functions must carry out Church policies. But he also admitted that some overzealous local priests may have exceeded their mandate and actively intervened in local political campaigns. Their instructions were limited to trying to ensure that voters elected believers to political office. When asked about Mečiar, Tondra, somewhat reluctantly, characterized his tactics as "undemocratic."

There were other signs of local conflict as well. On a visit to the Tatra National Park, just north of Poprad, local ecologists strongly denounced the government's efforts to get the 2002 Winter Olympics for Slovakia, saying the Slovaks were neither "economically, morally, nor physically prepared" to hold the games. Hearing that, Mayor Madáč snapped back: the only thing the ecologists were after is "to keep the Tatras safe for the bears to enjoy."

3

NA SLOVENSKU PO SLOVENSKÝ:
CRISIS OVER THE LANGUAGE LAW

November 17, 1990, was the first anniversary of the democratic revolution that had overthrown Communist rule. But the anniversary was marked in a strikingly different fashion in Prague than in Bratislava and showed how quickly events were moving in different directions in both parts of the country. In Prague's Wenceslaus Square, under the watchful eye of Václav Havel and visiting U.S. president George Bush, a ceremony celebrating the rebirth of democracy was held in a solemn atmosphere. In contrast, planned commemorations in Bratislava dissolved quickly into angry shouting matches between protagonists of the government's moderate policies vis-à-vis the Hungarian minority and those who heeded the nationalist calls of the day. These clashes were a harbinger of things to come.

After the June 1990 elections, Slovakia was governed by a coalition whose core was the VPN (Verejnosť proti násiliu or Public Against Violence) and the Christian Democratic Movement or KDH (Kresťanskodemokratické hnutie). The VPN was the first organized political force that emerged out of the wreckage of the Communist system. It was founded by intellectuals, including the actor Milan Kňažko, the environmental activist Ján Budaj, sociologist Fedor Gál, and the writer Ľubomír Feldek. In early 1990, the movement started to fragment. Ján Čarnogurský, a lawyer who had defended dissidents and who was himself a defendant in the notorious Bratislava Five case of five dissidents tried for subversion on the eve of the November 1989 events and freed from prison due to public pressure, took a group of activists from the underground Church of the Communist period and founded the KDH. The Slovak nationalists soon formed their own party to work for an independent Slovakia. The Hungarians broke into several groups, including MNI, the Hungarian Independent Initiative, the MKDH, or Hungarian Christian Democratic Movement, and Egyutelles (Coexistence), the predominately Hungarian catch-all movement for Slovak minorities. The MNI, although the smallest of these groups, was allied with the VPN and espoused a liberal line. Several of its representatives occupied prominent positions in the Slovak parliament or government.

The VPN also contained a number of political personalities and currents that would not long remain under one roof. One group felt that under Gál's leadership, the movement had neglected the "national" issue in its drive to acquire support from Europeans and Americans. Gál, who is Jewish and was born in 1945 in Theresienstadt concentration camp, understandably had difficulty in identifying with the nationalist emotions that fondly recalled an era when his family and brethren were persecuted and delivered to the death camps. Gál was opposed by Vladimír Mečiar, a former lawyer and one-time activist of the Communist-controlled Union of Czechoslovak Youth (ČZM or Czech initials ČSM). Mečiar so impressed a VPN commission looking for candidates for ministerial posts that he was named minister of interior in the first post-Communist government formed after November 1989. Mečiar became prime minister in August 1990, heading a coalition government that included the VPN, KDH, MNI, and the small Democratic Party—which was the reconstituted political organization that won the 1946 elections in Slovakia but was destroyed by the Communists after their 1948 coup.

After World War II, the Democratic Party had a short but glorious history. As the catch-all party that combined all non-Communist forces, in the 1946 elections it won 62 percent of the votes, compared to 30 percent for the Communists (prompting Slovaks much later to brag that the Communists lost the elections in Slovakia but won them in the Czech lands, where they received more than 40 percent of the vote, and formed the core of the first democratically elected government). The Democrats were subjected to various stratagems used by the Communists to bring them down by 1947, and by 1948 they had all but disappeared in the wake of the Communist coup (a small satellite party was allowed to maintain a precarious existence). In the 1990 elections, they barely polled the 5 percent of all votes necessary to return deputies to the Slovak National Council. One problem faced by the government that took over in 1990 was the fact that the Democrats and Hungarians received positions in the government and parliament that far exceeded their actual support in the electorate. When Mečiar bolted the

VPN in 1991, the remnant of that movement was forced to rely on political leaders who had a narrow base of support in the 150-person parliament.

After I arrived in Bratislava in October 1990, I was to know but a few short weeks of relative calm before the pot boiled over. That month, the twin issues of a draft bill on enthroning Slovak as the official language of Slovakia and Mečiar's determination to rid himself of a minister of the interior from the KDH (Christian Democratic Movement) provoked a political uproar. The latter case involved Anton Andráš, former district chairman of the Poprad (central Slovakia) National Committee (the national committee was the Czechoslovak equivalent of the Soviet, or local government unit). In 1990, local government was still based on national committees, but elections that fall established a system of local government units elected from below, along with the position of an appointed prednosta. In an October 21 speech, Mečiar accused Andráš of incompetence and demanded his resignation. Andráš refused, and Mečiar subsequently threatened to resign. Later reports suggested that Mečiar had deliberately made himself scarce for several days to create pressure—especially on his own colleagues in the VPN (Public Against Violence)—to support him. While the KDH later privately conceded that Andráš might not have been a world-class leader among ministers of interior, it feared that Mečiar's move was designed to get his hands on a ministry that was still quite sensitive in a country only a year removed from a police dictatorship.

While Mečiar used the tactic (repeated in later political confrontations) of tendering his resignation on October 31, the Presidium of the SNR announced on November 3 that it had declined to accept Mečiar's resignation, but had accepted Andráš's instead. Six months later, Mečiar's by now former colleagues in the VPN were slapping themselves hard; "what trouble we could have saved ourselves if we accepted his resignation then" was the refrain. Ján Čarnogurský temporarily took charge of the Interior Ministry, but his colleagues would not forget Mečiar's behavior. KDH sources then told the tale that Mečiar had threatened he could "dissolve" the KDH on forty-eight hours' notice, and they already felt he retained the "vindictive spirit" of the Communist Party of which he was a member until 1970. At the same time, it was clear that the VPN and KDH still needed each other. At the KDH congress that began November 3, Andráš was given the title of deputy chairman, a new position created expressly for him. Eighteen months later, Andráš would defect and join the nationalist wing of the KDH in a new party.

The real source of emotions, however, was the issue of a law establishing Slovak as the official language of the republic. But the issue involved much more than language. As has often been the case in East European history, the differences between the Slovaks and Hungarians were a case of two people who occupied the same space, and whose roles alternated between the bottom and the top of the political heap. The Hungarians had controlled what is present-day Slovakia for a millennium, and the last three-quarters century of their rule—prior to the establishment of an independent Czechoslovak state—was marked by oppression of Slovak national feeling and attempts at Magyarization.

Mostly concentrated in Slovakia, the Hungarians suddenly found themselves a dissatisfied minority in the new Czechoslovak state. In the prewar Czechoslovak Republic, Hungarians were the second-largest minority after the Germans, constituting 657,000 persons in 1921, 99 percent of whom lived in Slovakia. During this period, laws were passed allowing members of a minority constituting 20 percent of any district's population to use their native language in official dealings in the courts, applications, petitions, or other official business. Relations with Hungary were tense, as a number of Hungarian organizations followed the official Hungarian line at the time of challenging the validity of the 1920 Treaty of Trianon, which sharply reduced Hungarian territory. Immediately after the Munich *diktat* that stripped Bohemia of its mostly German borderlands, Hungary moved in for its share of the spoils. On November 2, 1938, in the so-called Vienna Arbitrage, Hungary received 10,390 square kilometers of Slovak land, starting just at the suburbs of Bratislava, and reaching all the way to the second largest city, Košice, in the east. Of the 850,000 persons who lived on that territory, 272,000 were of Slovak or Czech nationality. Many fled to the rump territory that was left of Slovakia, which declared its own independence on March 14, 1939.

When Czechoslovakia was liberated in 1945, retribution inflicted on the Hungarians was second only to that suffered by the Germans in the Czech lands. Until 1948, teaching in Hungarian was stopped, Hungarians were stripped of their citizenship, and the prevailing view was that the best way to "solve" the Hungarian problem was to export it—by sending ethnic Hungarians across the Danube to their motherland and inducing Slovaks living in Hungary to return home. According to official statistics, some 90,000 Hungarians went south and 72,000 Slovaks returned to Slovakia during this period. About 44,000 other Hungarians were coerced into moving to the Czech lands. Hungarian-owned property was taken over by trustees, and a "reslovakization process" was introduced to purge the population of any residual feelings of Hungarian identity. In 1992, when I met with Hungarian community representatives, one of them recalled that in those days,

Hungarians who wished to avoid deportation tried to purchase an official certificate stating that they had agreed to be "reslovakized."

After the Communist Party took power in February 1948, it introduced a more lenient policy toward the Hungarian population. It was not so much motivated by pro-Hungarian feelings as by the view that a quiet period in interethnic relations with the now "fraternal" People's Republic of Hungary was needed for the consolidation of political and economic power, including the collectivization of agriculture launched in 1949. Thus, Hungarian schools were reopened, Slovaks of Hungarian nationality had their citizenship restored, and Hungarian cultural life resumed. In 1949, the Communist Party permitted the formation of CSEMADOK—the cultural association of Slovak Hungarians and the only organization that allowed Hungarians to even remotely promote their interests. That year, the Party also established a Hungarian-language daily, *Uj Szo* (New Word).

After the 1968 Soviet-led invasion, initial efforts at establishing a firmer Hungarian identity in Slovakia were ended under the theory that society was developing as a "conflict-free" entity. While the Hungarians were well represented in government, they had no chance to make their views felt as an ethnic collective. The Hungarian population stabilized during this period, reaching 552,000 in 1971 and 559,000 in 1980 in Slovakia; about 18,000 to 20,000 additional Hungarians lived in the Czech Republic. During this period, the policy of concentrating development in urban areas meant the consolidation of schools in Hungarian-populated rural districts; thus, the number of Hungarian children attending elementary schools conducted in their native language rapidly decreased from 1970 to 1989.

At the time of the 1991 census, Hungarians composed about 10.8 percent of Slovakia's 5.3 million population, or about 570,000 people. Hungarians constituted the majority—sometimes the overwhelming majority—of the population in more than 500 towns and villages in the swatch of land that extends from the southeast of Bratislava east to the border with Ukraine. While guaranteed the rights to their own schools, newspapers, and culture, the Hungarians regarded themselves as second-class citizens, despite the fact that formal restrictions on their rights ended in the late 1940s. On the other side, many Slovaks felt that the Hungarians had too many privileges. Slovak-Hungarian relations in the early 1990s were essentially two conflicting views of the past, where each side saw itself as a victim of the wrongs perpetrated by the other, rather than as the aggressor. Thus, the Slovaks replied huffily to outsiders' questions about Hungarian rights by pointing to statistics showing the number of Hungarian schools, newspapers, and cultural institutions subsidized by the state.

While sociological surveys underscored the contradictory images Slovaks and Hungarians had of each other's situation, they also showed that the higher the percentage of Slovaks living in a region with Hungarians, the less likely they were to view the Hungarians as antagonistic. Thus, while 25 percent of Slovaks living in predominately Hungarian districts feared "Magyarization" pressures in 1990, 60 percent of those living with no or few Hungarians expressed that view. (One example of how Slovaks and Hungarians had a vastly differing view of reality is their answer to the question of whether there had been excessive pressure for assimilation, i.e., becoming Slovaks, since 1948. Of the Hungarian respondents, 55 percent said yes, whereas only 12 percent of the Slovaks agreed with that thesis.) What this suggested was that Slovaks who had more contacts with Hungarians were less likely to fear them, and vice versa.

Slovaks seized on an innocent remark by the late Hungarian Jozef Antall, then the country's prime minister, to the effect that he regarded himself as the "prime minister of 15 million Hungarians" (including five million outside of Hungary) as proof of Hungarian irredentism. Some Slovaks wondered whether their Hungarian brethren were a kind of fifth column waiting for the right time to respond to Budapest's blandishments. A sense of dialogue and compromise was absent.

After the November 1989 revolution, the political structure began to cleave, and three main Hungarian parties or movements arose. Egyutelles, the most popular, was headed by Miklos Duray, a fiery dissident whose imprisonment evoked a number of letters to me from American affiliates of Amnesty International while I was Czechoslovak desk officer in 1984 in Washington. Although Egyutelles was nominally an all-Czechoslovak organization devoted to the interests of all minorities, it was dominated by the Hungarians, who are the largest minority in Slovakia, and reflected Duray's combative spirit. I once ran into Duray at a Hungarian Embassy reception, and noted that his country's national holiday (then October 28) was coming up soon. He replied immediately, "it's not my holiday." Laszlo Nagy, the bearded former student leader from 1968, headed the liberal MNI or Hungarian Independent Initiative (later to become the Hungarian Civic Party) and was one of the deputy speakers of the National Council when the MNI was in coalition with the VPN and KDH. The third grouping was the Hungarian Christian Democratic Movement (MKDH).

A simmering feeling by Slovaks that they were being done in by the Hungarian minority erupted soon after my arrival in Slovakia. Many Slovaks feared that the Hungarian minority was separating itself de facto from the rest of the country by wrapping itself in a linguistic Hungarian ghetto.

Members of the minority, of course, spoke Hungarian to each other, but on more than a few occasions, they refused or were reluctant to use Slovak in communicating with the majority population. Slovak papers and speeches of some politicians were filled with stories about how Hungarians would reply *Nem beszelek Szlovakul* (I don't speak Slovak) when asked for something in stores or other situations. The Slovaks also feared that their brethren living in border regions were becoming aliens in their own country—surrounded by a Hungarian-speaking population that looked to Budapest, rather than Bratislava, or sometimes to Prague, as its reference point.

Operating through the Matica Slovenská, the Slovak Heritage Society, and armed with the battle cry *Na Slovensku, po slovenský* (In Slovakia, in Slovak!), they attempted to push forward a bill that would enshrine Slovak as the national language "without exception." The bill was designed, in part, to protect the interests of Slovaks who found, for example, that they could not even conduct business in state offices in their own language. The government introduced a competing bill that would allow minorities to continue to use their mother tongue in official business if they constituted 20 percent of the population of a given district, using the principle that had been in effect in the prewar republic. The law also stipulated that signs be in the official language. Typically, in mixed communities, signs were in both Hungarian and Slovak.

Thus, the issue that erupted was not whether there should be a language law stipulating Slovak as the official language, but what kind of law it should be. The Slovak government, headed at the time by Mečiar, argued that the 20 percent rule was essential for the preservation of minority rights. Fedor Gál, then chairman of the VPN, was especially active in championing the notion that without such a clause, Slovakia would not be accepted into the good company of democratic nations. More nationalist Slovaks argued that the Hungarians' rights would not be hamstrung by their version, and that the 20 percent clause allowed too many loopholes.

The real issue was distrust. If the Hungarians were really involved in a plot to separate from the republic, a language law would not have stopped them. The crowds demonstrating at Bratislava's main square were egged on by Jozef Markuš, an economist who had served briefly as deputy prime minister in the first post-Communist government in Slovakia. I first met Markuš in September that year, at a joint meeting with American and Czechoslovak economists in Washington, D.C. He had just been elected chairman of the Matica Slovenská, and showed little indication of the politician that was soon to emerge from within him.

Parliamentary consideration of the two bills was accompanied by high drama, including attempts by pro-Matica forces to storm the Parliament building. Public opinion polls showed that many young people were won over to the Matica side. Speaker Mikloško, who had begun his political career before the revolution as a mathematician and as an organizer of the Christian underground movement (including a memorable demonstration for religious freedom, on the same square where our consulate building stood, that was brutally broken up by Communist police in March 1988), struggled valiantly to keep order in an increasingly restive chamber. Although he finally prevailed and got the government's bill passed on October 26, it was a classic Pyrrhic victory, because he suffered a loss of prestige that led to his political downfall in 1992.

The political struggle was ugly. Viťazoslav Moric, the fiery chairman of the Slovak National Party (SNS), called the Slovak Parliament "illegitimate," demanded new elections, and announced that proponents of the alternative "Slovak without exceptions" bill would start massive protest actions, including civil disobedience. The Parliament building was besieged by Moric and Markuš supporters. In those days, Mečiar was on the government's side of the struggle, and he declined to accede to shouts by the crowd that he address them from the balcony of the building—the same balcony from which he would proclaim Slovak sovereignty twenty-one months later. Once the bill was passed, a number of hunger strikers camped in the main square, determined to do the last for "our Slovak language." Some press accounts suggested that the strikers were surreptitiously fed at night and paid for their trouble; at any rate, after gaining publicity for several weeks and making their point, they were eventually persuaded to use other means to advance their cause.

In a memorable television debate, Mečiar lashed out at Markuš for his dishonesty. Never one to lose a political lesson, however, Mečiar surely realized the emotional impact of the issue, and soon afterwards showed that he would be out in front on any issue where the Slovak soul would be aroused.

The lesson of the debate on the language law was that government and opposition in post-Communist Slovakia were going through a testing period in dealing with political disagreements and distributing power. While the episode showed that democracy was not so weak that its institutions collapsed in the onslaught, it was clear that development of a democratic political culture was still a long way off and that such an end would require help from the United States and other interested parties. Significantly, a message from the European Parliament on the ramifications of a language law that failed to provide for minority rights was not criticized as interference in Slovak affairs; indeed, it was welcomed by those closest to the government as support for their own goals.

Because of the legacy of almost fifty years of dictatorial or totalitarian rule in the republic, students had never acquired a political orientation or ability to analyze events in their own society, and they therefore fell easy prey to people such as Moric. Researchers concluded that the inability of the educational system to train young people to form their own opinions by a process of rational thought was one of its main failings. More than a year later, I would confirm this assessment at first hand, when I spent a day visiting a nearby school and talking to students in a civic education class. When I asked them what were the tangible results of the 1989 revolution in their lives, the first reaction was "prices have doubled." The idea that Slovakia was now a democracy was still a dim concept for them that had little practical meaning.

The VPN also lost ground because of its intellectually based policies; some of its spokesmen were good analysts of the domestic situation but poor communicators with the masses. The VPN's slogan, "Return to Europe," also bespoke a preference for looking at external issues before internal ones.

To further explore these issues, I spent one morning at the Center for the Study of Social Issues located in Comenius University in Bratislava. The Center was staffed by sociologists mostly assembled from the VPN, and it was headed by Fedor Gál, head of the VPN Coordinating Center. I had met Gál the previous summer, when he was visiting Washington, D.C. With his fiery eyes, grey beard, and fast tongue, Gál made an immediate impression. In March 1991, one of his colleagues marveled to me how a "bearded Jewish liberal intellectual" could remain so long as the head of the leading coalition party in Slovakia not known for its kindness to the Jews. A week later, the VPN split asunder and those prophetic words about Gál's position found their meaning as he was hounded from his job, and eventually from Slovakia, as ugly threats were made against his person.

I was interested in speaking to Gál's associates, because they had mapped political culture and public opinion in Slovakia; they could explain the soil out of which the surface phenomena observed every day were growing. Some of their conclusions included the fact that the sociopolitical climate in Slovakia was more tense than in the Czech Republic; there was considerable friction in relations with national minorities; political culture had been badly demoralized by Communist rule; journalists were inflaming rather than calming public opinion; economic uncertainty played on public fears; education, unlike in other societies, had the effect of making Slovaks less tolerant of others; and there was already a distressing lack of interest or care for what was happening in the Czech part of the country. When boiled down to numbers, some 57 percent of Czechs and 41 percent of Slovaks

polled in late 1990 saw Czech-Slovak relations as more negative than positive; some 86 percent of Czechs and 90 percent of Slovaks saw relations with
the Gypsies as "predominantly negative." In the latter case, tension was fed
by insecurities related to increasing crime, where Gypsies figured at a rate
considerably higher than their percentage of the population would indicate.
Researchers found a "victim's mentality" as being predominant in the Slovak psyche—the sense of being a victim of the machinations of others was
high, whereas the idea that some Slovak actions would give non-Slovaks
reasons for insecurity was not widely held. Slovaks tended to sympathize
most with those who held high positions, such as Alexander Dubček (then
speaker of the Federal Assembly), Slovak Prime Minister Mečiar, his predecessor Milan Čič, and Federal Prime Minister Marián Čalfa (whose popularity, however, would soon plummet). Those who were regarded more as "politicians," such as Ján Čarnogurský and his brother Ivan, Gál himself, or that
archdemon of most Slovaks, the Hungarian activist Miklos Duray, were at
the tail end of the list. (Even after he became prime minister, Čarnogurský
never acquired significant popularity, probably due to a widespread popular
feeling that he "stole" the position from Mečiar.)

Polls also showed Slovaks beset by significant fears for their future.
The Slovak National Party, to some extent, attracted support by playing
on fears of unemployment, especially due to conversion of military industry, which many believed was "dictated" by the Czechs. Surprisingly, while
university-educated people are expected to be more tolerant than the rest
of the population, one researcher sadly noted that the opposite was true
based on Slovak polling data. One sociologist explained that this was to
be expected; intake of students under the Communist regime was based
on political criteria. Moral values were not taught, and indeed, students
came out of their university experience often convinced that moral values
could be a detriment to them in society. One university lecturer told me
that already, her students were exhibiting more of a Slovak national con-
sciousness than one based on common citizenship and interests with the
Czechs. There appeared little sympathy or concern for what was happening
in the Czech part of the country, and she sadly predicted (without realizing
how fast the process would occur) that in "one or two decades" this process
would ultimately lead to a Czech-Slovak separation.

4

THE GULF WAR AND SLOVAKIA

The Gulf War's effects hit me at 3:15 A.M. on January 16, 1991. I was awak-
ened by a call from our administrative counselor in Prague, Frank Coulter,
who informed me that American planes had just started to bomb Bagh-
dad. In my semi-sleepiness, I muttered "good," and then went back to bed.
At that time, since we had to move out of the consulate building, and our
house was far from finished, we had made an arrangement to stay in the
apartment of my Slovak language teacher, who was still in Washington,
D.C. The apartment was located in a housing block dating from the 1960s
located a few miles outside of town. Since moving in a week earlier, I had led
a nondescript existence. However, this was soon to change.

Because I was deemed to be at risk due to my position as principal officer
of the post, I had to hide my official car in a nearby underground garage
and accept the offer of the Federal Protection Police to ride with them to
and from work. While I quickly became the envy of my colleagues, my predicament had both positive and negative aspects. I had not yet received
clearance to hire my own staff, but now found myself with the services of
a full-time driver and a full-time receptionist. Both were police agents, and
their sole purpose was to ensure that no unauthorized persons entered our
premises. The flip side of this assistance was the hassle of having policemen
dog my every step wherever I went in Slovakia. I wound up making up a
joke about my situation: "Question: What is the difference between being
an American diplomat in Slovakia in 1989 and being one in 1991? Answer:

twenty meters. Before, the police would follow you from twenty meters behind; now, they walk right next to you."

I sometimes wondered whether my police protection was self-defeating. If my neighbors had no inkling as to my identity, now it was no longer a mystery. A policeman was stationed in the building all night, and the black Tatra 613 limousine waiting each morning and returning me at night was quite conspicuous. I told the policemen that I felt like a real Communist Party boss, getting the treatment a local official would have during the old days. On weekends, we got some respite by driving our own car into Vienna. Naturally, the Slovak policemen would have been happy to protect me all the way to the Austrian capital—after all, how often could they travel there with all expenses paid? They mercifully agreed to leave us at the Austrian border, after providing the very essential service of leading us through the one lane open in the wrong direction so that we would avoid the usual two mile-long backup of Slovak cars waiting to exit the country on a Saturday morning. The hazards we faced were not simply cars and trucks coming from the other direction, but also angry Slovak drivers who had spent several hours waiting in line themselves and did not appreciate line-jumpers, whether diplomats or not. Our policemen were solicitous enough to provide transportation all the way to the eastern capital of Košice in March, when I was invited to visit Slovakia's second city. They knew the roads well, although they drove with full abandon, explaining that one regulation exempted them from the need to obey rules, such as speed limits, that were meant for ordinary mortals. Several months later, during the visit of our deputy defense secretary to central Slovakia to see some defense plants, I was quite impressed at the way the delegation's police escort simply swept forward, taking up most of the oncoming line of traffic and forcing unsuspecting drivers to swerve out of the way. At one point, one of them didn't make it, and an accident occurred.

Coincident with arranging with the Slovak Ministry of the Interior to assure my own safety, I was also responsible for briefing and reassuring the American community in Slovakia, or at least that part of the community that I could locate. Most of the latter turned out to be young (and a few older) volunteers from the Education for Democracy organization—a group created the previous year by an American woman from Alabama whose objective was to teach English to Czechs and Slovaks (and later other nationalities), and in so doing, impart something of our culture and democratic ethos. At the EFD headquarters across the street from our consulate, I engaged Col. Jaroslav Svěchota, a deputy interior minister who was in charge of the working group that insured against terrorist incursions in

Slovakia during that period. Actually, at that time, the situation in Slovakia was quite calm; the Slovaks were monitoring those Middle Easterners who might be suspected of causing trouble. Col. Svĕchota also exuded a confident, professional demeanor that calmed his audience. Only later did I learn that his experience included fighting against "Western agents" with the former Communist secret police.[1]

5

THE VPN IMPLODES

After a few months of quiet that followed the uproar over the language law, Slovakia exploded in its next crisis in early March 1991. As is true in any war, the causes of the crisis were both immediate and longer term. On March 3, Mečiar, accompanied by his foreign minister Milan Kňažko, was on his way to the Slovak Television studio to deliver his usual Sunday night message to the nation. But this time, he was met at the door by Slovak Television director Peter Zeman, who allegedly told Mečiar (in answer to Mečiar's query) that he would have to deliver a tape of Mečiar's remarks to the VPN (Verejnosť proti násiliu or Public Against Violence) before he could broadcast them. Mečiar, infuriated, refused to allow his remarks to be taped or broadcast, calling the order issued by the VPN Coordinating Center "immoral and unethical." He told Zeman that his own behavior was at odds with the principles of democracy and ethics. Warning that he would not be censored, Mečiar left in a huff. Instead of their prime minister, viewers that night heard Kňažko, who attacked the VPN leadership for being a Communist Party-like central committee. He openly accused the VPN Coordinating Center of trying to execute the will of "several federal political representatives" (a formulation that included Slovaks in the federal government, such as then Prime Minister Marián Čalfa). Mečiar's antagonists, as expected, disputed his version of events. When I spoke with him, Gál, for one, deplored Mečiar's (and Kňažko's) almost nonexistent relations with the higher bodies of the VPN, but denied that the VPN was trying to censor the prime minister.

Thus began the final round in the internal crisis in the VPN that soon pulled it asunder, and more important, resulted in the bottom dropping out of the movement's public support. There were really two issues at stake: first, the relationship between Mečiar and the rest of the VPN; and second, the position the VPN would take on the "national issue."

The March 3 incident was preceded by the February 23–24 congress of the VPN held in Topoľčany. While Mečiar had stated his disinterest in obtaining the chairmanship of the movement, his opponents claimed that he had not only lobbied hard for the position, but had also threatened to resign when delegates rejected his plan for direct election of the chairman. While some of his VPN colleagues may have considered Gál as a successor to Mečiar, in the end, political realism set in. Slovaks were not yet at the point where they could consider someone of Gál's origins as a "true Slovak." Given his background, it was understandable that Gál was less than fully enthusiastic about Slovak nationalism. In the crisis that ensued, Gál would be toppled and would find it so uncomfortable to remain in Slovakia that he would decide to move to Prague later that year.

There was also a nastier side to this political bloodletting. On March 4, the Czech daily *Lidové Noviny* carried an article by Ivan Hoffman, a Slovak journalist who said that Mečiar had accused Jozef Kučerák, deputy prime minister and one of his fiercest opponents in the VPN, of having been a collaborator with the Communist secret police (STB). In rebuttal, Kučerák disclosed that Mečiar had sent him a letter on February 26 that alleged that Gál had information to the effect that Kučerák was registered as an STB collaborator. The intimation that Mečiar was playing the secret police card against two of his opponents was unsettling. In this confrontation, Mečiar's strength, as always, lay in his strong base of popular support. A February public opinion poll gave the prime minister an 89 percent positive rating, far above that of any other Slovak politician, including Alexander Dubček. Those intellectuals in the VPN who coalesced around Gál had displayed a remarkable lack of understanding of the political realities. One faction thought of starting a signature campaign in Gál's favor, but recognizing its futility, soon had to abandon the effort.

At a marathon meeting of the VPN Council that ended at 3:00 A.M. on March 6, the organization formally split into two, after Mečiar and Kňažko walked out to protest the council's issuing a statement that failed to back up Mečiar's and Kňažko's charges of censorship. Kňažko and Mečiar were joined by thirteen other deputies from the Slovak Parliament and formed their own faction, "Democratic Slovakia." In time, this faction would evolve into a new Mečiar-led "Movement for a Democratic Slovakia" (HZDS).

When I met a harried Gál on March 6, he noted that five of the eleven VPN ministers had joined Mečiar's new group (in addition to Mečiar and Kňažko, Michal Kováč, minister of finance; Rudolf Filkus, minister of economic strategy; and minister of privatization Augustin Marián Huska). While fifty-five of the seventy-five members of the council remained in Gál's camp, he was acutely aware of the precariousness of his own situation, and refrained from pressing for a vote on his proposals to oust Mečiar and Kňažko from their ministerial positions. He talked instead of building a bridge between factions, such as had happened after the fragmentation in the Czech Civic Forum, and confessed that he needed to take Mečiar's undeniable popularity into account when planning his next moves.

In late March, KDH officials expressed the hope that Mečiar could be persuaded to take a three-month leave of absence from politics, and thus avoid a bruising political battle. At that point, the KDH had the largest number of seats—thirty-one—in the SNR, as opposed to twenty-six for the VPN and twelve for Mečiar, with several more leaning his way. The KDH regarded Mečiar as a petty tyrant who rejected any control by others, especially from colleagues within his own party. The ire of the KDH had been raised the previous October, over the Andráš affair. It feared that Mečiar was motivated by the desire to take over that key post, which he himself had held prior to the June 1990 elections. Mečiar had vowed to "crush the KDH in 48 hours" during that confrontation, and in the current crisis tried to induce the KDH to support him by dangling before them the lure of some additional ministerial positions.

The other method under consideration at the time (and finally adopted) was to have the SNR Presidium vote "no confidence" in Mečiar, allowing speaker Mikloško to then name a new government. The anti-Mečiar group could not be sure it could find a "smoking gun" to indicate that the prime minister had clearly acted in an unconstitutional fashion. Paradoxically, Mečiar had been helped by, of all people, Jozef Bakšay, federal minister of foreign trade, a Slovak who foolishly told the press that there was a "plan" to remove Mečiar in two weeks. In so doing, Bakšay ensured a resolution that was the exact opposite of what he had intended.

Mečiar's opponents in the VPN included some highly competent individuals—persons who were on comfortable terms with Westerners interested in the fate of democracy in post-Communist Czechoslovakia. Unfortunately, on the other hand, many of them lacked a sense of political realism. They forgot that politics is the art of the possible and thought too much in terms of absolutes. The Coordinating Center of the VPN, despite protestations to the contrary by its chairman, Juraj Flamik, tried to act more like a central committee than as the nonpolitical secretariat it claimed to be. While Mečiar believed that a nonelected body should not have control over policies that affect the nation, the Coordinating Center felt that Mečiar should be responsible to the movement that had put him into power. When I asked Mečiar about the controversy several months later, after some prodding, he admitted that anti-Semitism was undoubtedly a factor contributing to Gál's troubles. However, he attributed the lion's share of the contretemps to Gál's "arrogant personality." He recalled that he had offered to step down in place of Gál, but that his initiative was refused. Knowing his fellow countrymen only too well, Gál was aware that one thing they were not prepared for was a Jewish prime minister.[1]

During this time, Mečiar received support in an unexpected manner, from an unlikely source. Ivan Hoffman, the journalist mentioned earlier who had become known as the troubadour of the November 1989 revolution (he composed its theme song, "We Promised Each Other Love"), was also a correspondent for RFE and a columnist for *Lidové Noviny*. In the latter, he reported that Marcel Stryko, a VPN MP for the eastern capital of Košice, had had a recent conversation with Soviet Consul General Valeri Orlov. Orlov allegedly had told Stryko that (a) the USSR would "not shed tears" if Slovakia became a separate state, and (b) it supported Mečiar as head of the VPN. This conversation allegedly took place shortly before the March events. Orlov, however, said the statements attributed to him were absolutely false and the Soviet Embassy in Prague issued a denial. Hoffman was criticized for printing unverified information.

6

AMBASSADOR SHIRLEY TEMPLE BLACK:
THE PERSON AND THE FLOWER

My relationship with Ambassador Shirley Temple Black illustrates both the problem involved in dealing with a superior in a national capital when one is based in a provincial one, as well as the issue of how to cope with a noncareer ambassador possessing her own system of logic as well as a very strong personality. My first meeting with Shirley Temple Black outside of the silver screen was in the State Department's Office of East European and Yugoslav Affairs in May 1990, when she was home on consultations. As was expected on that occasion, I told her I looked forward to working as a member of her staff in Czechoslovakia and reviewed my background. The ambassador was gracious and friendly. She had to formally approve my appointment to Bratislava before my assignment could be realized. Career people paid her the compliment of remarking that, for a political ambassador, she was not bad, and could have been a whole lot worse. When I gingerly raised the issue of how my reporting was to be sent out, she replied immediately that, as she was responsible for policy, everything would be sent through Prague.

From the beginning of 1991, I tried to make a habit of going to Prague once a month to attend meetings of our Country Team (the ambassador, deputy chief of mission or DCM, section and agency heads). I was also responsible for her program, not to mention her well-being, when she came officially to Slovakia. The only exception was her first visit after my arrival, which took place on January 20. The ambassador had not yet had the opportunity to call on officials of the new Slovak government formed the previous August, and for protocol reasons, until she had called on the prime minister and speaker of the National Council (the two highest proto-col positions in the republic), I was not authorized to deal with them. She came down to visit Bratislava again two months later to sign a cooperation agreement between the Ministry of Industry and the Trade and Develop-ment Program (TDP) for a feasibility study on a project that, it was hoped, would be very profitable for U.S. exporters. She next came to Slovakia in June 1991, accompanying Vice President Dan Quayle, who was to deliver an address at the tenth anniversary meeting of the Institute for EastWest Studies in the northeast Slovak town of Bardejov.

Shirley Temple Black would always be seen as a person with two iden-tities and two career tracks. Her prodigious accomplishments as a child movie star had given her a worldwide reputation that contributed much to her image. This label remained a part of her public personality long after she started a diplomatic career which included stints as one of our ambassa-dors at the U.N., as chief of protocol, ambassador to Ghana, and at the very end of the Communist regime of Gustav Husák, as ambassador to Czecho-slovakia. As I remembered so well, she was visiting Prague at the time of the Soviet-led invasion in 1968, and exited the country as part of an embassy-organized caravan. At the time I was following Czechoslovak developments from my vantage point as a summer intern at RFE in Munich.

Having a national icon as ambassador sometimes involved me in the strangest of ventures. At one point, I was contacted by one of Slovakia's leading horticulturalists. He was a breeder of gladioluses, and owned up to the fact that the Slovaks had been capitalizing on the Shirley Temple name since 1935, with a hybrid variety named for the child star without her authorization. Now, nearly sixty years later, the Slovaks were trying to make amends. They wanted her to approve a new variety, which could have up to four words in the name. Knowing that I made periodic visits to Prague, the "gladiolus man," as the ambassador liked to call him, asked me to take four varieties in the back seat of my car. When I got to Prague, I first stopped at John Evans's DCM residence, across the street from the ambas-sador's. Together with our wives, we trooped across the compound to the ambassador's residence, where a reception was about to be held. As I under-stand it, the Slovaks can now purchase the "Ambassador Shirley Temple Black" variety of gladiolus, which is the grand flower of the original "Shirley Temple" version of circa 1935, and one that she herself picked out.

In Slovakia, as well as in the Czech Republic, she had a celebrity status that went beyond her ambassadorial role. To some, she was known affec-tionately as "Širlejka" or little Shirley—the youngster who had danced and sang her way into their hearts during the hard days of the 1930s. One elderly Slovak even came to my office to proudly show me a tattered membership card from 1935 in the Shirley Temple Fan Club. Her name at times also prompted some humor, since her initials in both Czech and Slovak—STB—were also those of the dreaded Communist secret police. It was tempting to capitalize on this coincidence on occasion. During our July 4 reception in 1992, a few months after Mečiar had withstood a media campaign that alleged he was a onetime police agent, I couldn't resist informing the audience that I was in possession of "photographic evidence of Mr. Mečiar's collaboration with STB." I proceeded to hand him a copy of a picture that had been taken during Ambassador Black's last visit to Slovakia several months earlier, standing next to a smiling prime minister. This was a week before she departed the country for good, and Mečiar signed the back of their joint picture, "Don't forget me."

On other occasions, though, it was clear that the ambassador viewed Mečiar with a certain distance, if not suspicion. In the summer of 1991, when we were planning our list of candidates for the following year's International Visitor program—Czechs and Slovaks who would be nominated to visit the United States as official guests of the U.S. government—I had gone so far as to have Mečiar fill out a biographic data form, which was essential for processing candidates. However, to my chagrin, I found that the ambassador had, in the end, vetoed my recommendation with the explanation that first, Mečiar was "too controversial" and his nomination would complicate our relations with the Czechs; and second, he would use the trip for his own political purposes. The notion that Mečiar needed us more than we needed him was a fallacy that was understandable when viewed from outside Slovakia, but one which had nothing to do with Slovakia's political reality. It was quite clear by mid-1991 that Mečiar's party was so far ahead in the public opinion polls that he would be returning to power the following year.

I felt that it was in our interest to expose Mečiar to the United States, to help broaden his outlook and get him used to dealing with Americans. When I had to break the news to him that we would not nominate him, I tried to do so as gently as possible. I played down any notion that his controversial politics were getting in the way, and suggested that when he returned to power he plan a working visit and be received at a level commensurate with his position.

After Mečiar's smashing election victory in 1992, I received another hard knock that showed how different the ambassador's perspective was from my own in dealing with him. Feeling it was very important to establish a working relationship with him and his new government as soon as possible, I asked for an appointment. To my surprise, he agreed to a meeting a few days later, during which he was accompanied by Kňažko. When I reported to Prague that I would be meeting Mečiar and asked if there were any questions to address to him, I received a response which was unexpected. Instead of being congratulated for getting an audience with Slovakia's leader so soon after the crucial elections, I found myself out on a limb again. One colleague in the political section curtly informed me later that the ambassador felt my meeting with Mečiar so soon after the election had been "inappropriate" because it meant the United States was "anointing him." The whole point of the matter had been lost. It was not our function to anoint Mečiar or not to do so. The people of Slovakia had spoken and returned him to power in a free election. Especially at my level, contact with Mečiar was marginal in sending any kind of message about being or not being in "favor" with the United States. I was disappointed that this simple fact had not been recognized, and felt that the notion that a meeting with Slovakia's new prime minister could possibly have anything to do with the degree to which he was regarded as politically legitimate at home was not based on reality. In defense of my action, I noted with a certain pride in my description of the meeting that Mečiar had expressed his "full confidence" in me (an event that was not to be repeated). When I recounted all of this to my colleagues back in Washington, they were, as usual, highly supportive, and quite pleased that I had gotten to see Mečiar so soon after the election, when Czechoslovakia watchers in Washington were eager for every scrap of information that would give them an indication as to where the country was headed.

Since we were to host a quick but important visit by Vice President Dan Quayle in June 1991, I suggested to Ambassador Black that we insert a few words in Slovak into his remarks that would impress his audience and make Slovaks feel he cared about them. When President Ronald Reagan arrived in Finland in 1988 on a stopover before the Moscow Summit, I convinced his staff to add in Finnish the greeting "I wish happiness and good luck to all the Finnish people" at the end of his remarks during a speech in Helsinki, and Reagan gamely attempted the words in an utterly unknown language. However, the ambassador was less trusting than I was about Quayle's ability to communicate in Slovak. Thus, in an impromptu speech he gave in the main square of Bardejov, she allowed only one word in Slovak, *ahoj* (hi!), which she was confident would not be flubbed.[1] The Bardejov meeting commemorating the tenth anniversary of the Institute for EastWest Studies (now the EastWest Institute) was a major production, including the heads of state of the Visegrad countries (Poland, Hungary, then-Czechoslovakia), as well as many leading lights in the field of international relations. It was marred, however, by one incident that illustrates the tension between the professional diplomat and the political officials to whom he or she is responsible. During a planning meeting on security, a twenty-something member of Quayle's staff made the unfortunate remark that when the vice president was in the center of Bardejov, the town must be "shut down as tight as a concentration camp." Some in the audience were survivors of Nazi concentration camps, and they were appalled by the insensitivity of the young staff member. A few days later, the remark was leaked to the *International Herald Tribune*. John Mroz, president of the Institute, asked me what could be done. But at this point there was nothing else to do except to apologize on behalf of people who knew little about the country they were temporarily sojourning in and who did not bother to ask what was or was not appropriate behavior.

In late 1991, after initial misgivings (and clearance from Prague), I agreed to join my consular colleagues in doing a "written interview" for a local weekly that was planning to print a story highlighting the work of foreign government offices in Slovakia. While none of my colleagues thought it either necessary or politic to do so, I specially emphasized the fact that our consulate operated under the ambassador's direction, and that several months earlier she had presided over the rechristening of our building. Her picture was on my desk behind me when my photo was snapped for the series, but it was cropped by the newspaper when it was inserted, so the readers were deprived of the graphic evidence of the lady to whom I reported. I knew that I might be aggravating the sensitivity of some readers about "Pragocentralism," but that was part of the job.

The ambassador liked to remind us of her "sixty years in public relations," and she indeed offered a very sound bit of advice in replying to journalists' questions: "If asked for your personal opinion, just remember that in this business we have no personal opinions." On the other hand, some of her reactions could at times be hard to fathom. For example, we had made it a point to participate each August in ceremonies in Polomka, a town in central Slovakia. The ceremony commemorated the December 26, 1944, capture of an OSS team led by an American Navy commander (the Green Mission), whose purpose was to aid the Slovak insurgents against their Nazi-backed government in an ill-fated uprising that the Nazis subsequently crushed with great brutality. All who were captured were imprisoned in Mauthausen, Austria, and executed on January 19, 1945. In the mid-1980s, Ambassador William Luers had begun a tradition of journeying to the town, and then hiking to the top of the mountain, to the reconstructed site where the team had been captured, to lay a wreath in memory of their sacrifice. This was a polite way of reminding Slovaks that it was not only the Soviet army that had sacrificed for their liberation. The people of the town gratefully remembered the U.S. role and welcomed us with open arms. To underscore the fact that Americans had shed their blood for the freedom of Slovakia, I drafted a press release for the Voice of America (VOA) to broadcast, noting the historical background and our presence at the commemorations. To my great surprise, our public affairs officer subsequently informed me that the press release had gone no further than the ambassador's office. When I made my next visit to Prague, she told me she felt the episode was "too sad" to remember. Unfortunately, it seemed that she had not recognized the significance of the event. It is just such tragedies that bring people together to acknowledge their common fate. For example, in the Philippines, we regularly commemorate the common struggle of Americans and Filipinos in the hopeless cause of defending Bataan and Corregidor against the attacking Japanese in 1942. Their tragic and ultimately unsuccessful story does not preclude us from recalling their heroism.[2]

What really upset me, however, was an official-informal cable our desk officer casually handed me in early January 1992 while I was on a visit to Washington. The message was a verbal reprimand addressed to me by the ambassador. It seems she had been given a fax message sent to a junior member of the political section, who had shown up without prior notice in the consulate a few weeks earlier and who now had two reports on Slovak Romanies (Gypsies) I was asked to clear. I was taken aback because I had done a report on the same subject myself, and reached very different conclusions from those of my colleague. How could I clear a report when I disagreed with its conclusions? While I suppressed my discomfort at having someone take over a responsibility that I believed had been given to me to report on Slovak developments, I limited my remarks to the statement that "the logical division of labor between us is for you to concentrate on Czech and federal matters and for me to do Slovak." I also suggested that if there were not enough items on his agenda to keep him busy, he should spend a longer time in Slovakia, but report under my direction. Before I left for the United States in December, the officer called me to apologize, and I thought the matter had been settled. The embassy did forward to Washington both the Prague-based officer's report and my own. In sending out two contradictory reports on the same issue, the embassy effectively nullified the justification for my sending reports through Prague ("the Mission must speak with one voice").

The ambassador had somehow interpreted what I thought was a common-sense allocation of responsibilities into an "order" to the officer not to come to Slovakia—an "order" which she now explicitly "countermanded." She also lectured me as to what the proper relationship was between an ambassador and consul—one gives the orders and the second implements them. In Washington, I felt as though a ton of bricks had been unloaded on me. Sympathetic colleagues in our Office of East European and Yugoslav Affairs recommended that, since it was the ambassador speaking, I had to take what she said seriously, but on the other hand, I should not take the substance of her remarks too literally. I was also advised there was no point in trying to explain to her that she had misconstrued the interchange, but instead to make the obligatory gesture of apology that would calm her. Regarding myself as a member of a team operating under the ambassador's direction, I felt my effectiveness would be compromised if colleagues were coming unannounced to Slovakia and producing reports which reached conclusions which I found erroneous. I also feared that the ambassador's own credibility would be questioned back home if she allowed out two contradictory reports on the same topic. She misconstrued this, however, as some kind of premature "declaration of independence." Shortly before her departure from Czechoslovakia, she sent me a "you're a good man, but . . ." letter.[3] I decided there would be no purpose served by rehashing old misunderstandings, but wished her well and told her the story of the elderly gentleman referred to earlier in this chapter—a story which I hope warmed her heart.

7

MORE HUNGARIAN PROBLEMS:
GABČIKOVO, THE CONSTITUTION,
AND THE ROAD SIGNS

Hungarian-Slovak relations were not just burdened by disputes over the use of language. What was originally a dispute between Czechoslovakia and Hungary over the fate of the Gabčikovo-Nagymaros waterworks project gradually grew to dominate the Slovak-Hungarian agenda. The project was jointly agreed to by the Czechoslovak and Hungarian Communist regimes in 1977. It involved construction on the territory of both countries, and entailed diverting most of the Danube into a new ship canal on the Slovak side of the border. The purpose of the project was to improve navigation on the Danube, to control periodic floods that inundate the area (then most recently in August 1991) through the construction of drainage canals along the river, and to reap the benefits of hydroelectric power. This electricity would be produced by one station located in Slovakia at the end of the channel at the town of Gabčikovo, and another in Nagymaros, in Hungary, 150 kilometers downstream (270 and 100 GWh respectively). In 1989, under the pressure of Hungarian dissidents, construction stopped on the Hungarian portions of the project. The new anti-Communist government in Budapest soon began to pressure Prague not only to stop construction, but in fact to demolish the entire structure. The justification given was that an "ecological disaster" was in the making, including allegations that sufficient water would not be flowing through the old Danube bed. The Hungarians soon found other excuses, however. Their spokesmen decried the project as "changing the borders" between the two countries, since most of the Danube would now flow north of the river bed. Actually, the 1977 treaty stipulated that the border would remain the midflow of the river. What had changed, however, was in the fact that Danube river traffic, now diverted to the canal, would be flowing at this point entirely through Slovakia.

Because Czechoslovakia had completed about 90 percent of its portion of the project and Hungary had completed only 40 percent at the time the Hungarians did their about-face, there was clearly much less economic rationale for Czechoslovakia, especially for Slovakia, on whose territory the project was built, to accede to Hungarian demands. As they moved closer to independence, the Slovaks became the custodians of the project for Czechoslovakia. Their principal concern was losing the economic benefits that would accrue with the full operation of the project, especially because the completed waterworks would add about 10 percent to Slovakia's electrical energy producing capacity, or produce energy valued at about $200 million annually. In 1989, Slovakia imported about 22 percent of its electricity needs; nine-tenths of these imports were from the Czech Republic. When it became impossible to compromise with the Hungarians, whose government negotiator was given no leeway by the Hungarian Parliament except to discuss the demolition of the project, the Slovaks considered various options, ranging from completion according to the original plan (Plan A) to stopping construction (Plan F) or dismantling the projects and restoring the area to its original state (Plan G). In the end, the government settled on "Plan C," which allowed it to partially operate the project by additional construction of waterways on Slovak territory and the provision of 2.7 billion kWh of power (as compared with 3.7 billion as foreseen under the original plans). Slovak environmentalists immediately attacked the plan, arguing that it would interfere with the flow of the Danube and adversely affect the environment in both Hungary and Czechoslovakia.

While there was a broad political consensus—except with the Egyutelles Movement of Miklos Duray—in Slovakia that construction should continue to completion, the Slovaks were also beset with doubts from Prague. Then Federal Minister of Environment Antonin Vavroušek had strongly criticized the entire project while working at the Czechoslovak Academy of Sciences in Prague, taking a more limitationist view about the possibilities of generating electricity and a more alarmist view about the effect on drinking water supplies. Vavroušek also warned about the consequences should the Hungarians make good their threat to blockade the Danube if the Czechs and Slovaks proceeded without their agreement. Even Václav Klaus, then the federal minister of finance, surprised the Slovaks by remarks suggesting that the whole project was designed to enrich the Slovak "concrete lobby," telling the Slovaks, in effect, to find their own funds to finish it.

But there were other considerations as well. Most of those citizens living on the Slovak side of the area affected by the project were Hungarians, and some local officials, reflecting concerns of their constituents, voiced fear that materials used in the waterworks construction were not fail-safe, and that there was a risk of inundation if the structures failed. One mayor wryly told me that "many a home" in the area had been built with materials stolen from the project.

Outside of Duray, most Slovaks appear to have regarded the issue as political, not economic or ecological. At the same time, the constant play given in the Hungarian media to critics of the project aroused fears—never far from the surface—that the real Hungarian objective was to destabilize Slovakia and prepare the ground work for irredentist movements. When Hungarian television prominently featured footage of demonstrators trying to block the project in August 1991, some Slovaks thought the coverage was deliberately provocative. While critics of the project called it the height of "totalitarian megalomania," its defenders retorted that the laws of engineering, physics, and biology know no politics. But, in any case, the reputation of the parents and circumstances of its birth caused the legitimacy of the child to be put in question.

In the end, the Slovaks took full responsibility for continuation of the dam project, and it opened in October 1992 after Slovak dump trucks, in a seemingly never-ending operation, poured enough sand and boulders into the Danube to effectively force it into the new derivation canal entirely on their side of the border. This act caused Hungary to formally denounce the treaty and to take the matter to the International Court of Justice in April 1993. However, for the Slovaks, the completed if truncated project was a source of national pride. Its chief engineer, Julius Binder, acquired something of the aura of a national hero, battling the Hungarians and other opponents of the project nightly on television not as a politician, but as an engineer who was ready with the facts and figures to refute any arguments.[1]

If in the fall of 1991 most politicians not firmly in the nationalist camp were still making public statements expressing hope that Czechoslovakia would continue as a single state, Miklos Duray was having none of that. When I met him in November, he said the question was not if but when the Czechs and Slovaks would go their separate ways. Hard-headed pragmatism pushed him to the view that the Hungarian minority, despite fear over how it would be treated in an independent Slovakia, should not try to block independence. This is not to say that the Hungarians were sanguine over their future. While the 1990 language law had allowed minorities constituting 20 percent of the population in a given district to use their language in official business with government agencies, Duray, as well as many other Hungarian spokesmen, felt that some officials had turned the intent of the law on its head. It was now interpreted to mean that where a minority did not constitute 20 percent, it had no right whatsoever to use its language. Indeed, a list was allegedly promulgated indicating Slovak towns where only Slovak was to be used.

Hungarians from such places as Košice complained that they could not even conduct burial services in their native tongue. Others told horror stories of how patients were told to "go to Hungary" if they could not communicate with local hospital staff in Slovak. Slovak officials were often sent to work in predominately Hungarian areas without regard to their own linguistic preparation. But ethnic Slovaks were equally dissatisfied with the implementation of the law; the Matica Slovenská, for one, complained that the situation of Slovaks in those areas in the south where they were outnumbered by ethnic Hungarians had consequently deteriorated. Even those who were nominally political allies, such as Prime Minister Čalfa, Duray lamented, had succumbed to cheap "Hungary-baiting" for their own reasons. Čalfa used the argument that an independent Slovakia would inexorably fall prey to "Hungarian expansion." Additionally, Slovakia's Hungarians objected that a government commission established to review the implementation of the language law was composed of nationalists who "found" what they were looking for—instances where the law had negatively affected the Slovak population. Actually, the problem was deeper. While only 30 percent of those over age sixty can converse in Slovak, most of those below that age have at least a conversational ability in the language. However, the concentration of the Hungarian population in compact areas where they come into contact mainly with other Hungarians limits the reinforcement necessary to keep up a certain level of competence in Slovak. Hungarians also felt shortchanged by the lack of a Hungarian-language university; the percentage of Hungarian Slovaks studying at Slovak universities is less than half the percentage of students from Slovak families. About half of all Hungarians in Slovakia who have higher education wind up going to Hungary for that purpose. The attractions of remaining in an ethnically and culturally comfortable environment, and the ease of assimilation in Hungary, are a powerful magnet.

The approval of Slovakia's constitution on September 3, 1992, also created rancor with the Hungarians. The preamble, which starts off, "We the Slovak Nation," caused Hungarian objections on the ground that the Slovaks are not the only nation inhabiting the country. At the end of the preamble, however, reference is made to the citizens of the Slovak Republic as adopting the

Constitution. Curiously, although I rendered my small service for Slovakia in helping correct an English translation made by the Slovak Foreign Ministry, the final version of the first words was translated linguistically incorrectly, but politically in a way more palatable to outsiders, as "We the Slovak People." Since the formulation is followed by the words "together with members of the national minorities and ethnic groups living in the Slovak Republic," and as the concept "Slovak people" already encompasses all the people living in Slovakia, the finally approved translation is a non sequitur.

Article 33 of the Constitution states that membership in a national minority or ethnic group (the last term refers to the Gypsies or Romanies) may not be used to the detriment of any individual. Article 34 allows minorities to develop their own cultural heritage, receive and disseminate information in their own tongue, form associations and cultural institutions, be educated in and be able to use in official communications their own tongue, and participate in making decisions that affect their specific interests. The Article's third paragraph, however, was particularly galling to the Hungarians, as it prohibits using these rights to threaten Slovakia's sovereignty or to "discriminate against other citizens." While no one has claimed that these are their objectives, the notion that minorities are budding irredentists or that the majority must be protected from the minority was seen as a slap in the face by many Hungarians. Of course, the roots of this paragraph go back to the Slovak fear that the Hungarian minority would deliberately cultivate use of its language with the ultimate aim of looking south for its loyalties. While the Slovaks saw such constitutional provisions as a defensive form of insurance, the Hungarians regarded it as placing in the highest law of the land the presumption that they are not deemed sufficiently "trustworthy."

The situation was further exacerbated by moves taken by Roman Hofbauer, minister of communications in the second Mečiar government, to implement provisions of the 1990 language law dealing with road signs. Hofbauer was a typical example of a politician who sought to find his niche in nationalism. The law stipulated that road signs were to be in the official language—Slovak—but did not rule out the possibility of using signs in the local language in addition, where warranted. Hofbauer decided to remove any Hungarian names from road and street signs in order to keep within his strict interpretation of the language law, as well as to "avoid confusion" by having a motorist see different names for the same town. The Slovaks agreed to some adjustments in Hofbauer's program as the price for admission to the Council of Europe in June 1993, but he persisted until the realities of Slovakia's external relations forced some compromise.

When I asked Mečiar about the matter shortly after his election victory in 1992, he asserted that nowhere else in Europe did minorities have the right to signs in their own language. I politely recalled the Finnish case, where localities with a minority population have signs with two names for towns—the upper name for the majority in the town and the lower name for the minority (the upper name in some towns in northern Finland is not Finnish but the language of native Lapps). But to him, such logic was irrelevant, even when the Hungarians pointed out that Slovaks used signs in their own language in some Hungarian villages where they lived. The Slovaks also feared that the legalization of Hungarian names—especially those that had been used before 1918—was a kind of creeping "linguistic annexation"—a prelude to the real thing. While Hofbauer did not touch bilingual street signs (as opposed to road signs), his minions wanted to be sure that street signs were only the Hungarian translation of Slovak names, rather than entirely different names.

As so often in recent history, the Slovak position on the road sign issue was one of being penny-wise and pound-foolish as far as their political capital was concerned. The result was that, as Slovakia was looking forward to full acceptance in Europe and elsewhere, its government's refusal to give the Hungarians their due on road signs was giving it the aura of a country whose leaders obstinately fought for a policy that was inconsistent with standards followed elsewhere in Europe.

8

CZECH-SLOVAK RELATIONS

The question of the Czech-Slovak relationship underlay everything that transpired during my tenure in Slovakia. The attempts to reestablish that tie in a way that would be acceptable to both nations caused much of the political drama of the period, and it was the foundering of those attempts that led to the political breakup of the country in 1993.

Despite the ethnic, cultural, and linguistic similarities between Czechs and Slovaks, the two nations that made up nearly nine-tenths of the population of the country saw their identity in very differing ways. For the Slovaks, their identity as a nation was the primary one; for the Czechs, their identity did not exist outside that of the Czechoslovak state. Although the only reform of the Prague Spring of 1968 that the Soviets allowed to go ahead after occupying the country was federalization, the "Czechoslovak Federal Republic" approved in October 1968 and that went into effect in January 1969 actually was a unitary state by another name. While a number of ministries (e.g. culture and education) reverted to the republics, the reimposition of totalitarian control meant that a strong center would concentrate all power in its hands regardless of the intention of the federalization law. The federalization idea had been a response to ferment in Slovakia that was in evidence since 1963, when Slovaks—especially writers and intellectuals—demanded a loosening of strict control emanating from Prague. Had the invasion and the following "normalization" not occurred, federalization might have evolved into a meaningful new relationship between Czechs and Slovaks. Since that did not happen, the issue of the

Czech-Slovak relationship was bound to reappear once the lid of totalitarian control had been lifted.

Even in the post–November 1989 days of political liberalization, many Slovaks continued to feel that the Czechs were dominating the relationship. In the main, the Slovaks believed that their deteriorating economic position relative to the Czechs after economic reforms began in 1990 was due to the view that these reforms reflected Czech, not Slovak, priorities. But there were other instances of perceived hurt. One noted doctor, who was far from being a nationalist, complained to me that opportunities for participation in exchanges were often monopolized by the Czechs. He said the Slovaks were informed of opportunities to go abroad usually a few days before a program began, and by then there was insufficient time to pick candidates and make arrangements.

Two university student leaders who visited my office in November 1990 also used the opportunity to vent their displeasure with the way their Czech colleagues were treating them. They came to complain that they had not been invited to President Havel's reception for President George Bush two days previously. According to their account, twenty student leaders were supposed to have been included on the invitation list, but the Czechs kept the invitations for themselves. I regretted the incident but assured them we were not responsible for invitations issued by President Havel's office. I also assured them that an important reason for reopening our consulate was to assure that the Slovak point of view was adequately considered in our relations with their country.

Another problem that really bothered them was the passage of a law on November 16 by the Federal Assembly that turned over properties of the former Communist-controlled Socialist Youth Movement (ZSM) to the state. They felt the law had been passed almost in secret, and that the decision not to place these properties in the hands of local student organizations was a mark of insensitivity that would cause more political ferment that surely was not needed. Typically, their reaction failed to take into account the fact that the Assembly's move affected the interests of Czech students as much as their own. The problem was not so much Czech versus Slovak as federal versus regional. The Slovaks had insisted on separate representation in the European International Student Bureau, and on alternating representation with the Czechs in international bodies when separate Slovak membership could not be arranged. They also noted, not atypically, that they had their own problems with colleagues from Košice, the capital of eastern Slovakia, where Prague was seen in more benign terms than Bratislava, and where compromise with "Pragocentralism" was more likely.

Under Čarnogurský's guidance, his Christian Democratic Movement (KDH) conceived the idea of a state treaty between the Czech and Slovak republics to regulate their future links. This notion was intended to meet the Slovak desire to show that relations were being determined by two sovereign states that would then voluntarily cede some of their sovereignty to a federal entity. The KDH leadership expressed the view that a state treaty was the "last chance" to save the federation, and feared that the out-of-hand rejection of the idea by some Czech officials meant that the project would move nowhere. The Christian Democrats, while leaning somewhere toward the middle of the Slovak spectrum of opinion on the federal issue, strongly rejected Havel's idea of a federal constitution, seeing it in effect as putting the cart before the horse. The idea of a treaty was to ensure that mere political declarations signed in the past by both sides, such as the Pittsburgh Declaration of 1918 between Czech and Slovak leaders signed in the United States, or the 1945 Košice Declaration (which reestablished the Czechoslovak state at the end of World War II, and was signed in that eastern Slovak city shortly after its liberation), would not be subsequently broken. In my discussions with KDH leaders, I recalled that the problem was not so much that a "treaty" would have a higher force than a declaration. Instead, the issue was that totalitarian states had a history of breaking any agreement they chose to, no matter what level it was signed on.

While 1991 public opinion polls gave strong backing to a common state even among Slovaks, the KDH argued that these polls begged the essential point. The nexus of Slovak opinion was in favor of equality with the Czechs; if an adequate feeling of equality could not be achieved under a federation, then other solutions would come into play. For the Slovaks, the federal government in 1991 was regarded as a Czech show with some token Slovak participation; the Czechs clearly did not share that view. While one might point to the inclusion of such Slovaks as Prime Minister Marián Čalfa in the federal government, other Slovaks argued that Čalfa, who went to Prague at the age of eighteen and has a Czech wife, is himself more Czech than Slovak (after the 1992 elections, Čalfa decided to make his home in Prague rather than return to Slovakia). Some members of the KDH also perceived Slovaks such as Foreign Trade Minister Jozef Bakšay as an individual who allowed himself to be manipulated by Czechs, whereas Minister of Economic Strategy Pavol Hoffmann was regarded as more attuned to the international rather than the Slovak dimension of his portfolio because of his Jewish origins. To be sure, those holding this view would quickly argue that it was not anti-Semitic; however, its prevalence does indicate that some Slovaks felt that members of their Jewish community could not be relied upon to have a true-blue "pro-Slovak" outlook. What was interesting from this conversation was the remark expressed by a nominally pro-federalist party official implying that unless the Slovaks were able to negotiate a solution that afforded them a sense of their own statehood, they would take unilateral measures to achieve that end. In such a case, rational arguments, such as the certainty that a hefty economic price would have to be paid, were lost in the wind.

In March 1991, a group of nationalist-oriented intellectuals tried to force the issue by coming out with a detailed program for a declaration of Slovak sovereignty. Taking similar pronouncements that were erupting in Yugoslavia and the then Soviet Union as a point of departure, if not an actual model, the purpose of this measure was to assert that the Slovaks could do anything they wanted to without being subject to the will of the Czechs. Already in January, in a conversation with Ambassador Black in Bratislava, Čarnogurský remarked that some Slovaks were arguing, "If the Baltics can declare their laws superior to Moscow, why cannot we do the same vis-à-vis Prague?" In my own later conversations with Čarnogurský, he kept returning to the examples set by the Soviet republics and Yugoslavia: individual republics in both federations were declaring their sovereignty and getting away with it. This reality emboldened Slovak nationalists and created a new bottom line against which the discussion about future relations with Prague would be conducted. Whatever their feelings about a declaration of sovereignty, Čarnogurský reasoned, the Slovaks overwhelmingly supported the view that the sovereignty of the republics came first, and that the sovereignty of the federation was only derivative.

The language of the proposed declaration blurred, if not erased, the distinction between the constituent of an independent state and an independent state itself. All the attributes demanded were those associated with independent states: an independent member of the European and world community, having state rights "in accordance with the norms of international law," having the sole right to grant citizenship and speak in the name of its people abroad, having its own banking, financial, credit, and customs system, having Slovak laws take precedence over any other laws, creating a separate armed forces, and making future relations with other states (read: the Czechs) the subject of the "free and voluntary decision of the Slovak republic."

From that time on until independence, the battle over a sovereignty declaration was part of the semantic war against the Czechs. By choosing a less offensive nomenclature for independence, the Slovaks could avoid using the dreaded I-word and absolve themselves of the accusation of being separatist. Indeed, the constitutional law of 1968 itself had referred to the two republics that made up the federation as being "sovereign states." The Slovaks were simply fulfilling a promise of 1968 that had not been kept. Of course, the 1968 law was meaningless on this score, because all aspects of policy were controlled by the Communist Party.

The attitude toward a declaration of sovereignty soon became a litmus test of where a politician stood. The pro-independence Slovak National Party (SNS) warned that any doubting of the rights contained in such a declaration would be a "betrayal" of Slovak national interests. Čarnogurský, then prime minister, said he was in favor of Slovak sovereignty, but wanted it achieved by constitutional means, through a treaty with the Czechs. Fedor Gál, the embattled chairman of what was still the majority wing of the VPN, dismissed the idea as the work of "a few extremists" when we met on March 6, but admitted that a demonstration organized by Markuš and the Matica five days hence "would cause us pain."

In reporting back home, I tried to make clear the implications for the United States. While our policy at the time was tilted in favor of continuing a common state, I observed that the federal republic which we supported would not survive the implementation of a declaration of sovereignty. The concept of a constituent republic nullifying national laws, having its own military, post, and customs, and entering into diplomatic relations with other states and international organizations was incompatible with the maintenance of a common state.

Soon after forming his Movement for a Democratic Slovakia, Mečiar joined the bandwagon for a declaration of sovereignty. Because the Slovak National Party minced no words in coming out directly for independence, he was conveniently able to depict his HZDS as centrist on the issue. Mečiar's program came out for a confederational relationship between the two republics—it maintained loose ties but allowed them to act, for all practical purposes, as independent states. When I translated for him verbatim guidance from our European Bureau in Washington on Yugoslavia—underscoring that the United States would accept any framework that respects the free and democratic choice of the people of that country regarding their future—I also pointed out that the general drift of U.S. policy in Czechoslovakia would be consistent with that statement. Mečiar was clearly pleased that the United States was signaling an alteration in its previously absolute opposition to any changes which would jeopardize the existence of a single Czechoslovakia. Not too long thereafter, he began to taunt his opponents, noting that the United States itself was not wedded to a continuation of the federal republic. Of course, the United States still hoped that the Czechs and Slovaks would opt for a continuation of a single state. Up until several months past the 1992 elections, he would continue to use the "confederational" language, although for tactical reasons, he would sometimes obfuscate the issue, talking about "several models, including the federal," which could determine the future course of Czechoslovakia.

Developments in Yugoslavia also convinced those who were dissatisfied with the status quo in Czechoslovakia that their instincts were correct. In June 1991, I had a private meeting with three HZDS officials who had served in the first Mečiar government and would attain high positions after the HZDS election victory a year later. At that point, Slovenia was on the verge of declaring its independence, and the breakup of Yugoslavia was on the horizon. During a visit to Yugoslavia, then Secretary of State James Baker made statements condemning Slovenian and Croatian moves toward independence, and at a June 1991 CSCE meeting in Berlin, he uttered the famous phrase "we don't have a dog in that fight," to indicate that the United States had no intention of getting involved in the Yugoslav imbroglio. Several of my interlocutors considered those remarks to be ill-advised, only encouraging military intervention by a Communist regime in Belgrade that aimed at preserving its hold on the country by military means. Significantly, at this point even Čarnogurský was moved to note that the impact of the events in Yugoslavia would be "more than incidental" in his own country.

The general view expressed was that the Czechs still held too much power in the country. When Federal Finance Minister Václav Klaus, a Czech, was asked to set up a separate bank for financing conversion projects in Slovakia, he curtly dismissed the idea as "not needed." One of my HZDS interlocutors referred caustically to a meeting that had just been held in Bratislava, sponsored by the U.S.-financed Charter 77 Foundation, which had noted the price that Slovakia would have to pay if it became independent. "Cooked to order" was the verdict about these conclusions. The notion that the European Union (then the European Community) would not accept a separate Slovak entry was also rejected.

On October 28, 1991, President Havel returned from a trip to the United States directly to Slovakia, to participate in ceremonies marking the country's seventy-third anniversary of independence, and to strengthen federalist forces in Slovakia. The visit was a near-disaster. I joined my consular colleagues at the Lion Monument on the banks of the Danube, which was the traditional gathering point of those celebrating Czech-Slovak brotherhood. Havel came to lay a wreath at the monument, and he was joined by a number of federal ministers. But except for the ministers and consuls, almost no one showed up for the occasion. For the first time in my life, I had witnessed a ceremony taking place almost entirely without bystanders. Where were all the Slovaks?

Havel next went to the Slovak National Theater, where he was guest of honor at a ceremonial program, which was followed by a short trip to the SNP Square two blocks away for speech-making. The Square, however, had been taken over by the opposition, as had already so often been the case. Many of the estimated ten thousand persons who assembled to hear the president sympathized with the independence movement, which mounted its own counter-rally. This group threw eggs at the podium, hitting several speakers. By the time Havel arrived at the podium, the situation had gotten out of hand. In an effort to calm the crowd, Havel appealed for two minutes of silence in memory of all those who had lost their lives for the freedom of the Czech and Slovak nations. However, his call went unheeded, and was interrupted by a barrage of catcalls and fisticuffs. After two minutes, Havel was forced to leave the stage, and that was the last time he ever attempted to address a rally on the main square in Bratislava.

By February 1992, the Czechs had come quite a distance from their original insistence that any kind of Czech-Slovak arrangement based on a treaty would be tantamount to destroying the federation. However, the KDH position on the issue was badly split. Ján Klepáč, who represented the nationalist wing within the movement (from which he would soon split off), said he would not accept the treaty, and further efforts to find a negotiated arrangement that would preserve the common state were doomed to failure. A proposal to the 105-member KDH council in late February failed by one vote to gain the necessary two-thirds majority for support. The KDH wound up in a deadlock, with Klepáč unable to get the movement to denounce the Milovy agreement,[1] and Čarnogurský unable to get a forthright approval. Shortly thereafter, the SNR Presidium deadlocked 10–10 on the issue, and that was the end of negotiations. A government that could not command a majority in Parliament could not take a step on this crucial question. At this point the Hungarians began to hedge as well, and eight of the fourteen Hungarian deputies in Parliament threatened not to vote for the treaty unless it contained a clause guaranteeing the collective rights of minorities. Such a clause was politically impossible for the Slovak leadership to incorporate.

But there were other problems. The draft treaty contained nothing that referred to the two republics as its subjects; the best the Slovaks could get was the "implication" that this was so. Secondly, Klepáč found a strange bedfellow in Czech National Council Deputy Chairman Ján Kalvoda, who argued that the draft could not be characterized as a treaty, but only as a "legislative initiative." With both the Czech and Slovak opposition agreeing that the basic requirement of the Slovaks was not incorporated in such an important document, it had nowhere to go in Slovakia. One of my interlocutors from the KDH, who had just returned from the negotiations, bitterly remarked that the Czechs "had not learned any lessons from the past" and were still in a "take it or leave it" mood. Some Slovaks who fought hard for a treaty felt that they were also undercut by other Czech politicians. Václav Klaus, later Czech prime minister and president, was reluctant to accept the treaty idea. Several Slovak officials at the time complained that their Czech counterparts were behaving as cold-blooded economic pragmatists who saw centralization of administration and economic power in Prague as the best way to achieve their economic goals. The Slovaks felt these officials lacked understanding of the political dimension and could not grasp the depth of Slovak yearnings.

However, the KDH leadership also failed at a crucial moment. It had admittedly not been sufficiently alert when the SNR Presidium deadlocked, and four of the six KDH members on the Presidium voted with the opposition. At the last moment, the ever-calculating post-Communist Party of the Democratic Left (SDL) also joined the opposition, despite its avowed approval of a common state. In March, Klepáč and Čarnogurský had their political parting of the ways, with Klepáč bolting to form his new Slovak Christian Democratic Movement (SKDH).

With the SKDH both in the government and in opposition, the drive for a declaration of sovereignty became another of the surreal features of Slovak politics. On April 1, 1992, Minister of Forestry and Water Economy Viliam Oberhauser, acting for the SKDH, introduced a measure in the SNR to declare that "The Slovak Republic is the sovereign state of the independent (*svojbytneho*) Slovak nation, a state which secures for all its citizens equal rights and freedoms without regard to nationality, ethnic background, race, religion, and world outlook. At the same time, we declare that we will continue to respect the legally valid constitutional situation and that further steps will be taken in accordance with it." Čarnogurský's government regarded the move as just so much political mischief, and resorted to the tactic of walking out of the SNR to make sure a quorum was not present and that voting could not take place. But Oberhauser reintroduced his measure in the next session of Parliament, which began on April 27. On May 7, at its last session before the elections, the declaration was the last item to be taken up. On a motion introduced by the Greens and supported by the SDL, it was decided that a three-fifths margin would be needed for passage, whereupon the SDL voted for the measure, knowing that it would not pass. The debate was fierce and emotional, but in the end, the matter was left for the Parliament that would be elected in June to sort out the matter, and a month later, finally pass its own sovereignty declaration on the HZDS's watch.

Some of Čarnogurský's political allies—especially in the ODÚ (the successor party to the VPN, which for a short time used the transitional title of ODÚ/VPN)—evinced a certain degree of irritation over what they felt to be his constant shifts toward or away from a pro-independence stand. In one interview, for example, the KDH leader talked about the Slovaks entering the European Community on their own—surely a reference to independence. Jozef Kučerák, then ODÚ deputy chairman, expressed exasperation that Čarnogurský was carrying out a contradictory policy—supporting the common state in negotiations with the Czechs, but surrounding himself with politicians who negated that stand (shortly before the break with Klepáč when Čarnogurský assumed a more forthright pro-federalist stand).

9

★ ★ ★ ★ ★ ★ ★

COUNTDOWN TO THE 1992 ELECTIONS

In early 1992, the VPN (now using its transitional name of ODÚ/VPN) stood at a precarious four percent in the public opinion polls—somewhat higher than the nadir reached after the split with Mečiar's forces, but insufficient to return to Parliament. The national and leftist opposition—the HZDS, the SDĽ, and SNS—benefited from the existing downturn in the standard of living and exploited uncertainties over Slovakia's economic future to maintain their strong lead over the government coalition. Within the coalition itself, commitment to a common state in cooperation with the Prague-based Civic Democratic Party (ODS) and Civic Democratic Alliance (ODA) was the cement holding them together. On the other hand, there were differences of policy and philosophy that separated the ODÚ from their main coalition partner, the KDH.

Pro-government political forces based their dwindling optimism about the June elections on the hope that privatization would proceed far enough to give rise to an entrepreneurial class that would look to the governing coalition to protect its interests. ODU/VPN leaders in early 1992 voiced the fear that a right-wing victory in the Czech Republic, along with a left-wing victory in Slovakia, would vitiate prospects for the federation's survival. They feared that Slovak leftists—among whom they included Mečiar and his HZDS—would try to annul privatization, property restitution, agreements with the IMF, and coupon privatization (transfer of assets of state-owned firms to private citizens, who could then use them to become shareholders or sell the coupons to others). The ODU/VPN hoped that Slovaks would understand that separation would have negative consequences not only in their own personal pocketbooks, but also in the political and geopolitical realms.

As Prime Minister Čarnogurský explained it in early 1992, the KDH's point of departure was the insertion of the social dimension into the political and economic plan for the transformation of the country. He wanted a broader spectrum of people to wind up as property owners and intended to limit the participation of investment funds which were then springing up. Of particular concern, not only to Čarnogurský but to Slovaks in general, was the fact that the republic had attracted a small fraction of total foreign investments to Czechoslovakia. While he bandied about the figure of 5–10 percent, others suggested it was about 15–20 percent.

Klepáč's idea in forming the SKDH was calculated on the assumption that his new party would attract the bulk of KDH supporters, who he felt were more nationalist than their leadership. He also banked on becoming an attractive coalition partner or at least political ally of Vladimír Mečiar. However, my conversations with some of Mečiar's associates showed that they were keeping the SKDH at arm's length. They considered the new party to be "too clerical," but might have added that Klepáč, by trying to rehabilitate Father Jozef Tiso (the wartime leader of the puppet Slovak state who was executed as a war criminal in April 1947) and by bringing into his campaign such questionable figures as the Australian-Slovak Tiso apologist František Vnuk, was making himself more of a liability than any potential asset. One of our employees attended a campaign rally at which Vnuk spoke, where he argued unconvincingly that "Tiso was not on the list of war criminals" and that his trial was "politically motivated." Other speakers included Deputy Minister of Finance Marián Tkač, a former Communist who would become the temporary head of the Slovak National Bank after independence, and who now argued that there was no risk of economic collapse after a declaration of independence. But Mečiar paid as much attention as anyone to the polls, many of which were done by his own HZDS polling unit and which correctly predicted that Klepáč would not return to the SNR.

One of the clear disappointments for Mečiar was Alexander Dubček's decision to join the Social Democrats. Dubček had first assured him that he would announce his candidacy on the HZDS ticket, but at the last minute, he reconsidered. When Ambassador Black met Mečiar on February 19, he was quite confident that Dubček would join his team, and expected (without saying so directly) that Dubček would eventually become Slovakia's first president. Mečiar, according to one source, had promised Dubček that the HZDS would campaign on a line of "freer association" with the Czechs, but in the end, Dubček felt the HZDS was too far from his conception of keeping a common state. Dubček's decision also was disappointing to Peter Weiss and the SDĽ, because Dubček ruled out a coalition between the Social Democrats and Weiss's group. This position was dictated by the feeling that the SDĽ was still not purged of its taint as a Communist, albeit reformist, party, despite the expressed desire of its leadership to win acceptance as a genuine socialist party. As it turned out, the much-vaunted "Dubček effect" proved to be a chimera. While the Social Democrats were able to win election to one house of the Federal Assembly, given the fact that the institution was already in a phase of self-destruct, they could do little to influence events. When the results were counted, it appeared that Dubček's influence had severely waned, and that he was regarded more and more as a relic of the past than a symbol of the future. I had the opportunity to meet Dubček both in Washington, D.C., when he received an honorary degree from American University, and again in Slovakia. While no one could doubt his honesty—he had paid a considerable personal price in 1968 and after for his refusal to compromise his views—in 1989, he represented a link with the past that was essential to the transition to a democratic government but whose relevance rapidly wore off thereafter. While he was also a strong believer in the idea that Czechs and Slovaks should stay together, his views increasingly became less and less relevant to the political realities that were shaping the Czech-Slovak future.

Perhaps more in sorrow than in anger, Mečiar had to address the painful fact that Dubček, in the end, declined to join the HZDS team, and instead took over the chairmanship of the fledgling Slovak Social Democratic Party (SDSS). He predicted—quite correctly—that the much-vaunted "Dubček effect" would be of much less help to the SDP than it thought. He believed Dubček's mind was weakening, and criticized the venerable hero of 1968 for living in the past—trying too hard to pick up the pieces left by the Soviet invasion, rather than starting from the real situation of 1992. When Dubček died in November as the result of complications suffered from an automobile accident on the Prague-Brno highway that summer, Mečiar and many other Slovaks mourned his passing. However, I felt that Dubček had become something larger in death than he had been in life—a phenomenon similar to what followed in the United States with John F. Kennedy in 1963 and in the Philippines in 1983 with Ninoy Aquino, after both fell victim to assassins' bullets.

Mečiar and Kňažko, along with journalist Milan Augustin, came to the consulate general on March 31 to get visas for a trip to the United States. They had been invited by Leo Danihels, a Slovak-American millionaire who would soon become the new president of the Slovak World Congress. The trip was scheduled to take place in April, but was canceled at the last minute. According to Mečiar, it was because the government was planning to "arrest" him when he got back. In truth, any government that contemplated arresting Mečiar in the spring of 1992 on any charge would have found itself with its back to the wall in face of a storm of protest and sympathy that would inevitably follow. At issue were allegations that Mečiar was a mysterious police agent, code-named *Doktor*, who had, among other things, been assigned to keep tabs on Alexander Dubček during the old days.

The previous day, Mečiar had called a press conference to denounce the charges as manufactured, and to hint that the trail of those charges led directly to the Prague Castle. Referring to President Havel's possible re-election later that year, he asked how he could even think of voting for someone who was involved in the "campaign" against him. Mečiar brought to his press conference no less a personage than Richard Sacher, former federal interior minister, who supported his claim that there was no substance to the accusation. As far as Mečiar was concerned, the charges were "ordered" by federal officials to effectively destroy his chances of running in the 1992 elections. Additionally, the desire to keep out members of the president's office made him decide to close the congress of the HZDS to outsiders. I had previously approached some members of the HZDS with the suggestion of inviting accredited foreign diplomats to the congress to promote closer contacts between the movement and its counterparts in various foreign countries. There was still extreme sensitivity over "information leaks" and the decision was made to invite no one. Mečiar also displayed a feel for realpolitik, noting that Václav Klaus had recently distanced himself from the HZDS, commenting that Klaus "had to do that" to get reelected in Prague. What did register with Mečiar, though, was that Klaus had resisted the temptation to get on the "anti-Mečiar bandwagon."

Even before the 1992 campaign was officially launched, the HZDS kept itself in the public eye through a series of mass public meetings. One of these, which took place March 4, attracted some 2000 participants to the Park of Rest and Culture on the banks of the Danube near the center of Bratislava. The HZDS explained these meetings as necessary because of its alleged "exclusion" from the mass media. All the big guns of the movement were there, from Mečiar, to his deputies Huska and Kňažko, writer Dušan Slobodník (already correctly rumored to be the next minister of culture), former Bratislava mayor Roman Hofbauer, and Gabor Zelenay, father of the controversial Roman, who had been Kňažko's deputy at the Slovak Ministry of Foreign Relations. Mečiar opened the proceedings, using the occasion to vent Slovak "national feelings," and HZDS officials received a maximum of three minutes to answer questions submitted from the floor. They used short, simple answers, addressing the man in the street in his own idiom. They showed interest in people's problems and resorted to similes and folk language. Kňažko was especially effective; toward the end of the meeting, he got up and announced to the delighted crowd that "I have to go in a few minutes to help my wife with the baby and to wash the dishes."

At another rally the following day, a carefully orchestrated meeting began with a women's choir from central Slovakia singing the Slovak portion of the national anthem, omitting the Czech portion. Mečiar was presented with a cake by two girls in folk costumes and lit a candle on it to symbolize the HZDS's first anniversary. On substantive questions, speakers referred to Slovakia as already a sovereign state, sought to implement cooperation with the Czechs following the model used by the Benelux countries, and said a declaration of sovereignty would come first, followed by a Slovak constitution, and only then, a treaty with the Czechs. Mečiar promised to fight unfair policies such as returning property to former nobility or wealthy persons, and promised job opportunities to all (the original HZDS program draft promised, Communist style, the "right to work" to all, but a looser formulation was later adopted). Mečiar warned about more "fabricated stories" about him and refuted accusations of collaboration with the former secret police. He announced that former Trade Union chief Roman Kováč, former federal prosecutor Ivan Gašparovič, and Alexander Dubček would be on the HZDS candidate list and appear at future meetings (as explained above, Dubček shortly thereafter declined Mečiar's offer and decided to head the Social Democrats instead).

I was on the scene in the auditorium of the Technopol foreign trade enterprise building in the Bratislava suburb of Petržalka in mid-May to watch the HZDS kick off its campaign. When my presence was noticed, I was immediately invited to sit in the front row. I declined, in order to avoid being identified as a participant, rather than an observer, in the proceedings. In keeping with the HZDS's populist tune of the times, I explained to the audience's delight that I would rather stay with the "ordinary mortals." The scene began on a surrealistic note, when all the lights went out, keeping the audience sitting for a time in total darkness. Outside, in the lobby, HZDS campaign paraphernalia were quickly swept up. The first to go were pictures of Mečiar. On the other hand, those of his legal expert (and soon to be foreign minister) Jozef Moravčik or future minister of privatization Augustin Marián Huska were available for the taking. I heard one man sigh: "If you haven't got a picture of Mečiar, at least can I have Filkus?"

Rudolf Filkus, the economist who was minister for economic strategy in the Mečiar government of 1990–91, and who incurred Mečiar's wrath for his excessive closeness to the Czechs and Mečiar's Slovak opponents, was in good form as the main speaker. Referring to the slick billboards put up by the ODÚ featuring the faces of various ministers, Filkus told the crowd, to loud cheers, that the HZDS could not afford such luxuries as billboards (ultimately, it wound up matching the ODÚ effort), and would donate any excess campaign contributions to charity. The HZDS, which "does not have access to media" (allegedly because the state-controlled radio and television were disregarding Mečiar and the HZDS), needed to get its message "directly to the people." Filkus was interrupted by a man who claimed to have found two trucks with ODÚ campaign literature signed by Minister of Privatization Ivan Mikloš, which used computerized databases supposedly kept in government offices and now misused for political purposes. The HZDS gained much political mileage by criticizing the Mikloš effort; Mikloš claimed that he had used private databases, but was hurt by such scenes as HZDS supporters complaining that their deceased relatives could not sleep peacefully in their graves because he had sent campaign literature to them, unmindful of the fact that they had died since their names were entered. But the absence of the most prominent star—Vladimír Mečiar—irked some of the audience. One woman asked why Mečiar was not there; she and others were heartened when they were assured that he was busy campaigning in central Slovakia and that "we will let you know when he comes to Bratislava."

Despite its internal divisions, the HZDS showed great skill in carrying out its political campaign. Besides its populist campaign on the billboard issue, the HZDS also used imaginative means to put forward the idea that it was a closely coordinated team working in unison. A week before the election, it invited the public to a football game in Petržalka. All of the HZDS's front-running candidates showed up wearing T-shirts emblazoned "I love [in the form of a heart] Mečiar." A local women's team was picked to face off the HZDS regulars. The purpose of the game, of course, was to ensure that the crowd enjoyed itself, and would cast its votes for the HZDS. Despite the fact that the game started several hours behind schedule, it accomplished all its objectives. Mečiar claimed that the government was trying to shut him off from television coverage as much as possible, and that he therefore had to "go everywhere and show myself to the people."

During the campaign, I met with one of the HZDS advisors to see how the movement itself assessed its successes. The HZDS carried out its own polling, and treated the results as confidential, to be shown only to the movement's top leadership. However, the main findings of these polls in general were in agreement with those of the official Institute for Public Opinion Research, which carried out monthly assessments of political support for different parties. HZDS polls showed, for instance, a solid base of support that had not fluctuated significantly since its founding in mid-1991. They predicted (as it turned out, fairly accurately) a poll of some 35–45 percent of the vote. They saw the Slovak Nationalists as losing ground, and accurately predicted the support levels of the KDH and the mostly Hungarian Egyutelles. The HZDS also knew that its arch rival, the ODÚ, would not reach the minimum of 5 percent required to return candidates to the Slovak Parliament.

Why was the HZDS so strong? Two factors explained this. The first was Mečiar's continuing popularity. He had become the butt of so many allegations about his alleged misdeeds that the public began to weary of "another bombshell." Secondly, the deteriorating economic situation, which saw unemployment in some Slovak districts nearing levels not seen since the Depression, worked to the advantage of the HZDS. Slovaks in 1992 were mostly interested in prices, job prospects, and living standards. The national issue, according to the HZDS's own data, was of lesser concern to voters, although there was an increasing emphasis on the need for "equality" between the two republics. While the ODÚ clung to the hope that a late surge would bring voters back to them, the HZDS dismissed such a notion as "naïve." In contrast with the 1990 election when such a surge did take place, the political situation had mostly solidified.

While conventional wisdom in 1992 was that some 70 percent of the electorate still favored federation and 30 percent independence, when the HZDS experimented with different kinds of questions, it found a significant difference in opinion. For example, given various alternatives for the future, 40 percent of Slovak respondents opted for "a confederation of two equal republics," while only 20 percent wanted "a federation with enhanced competencies for the republics." Part of the problem, of course, was the fact that political rhetoric was expounded without a clear understanding of meanings, nuances, and implications of certain terms. While the HZDS came out with the idea of confederation as a halfway house between federation and independence, its definition of the attributes of a confederation looked suspiciously like a relationship between independent states. Slovaks wanted combinations of things that could not coexist—an independent army or separate membership in international organizations coupled with continuation of a federation.

10

SLOVAKIA'S SECOND REVOLUTION:
MEČIAR'S TRIUMPHANT RETURN

In the 1992 elections, the HZDS was swept into power with a vengeance, winning 74 seats in the 150-member SNR, as opposed to 29 for the SDĽ, its closest competitor. With 16 seats, the KDH had become a remnant of its former proud self. The SNS and the Hungarian coalition parties wound up with 14 seats each. Of the remaining parties, only the Social Democrats were able to barely cross the 5 percent threshold to gain seats in one of the two houses of the Federal Assembly. They had gambled on the "Dubček effect" and badly miscalculated the degree to which the hero of 1968 could still bring them votes in 1992. The SDĽ, which had planned to join an election coalition with the Social Democrats but had to pull out because of Dubček's opposition to the idea, was wistful in describing what "might have been." The KDH, which did somewhat better in eastern Slovakia, was decimated in Bratislava, and overall garnered only half the percentage of votes it attained in 1990. Of some small satisfaction was the fact that Klepáč's faction in the SKDH failed to gain enough votes to be elected to any legislative body. So too was the fate of the ODÚ, which collapsed entirely soon after the elections. Its coalition partners, including the Hungarian Civic Party and the Democrats, also became political has-beens. One of the real surprises was that Miklos Duray's Egyutelles and the Hungarian Christian Democrats, joined in a coalition, received more than twice the percentage of votes predicted by the polls. However, this was still irrelevant to the post-June 1992 political equation, dominated as it was by the HZDS. Only two seats short of a majority, the HZDS was able to easily determine the course of future Slovak politics through informal coalitions with the Nationalists and the SDĽ. Although the Nationalists lost a third of their support compared with 1990, they could take some consolation in the knowledge that much of their program, not to mention their thunder, had been appropriated by the HZDS.

While Mečiar had fudged the fact that the HZDS program stood for a confederation with the Czechs during the latter part of the campaign, and even proposed a referendum with five alternatives, including a federation, the voters did not appear to back, or understand that they were backing, someone who would lead them to independence. Mečiar had skillfully tapped fears that the Čarnogurský government was being manipulated from Prague, and few believed assertions of Mečiar's opponents that the quasi-independence he offered would mean economic hardship for Slovaks. On the contrary, many felt that the relationship with the Czechs had meant economic gains for the latter, along with extra hardship for Slovaks, especially when measured in terms of unemployment, then running four times the level in the Czech part of the country.

I watched a triumphant Vladimír Mečiar stand before the cameras in the old Trade Union House on Sunday, June 7, 1992, a day after his HZDS swept to victory in the general elections. While the "morning after" in the United States is typically a time when vanquished congratulates victor and both pledge their efforts—if only during a honeymoon period—to work together for the good of the country, for Mečiar victory meant the chance to complete the job of crushing his enemies. First on the list were federal radio and television, which he felt had acted in a partisan way against him during the campaign, "violating law and decency," and whose existence should be put to an end by cutting off further appropriations. Close behind were Václav Havel, whom he deeply distrusted, and the KDH, which owed whatever votes it did get to alleged support from the Catholic Church.

Flushed with victory, Mečiar enunciated his positions as part of a new political order.

—A declaration of Slovak sovereignty, which Mečiar had supported since he formed the HZDS in early 1991, but wanted promulgated only after he returned to the helm of government, would be issued soon after the Slovak Parliament reassembled. It would be followed by a Slovak constitution including "full powers" (i.e., that of an independent state), and providing for a president, by the end of August. Mečiar promised a referendum to decide on the future of Czech-Slovak relations, but noted that those relations should be between two international "subjects" (i.e., independent states), and that the Slovaks would decide their own fate regardless of what the Czechs decided for themselves.

—President Havel was pronounced as having "minimal chances" of being reelected as president of Czechoslovakia. Mečiar, still smarting from Havel's "prejudicial" remarks before the elections, said he would call on his deputies not to vote for Havel, who had urged voters to approve parties that favored the common state and to reject those whose "own power is more important than the future of their nation." At this stage, he suggested that the future president be a Czech, with the federal prime ministership and position of Federal Assembly speaker going to the Slovaks.

—Whatever his prescriptions for heading a federal government, Mečiar considered the formation of such a government to be temporary, pending a final decision on whether a common state would remain. However, he left no doubt of the direction where his thinking was heading, recalling that HZDS policy favored two "international subjects" and noting that Paragraph 142 of the then existing federal constitution stipulated that the document would cease to exist once the Slovaks (actually, the republic) formulated their own constitution.

—One of the few persons for whom Mečiar had kind words was Václav Klaus. Klaus had avoided the urge to earn "cheap political points" by picking on him during the campaign, and Mečiar vowed to reciprocate. In so doing, he was exhibiting a pragmatic political sense, knowing so well that he would have to deal with Klaus in deciding the fate of the country.

Mečiar was particularly hostile toward the Hungarians. He pronounced their unilateral abrogation of the treaty on construction of the Gabčikovo-Nagymaros project "legally invalid," and called for "revisiting" the controversial 1990 language law to assure that Slovak would be the language of communication both for the majority and minority. During my post-election tour of one of the Hungarian-speaking regions around Bratislava, it was clear that Mečiar's remarks had considerably raised the anxiety level.

When one journalist asked about U.S. reaction to Slovak independence, Kňažko, one of the many HZDS officials who joined Mečiar for this session, quickly replied that the United States was concerned that the Czechs and Slovaks decide their future by constitutional means and preserve a democratic system, rather than being committed in the abstract to the continuation of a common state. He had learned his lines well.

In retrospect, it appears that Mečiar's political opposition was increasingly living in its own fantasy world. After I attended a March 29 congress of the ODÚ, in which government ministers confidently proclaimed their chances of victory, I sent a message back to Washington entitled: "Titanic sinking, band still plays on." Hopes that the coupon privatization process would give each citizen a stake in preserving the KDH-ODÚ government were not realized. On June 5, the first day of the elections, I met a group of local politicians in Košice and was struck by their insistence that the government coalition would be returned with 40 percent of the seats in Parliament that would allow it to block constitutional changes and that it would be in a position to "decide" whom it would take on as a partner in a future government. The government's propaganda, warning against a "national socialist coalition" that would reverse the course of economic reform, fell flat with the voters. A colleague following the polling in Poprad and Banská Bystrica in central Slovakia, however, found local officials much more skeptical about the chances of stopping Mečiar. Frustration at the results was also directed at the voters for not "getting the message," causing some of Mečiar's supporters, with some justification, to remember Bertolt Brecht's famous sarcastic line from his poem "The Solution," penned after the abortive revolt in East Germany in 1953, recommending that the Communist Party "dissolve the people and elect another" after they had lost the Party's favor.

Three days after Mečiar celebrated his triumph, I called on František Mikloško to say farewell to him in his capacity as speaker of the Slovak National Council. Mikloško had held the job since shortly after the 1990 elections. Protocol-wise, he was the highest-ranking official in Slovakia, outranking the prime minister. However, he was at the center of controversies surrounding the future of the country, and his prestige had suffered first during the controversy over the language law, and next, over his role in deposing Mečiar in 1991. Mikloško had been a leader in the underground Church before 1989, and had organized the 1988 demonstrations in Hviezdoslav Square, just below our then-unoccupied consulate building, that were brutally suppressed by policemen wielding clubs and water cannons. Mikloško's values were moral absolutes; he would no sooner make moral compromises than he would compromise with the devil. It was almost by accident that he joined the VPN in 1989; by early 1992, he saw no future in continuing with the VPN, and moved to the KDH, where his natural political roots lay in any case.

Mikloško was never a person to mince words. When I met him, he was still reeling from the election defeat—though by switching to the KDH he was able to ensure his continuation in the SNR as a member of the now opposition party. He regretted that people did not take Mečiar seriously; when he called for "international subjectivity" in 1991, few accepted the fact that this meant independence. Mikloško was the picture of pessimism that day. A common state could not be preserved. Mečiar would begin an assault on press freedom by behind-the-scenes manipulation. Mikloško was concerned over the fate of thousands of Slovak workers in the Czech lands, as well as Slovak ability to finance completion of the Gabčikovo project. He also feared that moderates in the HZDS, such as Rudolf Filkus, had little influence. At a time when moderate Slovaks were still discussing the idea that a joint state could continue, Mikloško predicted the end would come in a few months, as there was no room for compromise between the vastly different Czech and Slovak conceptions on constitutional issues. He felt the Czechs were themselves partly to blame for this state of affairs; they had proven themselves unable to understand the situation faced by the outgoing government and failed to make compromises necessary for the Slovaks to sell a constitutional agreement to their own people. Mikloško was now also near the top of Mečiar's "enemies list": that same day, Mečiar's spokesman, Bohuš Geci, announced that Mečiar would be sworn in by the new speaker of Parliament, Ivan Gašparovič, to avoid the embarrassment of having Mikloško preside over the ceremony.

As she was due to end her mission in Czechoslovakia July 12, Ambassador Black, accompanied by her husband, Charles, came to Slovakia to say farewell to its leading personalities on June 22. It was a subdued Vladimír Mečiar whom we met at our residence that evening. Mečiar had been taken aback by the firm position of his Czech counterpart Václav Klaus, who firmly told him that there was no middle road between federation and the formation of two independent states. Mečiar accused the Czechs of not wanting to agree to a common market or currency; that their attitude was "divide the country first, then we'll negotiate a customs and currency union." Depicting himself as "confused" by the Czech stance, Mečiar said he had declined to get into public debates with the Czechs over their disagreements, or to allow his supporters to begin public agitation campaigns. He admitted that Slovakia was not ready to manage a whole host of problems on its own, including unemployment, the structure of exports, and dependence on eastern markets. He said that Slovakia needed friends, and that good relations with the United States would be a priority in the future. When the ambassador reminded Mečiar that human rights, including those of minorities, are important to the United States, he quickly countered that relations with Hungary were easier after the elections than they had been before. He also assured the ambassador that Slovakia would not sell armaments to countries blacklisted by the United States for supporting terrorism. Mečiar also softened his insistence on "international subjectivity" for

Slovakia, noting that Czechs and Slovaks could sign international treaties as one, but that the separate republic parliaments would have to ratify them. Common embassies could also be preserved in many cases. Of
course, as negotiations continued with the Czechs, these ideas quickly fell
by the wayside.

The cold pragmatist in Mečiar gave voice to the comment that Klaus
would be "destroyed in three days" if he took a more conciliatory attitude
toward the Slovaks; on the other hand, he had been criticized by his own
people for trying to "help" Klaus by declining the post of federal prime
minister, allegedly offered to the HZDS. Mečiar had assumed that he
could continue to control the direction of the Czech-Slovak relationship,
and appeared surprised that Klaus had his own priorities. The Mečiar who
packed in the crowds had to give way to the leader who was able to find
productive relations with the Czechs and with other nations important to
Slovakia.

Once inaugurated on June 25, Mečiar practically wiped out the government secretariat and instituted a purge that would lead to the emergence
of many new faces in Bratislava and the provinces. Despite the assurance of
his minister of the interior, Jozef Tuchyňa, that only those found guilty of a
punishable offense would be removed, a systematic effort to recall local pre-
fects (prednostovia) was begun. In the areas of education and health management, a similar process took place, with incompetence or malfeasance
usually used as an excuse to make a politically motivated dismissal. This
purge was facilitated by the fact that Slovakia had no civil service law giving
job security to government employees.

Ambassador Basora's first visit to Slovakia in late July provided an
opportunity, among others, to get acquainted with Mečiar's economic
team, to ponder where the republic was headed economically, and to analyze the quality of the team making economic policy. The ambassador was
not left with a glowing feeling of optimism. We met with Finance Minister
Julius Tóth in one of the few air-conditioned offices in Bratislava. I had
first gotten acquainted with Tóth the previous year when he was deputy
chief of the giant East Slovak Iron and Steel Works. The problems Tóth was
facing in the summer of 1992 included a drop of as much as 25 percent in
some productive sectors over the previous year, nominal unemployment
of 12 percent (the true figure was obscured by such measures as social
assistance that kept people working at least nominally and therefore off
the unemployment rolls). In addition, depreciation of the terms of trade
with the Czechs by as much as 20 billion crowns (about $700 million) had
come about because rises in prices of mostly finished Czech products had
not been matched by similar increases for the more typical semi-finished

products and raw materials which the Slovaks sent to the Czechs. Tóth complained that decisions concerning the arms industry—basically made in Prague—had cost the Slovaks close to a billion dollars.

There were other problems: a lack of new capital, a weakened credit system, and unpaid enterprise debts amounting to 60–80 billion crowns ($2.1–2.7 billion). Unpaid enterprise debts precipitated a chain reaction. When a firm in financial straits failed to pay its debts, it placed otherwise healthy firms in a precarious position. Without the inflows they expected, other firms had to renege on their debts as well. The matter could be addressed only by passing a law on bankruptcy that would allow a firm to be liquidated if it was financially unable to meet its obligations. However, bankruptcy would add to the already spiraling unemployment. When Tóth spoke in terms of balancing the budget, he noted that while expenditures were down 2 percent, revenues were running 10 percent less than in 1991. While he expected free movement of labor and capital after independence, he knew that monetary union was a concept with a limited time frame.

The pending breakup of the federation into two separate states also had its echo in the local political sphere. At the Fourth Congress of the SNS, held October 10–11, the Party elected Ľudovít Černák as its chairman, replacing the more fiery Jozef Prokeš. While the SNS, in a show of unity, proposed Prokeš as its favorite son candidate for the future post of Slovak president, there were obviously many views about the direction of the Party's future. Some wanted the SNS to become a right-wing party, whereas others pressed for retaining a "social accent." Another issue was the future relationship with the HZDS. Putting Černák, the minister of economy, at the helm was clearly a sign that the Party would emphasize economic matters in the future. However, as Černák noted, both publicly and privately, he intended to make the SNS into a "guarantor" of democracy in Slovakia. While this may have been a laudable goal, we were struck by the fact that the SNS remained unsympathetic, if not hostile, to complaints by the Hungarian minority about unequal treatment. It also failed to support its own member, Vladimír Miškovský, the short-lived chairman of the State Council for Television, who was fighting an attempt by the HZDS to replace the Council with a "non-political" body that would then purge the general director of Slovak Television, Marián Kleis—a job that was soon carried out.

At about this time, Klepáč's Slovak Christian Democratic Movement (SKDH) rechristened itself the Christian Social Union (KSU). Likewise, it also plugged itself as a champion of human rights. However, remembering Klepáč's tirade against our human rights report the previous February, we were not about to hold our breath (explored in more detail in Chapter 12, pp. 99–100).

In early November, I had the opportunity to visit the eastern Slovakian town of Lučeňec to meet with local officials and see how the "Mečiar revolution" was proceeding in the provinces. The trip was arranged by the prefect of Rimavská Sobota province, Ján Ostrica. Ostrica, who had been appointed during the previous administration, was well aware of the fact that people in his position were falling right and left, usually due to "charges" that had been levied against them for imagined petty sins. My expressed interest in hearing about minority problems in this strategically located territory evoked a torrent of discussion, with little agreement. Representatives of Miklos Duray's Egyutelles movement, for one, protested that the new Slovak Constitution was biased against the Hungarians because it contained a clause that suggested the Slovak majority needed to be protected against the Hungarian minority. Others from the HZDS and Matica Slovenská sharply disagreed, arguing instead that the real problem was that the Hungarians refused to be integrated into Slovak society, and looked beyond the border for their political cues. A teacher, the local HZDS representative, claimed that Hungarian children came to her high school woefully unprepared in Slovak (some attend Hungarian-language schools). I later learned that, once the HZDS had found a pretext to ease Ostrica out of his job, she was the person anointed to succeed him.

When I asked about freedom of speech issues, one young journalist who wrote for the opposition daily *Telegraph* told me she needed to be careful about the way she addressed certain issues and complained about government attempts to control the press, including proposals to require people who submit to interviews to approve them before they could be printed. She was especially scathing in her criticism of the pro-regime daily *Koridor*, noting that a colleague of hers who joined the paper's staff was asked to insert pro-nationalist commentaries into his articles, despite the fact that he wished to steer away from politics. The discussions were summed up by the moderator, who was head of the Office of Regional Cooperation. Annoyed by the answers given by the Hungarians, he tried to cut them off, and in his final summary of the proceedings, he argued that any assertions that the Hungarians were mistreated were simply "not true." My visit to Lučeňec coincided with an annual seminar on regional cooperation, which included participants from Ukraine and Hungary. The Hungarians originally planned to send their state secretary for foreign affairs; instead, the Slovaks had to settle for the state plenipotentiary for the Hungarian province just across the border. The Hungarians downgraded their representation because of continuing tensions between the two countries.

Hviezdoslav Square, with the Radisson SAS Carlton Hotel on the left and the U.S. Embassy in the middle, September 6, 2007. Courtesy of Julie C. Van Camp.

The Slovak League of America presents a portrait to Senator Claiborne Pell at the U.S. Consulate in Bratislava on May 27, 1991. From the left, John Hvasta (who, before his arrest in 1948, worked for Pell at the Consulate Slovak League), President Daniel Tanzone, Senator Pell, and Ambassador Shirley Temple Black.

Senator Claiborne Pell in animated conversation with Augustin Marián Huska, deputy chairman of the Movement for a Democratic Slovakia (HZDS). The photo was taken during a luncheon in August 1992 with Slovak parliamentarians held at the consul general's residence.

The author's son Alex, then nine months old, at the July 4, 1993, U.S. National Day reception.

Senate Foreign Relations Committee Chairman Claiborne Pell and his wife, Nuala, bid farewell to the author's wife, Eeva (center), at a hotel in Vienna, August 1992. Senator and Mrs. Pell were part of a senatorial delegation that had just visited Slovakia.

The author's mother, Annie Hacker, with his son Alex, June 1993, at the Embassy Residence. The Danube River is in the distance, with views to Austria. The old Iron Curtain was roughly at the river bend in the picture.

Ambassador Shirley Temple Black and her husband, Charles (who died in 2005), meet Czechoslovak President Václav Havel (center) at the Embassy Residence in Prague, 1991.

Ambassador Shirley Temple Black has a final meeting with Slovak Prime Minister Vladimír Mečiar prior to her departure from Czechoslovakia in July 1992.

Czechoslovak Foreign Minister Jiří Dienstbier addressing a May 27, 1991, gathering called to rededicate the U.S. Consulate in Slovakia. To the right are Consul Paul Hacker, Speaker of Parliament František Mikloško, Prime Minister Ján Čarnogurský, and Bratislava mayor Peter Kresanek.

The author at work, October 1991. The portrait of Ambassador Black was placed strategically so that this photo, taken for a series showing the work of consuls general in Slovakia, would underscore that consuls are responsible to their ambassadors.

Consul Paul Hacker says farewell to Vice President Dan Quayle at Poprad Airport, June 7, 1991. Courtesy of the George Bush Presidential Library.

František Mikloško, speaker of the Slovak Parliament, and Ján Čarnogurský, prime minister, receive the first visas issued at the U.S. Consulate, October 1991.

Adrian Basora (second from left), the last U.S. ambassador to Czechoslovakia and later the first U.S. ambassador to the Czech Republic, visiting Nitra, August 1992. His wife, Pauline Barnes, holding flowers, is second from the right.

In late August 1991, Consul Paul Hacker remembers the sacrifice of members of the Green Mission, sent by the Office of Strategic Services to aid the Slovak National Uprising in 1944. The cabin is a replica of the hut in which they took refuge until they were captured by pro-German Slovaks from the Edelweiss Brigade on Christmas Day, 1944. Ironically, the author worked as an intern at Radio Free Europe with Ladislav Nižňanský, who was part of the same unit that captured the Americans and delivered them to their eventual deaths the following month. The mayor of Polomka, the town closest to the site, is third from left. Other participants include Slovak veterans and members of the Defense Attaché's Office in the U.S. Embassy in Prague. The author's wife, Eeva, is on the right.

President Michal Kováč meets Chargé d'Affaires Paul Hacker and his wife, Eeva, on July 4, 1993. Eleanor Sutter, who would assume charge of the U.S. Embassy three days later, looks on.

The author welcomes former president Jimmy Carter to the U.S. Embassy library, June 1993.

Chargé d'Affaires Paul Hacker and his wife, Eeva, greet Speaker of the Slovak Parliament Ivan Gašparovič and his wife, Silvia Gašparovičová, on July 4, 1993. Gašparovič was elected president of Slovakia in 2004.

Eeva Hacker, the author's wife, introduces (right) Gail Klevana, wife of the head of the U.S.-Czechoslovak Enterprise Fund, Leighton Klevana, and Dr. Kaija Frecerová to Emilia Kováčová, first lady of Slovakia, in 1993. Mrs. Hacker was first president of the International Women's Club of Bratislava; Mrs. Klevana, an American, was in charge of public relations; and Dr. Frecerová, a Slovak, was vice president.

Theodore Russell, first U.S. ambassador to Slovakia, shares a light moment with Public Affairs Officer Helen McKee (left) and Public Affairs Assistant Jana Illešová, 1995. Courtesy of the U.S. Embassy, Bratislava.

President George W. Bush, hosted by Slovak Prime Minister Mikuláš Dzurinda, addresses a gathering at Hviezdoslav Square, February 24, 2005. Behind them, from left to right, are Mrs. Eva Dzurindová, wife of the prime minister; Silvia Gašparovičová, the first lady of Slovakia; and President Ivan Gašparovič. Courtesy of the U.S. Embassy, Bratislava.

11

AFTERMATH OF THE 1992 ELECTIONS:
THE BREAKUP OF THE FEDERATION

The history of Slovakia in the second half of 1992 is the history of two simultaneous processes: first, Mečiar's consolidation of power and the development of Slovak political institutions; and second, the inexorable process of shaping an agreement with the Czechs on a modus operandi for dismantling the federation and forming two separate states.

When Václav Klaus and Vladimír Mečiar met for the first time as victors in the elections in their respective republics on June 8–9, they met as two political realists. Their first meeting, however, merely confirmed the reality of how far apart they were in their respective views of a future Czech-Slovak state. Klaus was willing to tinker—up to a point—with the federal republic. Mečiar wanted a confederation, which would give him "international subjectivity" and the attributes of an independent state without using the "independence" word. The Czechs, however, objected that his formula for confederation amounted to "independence with a Czech insurance policy."

Bohuš Geci, an editor at *Radiožurnal,* the main Slovak radio news program, became Mečiar's press spokesman. He told a press conference on June 9 that the HZDS wanted the final solution as to the future of the country to be decided in a referendum. While Klaus had characterized the Slovaks as coming to the meeting with a proposed "defense and economic community," the HZDS wanted more encompassing arrangements, including free movement of people, minority guarantees, and coordination of foreign policy. The HZDS agreed that the president of a future Czech-Slovak state should be a Czech, but was clearly opposed to Havel's continuing in office. Other HZDS officials, such as Milan Čič (Mečiar's predecessor and the last Communist minister of justice, who presided over discussions that peacefully brought Communist rule to an end in Slovakia), expressed the "private" view that Havel could stay if he "changed his ways." As it turned out, Mečiar's strong aversion to Havel, including the feeling that Havel had actively plotted his downfall, led the HZDS to oppose the president's continuation in office. The following day, Geci qualified the HZDS position by explaining that his movement "favored a confederation" with the Czechs.

Amidst intense interest back home over the meaning of the elections for the future of the Czechoslovak state, I called on Mečiar and Kňažko on June 12. Our meeting took place after the first round of discussions between the Czech and Slovak leaderships. At this point, neither had been sworn in to a new position. I started off by telling Mečiar that I was carrying no message of any kind and that my purpose was to find out the status of negotiations with the Czechs. At this early stage, Mečiar summarized the dilemma by recalling Klaus's remark that his election mandate was either to preserve the federation or to prepare for two independent states; Mečiar retorted that he had no mandate to either keep the present federation or to break up the common state. He objected that Klaus was trying to retain the current federation in as untouched a form as possible. Klaus wanted to retain a strong central role over the economy, whereas Mečiar said he argued that even in the U.S. individual states have their own taxation and investment policies.

Mečiar confirmed his adamant opposition to Havel's continuing in office as federal president. He denied that Havel's pre-election speech, widely interpreted as a signal not to vote for the HZDS, was the crucial issue. Rather, the problem was that Havel was simply "incapable" of governing. He was too much a creature of his advisors, and too often said one thing and did another. Mečiar agreed to call on Havel during the following round of negotiations in Prague, but would do so only if accompanied by Klaus. Mečiar was not worried over the future of the Gabčikovo project; the Slovak government, if need be, would take over the burdens of financing, together with foreign investors. At the meeting, Kňažko confirmed that the two sides had come to an agreement over a transitional federal government including foreign affairs, defense, economy, finance, and interior. At this point, the Slovaks were arguing for dividing the country into two military districts with a unified general staff in command. However, the Czechs accused the Slovaks of wanting a separate army with only a "roof organization" joining the two republics' defense.

While Mečiar still talked of a referendum in which federation would be a possible choice, his other criteria belied the notion that a federation was feasible. He would soon be introducing a declaration of sovereignty, followed by a constitution with "full powers." When he also mentioned separate Slovak membership in international organizations, I demurred, noting that once he crossed that river, he was talking about an independent state, and nothing else. He listened carefully but did not react. A master of saying two things at the same time that did not necessarily agree with each other, Mečiar kept people guessing about his final intentions.

What Mečiar was really after was independence coupled with the maintenance of certain institutional relationships with the Czechs that would preserve some semblance of a common state. Of utmost importance to the Slovaks was the preservation of a free trade area and free flow of labor. In the end, they received these benefits in the context of two independent states. Mečiar professed admiration for Klaus, but also complimented him, in an offhanded way, for his "arrogance," noting that "I met his arrogance with my arrogance." While Mečiar claimed that Klaus was negotiating with him because "he had no other choice," the same could be said for Mečiar's own relations with the Czech prime minister. I reported that Mečiar had "met his match" with his Czech counterpart, and that Mečiar's major motivation at this point seemed to be deflect the onus for a split away from his leadership.

I also asked Mečiar about his intentions vis-à-vis the Hungarians. Presaging what would turn into a nasty campaign to eliminate Hungarian-language town names, he assured me that the Hungarians could keep their schools and street signs, but would have to use Slovak for town names, "in accordance with internationally accepted usage." I reminded him that in places such as Finland, towns with a majority population of a minority nationality (e.g., Swedes) are listed in the minority language first, the majority's language second. This is also true in other areas, such as Croatia and Italy. One area, however, where Mečiar positively registered U.S. policy was in noting our "restrained" approach to the future of the country; we were not trying to impose any prescriptions on the Czechs and Slovaks, but wanted them to peacefully decide their own future.

Later that day, USAID Office Director Pat Lerner and I met with Michal Kováč, who was destined to be the new speaker of the Federal Assembly. Kováč hewed closely to the HZDS line of stating that the HZDS had "no mandate to break up the common state," but then referred to Czech desiderata as amounting to a "centralized federation." There were still disagreements on political vetting of former police agents, the transformation law on agricultural co-ops, and the future of federal television, as well as Slovak interest in two separate central banks that would have closely coordinated policies. At this point, Kováč still looked forward to a referendum as the final arbiter of the fate of Czechoslovakia. Four days later, we called on Rudolf Filkus, who was his usual outspoken self. He expressed himself strongly in favor of mutual concessions that would allow the continuation of a common state. He said a politician must refer to his "heart, his head, and his label," indicating that party programs should be a point of departure, not an absolute straitjacket. Although Filkus soon joined the HZDS negotiating team, as Mikloško's predictions proved out, Filkus was a lone voice whose views were summarily dismissed by Mečiar as being "too close to the Czechs."

By the third round of their discussions on June 17, Klaus and Mečiar agreed on the formation of a federal government that, although not yet formally labeled as such, was in effect a caretaker administration to carry on joint functions until a mechanism for dismantling the state could be agreed upon. While at this stage, Mečiar still spoke in terms of continuing the government's activities for eighteen months, Klaus immediately argued that a resolution of the Czech-Slovak future would have to come much sooner. Klaus also announced at this time that he would be the candidate of his ODS Party for the Czech premiership. At this point, his lieutenant Petr Černák saw the handwriting on the wall. He announced that the move "means that the ODS has lost hope of maintaining the federation." At that time, however, a lot remained unclear. Neither side could agree on Havel's political future. Klaus wanted to continue federal television broadcasts, while Mečiar wanted them abolished. Mečiar got in one parting shot at Havel, accusing him of organizing an unconstitutional "second power center" in the Prague Castle, causing Havel to issue a formal protest in return.

By mid-July, the die was cast and the decision was made to split the federation into two separate republics by the first of the new year. But first, the long-delayed Slovak declaration of sovereignty had to be formally promulgated. At a ceremonious session of the SNR on July 17, the declaration was approved by an overwhelming vote of 113–24, with ten abstentions. The naysayers were all seventeen of the KDH deputies, together with seven Hungarians. The remaining Hungarians abstained, along with three SDĽ deputies. This was a special occasion, and upon the motion of a Nationalist deputy, it was determined that the vote not only be open, but that each deputy rise when called, stating name and vote, in the glare of the television cameras. In order to avoid being labeled as traitors during this high point of nationalist fervor, each KDH deputy, rather than simply stating "no" in voting, instead answered, "no in this form," to stress that they were not opposed in principle to Slovak sovereignty.[1]

The declaration proclaimed the "natural right of the Slovak people to self-determination," pledged to protect the rights of all citizens of Slovakia, and proclaimed Slovak sovereignty "the basis of the sovereign state of the Slovak people." The declaration also affirmed that the "millennium-long effort of the Slovak people to achieve their independence has been fulfilled." In this passage, however, the word chosen, in keeping with the tenor of the day and the political discussions still going on with the Czechs, was *svojbytnost* rather than the more political *nezavislost*. The first of these words connotes "self-existence," the second "independence" in the political sense. Slovaks serving in federal positions held a place of honor on the podium, in order to emphasize the point of Slovak unity, irrespective of where Slovaks were serving. Ján Cardinal Korec, the first primate of Slovakia, was a guest, along with the Canadian Slovak hockey player–turned-politician, Marián Šťastny, then the chairman of the Slovak World Congress. That evening, traditional bonfires were lit on mountains across Slovakia, with the largest one near Kremnica, in central Slovakia, at the point reputed to be near the geographical center of Europe.

While there will be many interpretations of the time when Czechs and Slovaks crossed the dividing line that led from a common state to two separate ones, the sovereignty declaration prompted KDH deputy Ivan Šimko— Slovak minister of justice in the 1991–92 Čarnogurský government—to write a comment that "we have crossed the Rubicon," meaning that the dividing line had already been breached. While Čarnogurský protested that the Slovak state was sovereign already and the declaration was a "gamble," the Catholic bishops issued a statement welcoming the step, calling this the moment of prayers to make a "life of freedom" for the Slovak people.

A few minutes after Mečiar proclaimed the declaration to jubilant crowds outside the SNR building, Václav Havel took the next logical step and announced his resignation from office. He chose the moment of his resignation to reinforce the view that he could no longer remain president of a federation one of whose parts had now declared itself to be sovereign. The president, however, deliberately postponed the effective date of his resignation by three days, so that as one of his last official acts, he would be able to accept the credentials of Adrian Basora, a career Foreign Service officer, who on July 19 replaced Shirley Temple Black as U.S. ambassador to Czechoslovakia.

Five days after the sovereignty declaration, Klaus and Mečiar held a fifth round of negotiations in Bratislava, and agreed to end the federation. They declared that it would be their task to divide the federation in optimal fashion, to respect civil and human rights, and to coordinate foreign policy and maintain stability. They agreed to form a customs union and a free trade area, and pledged to allow free movement of labor and capital, and a common payments system. Questions of currency, banking, and payments were left to decide later. From the historical viewpoint, this political declaration made by Klaus and Mečiar in their capacities as chairmen of their respective political movements was the first public mention of an agreement to divide the country, and it contained some basic principles for the coexistence of the two republics after independence.

By early August, it had become clear that those still favoring some step that could forestall independence (e.g., a referendum) were a dying breed. Even Ján Čarnogurský, while voicing misgivings as to what was going on, declared that the KDH would not act as a "Don Quixote"—tilting at windmills in a hopeless attempt to delay the inevitable. On August 26, teams of Mečiar's HZDS and Klaus' ODS met in Brno and agreed that the federation would formally dissolve at midnight on January 1, 1993. The two sides agreed on a timetable until then, including presenting to the Federal Assembly a bill on the ending of the federation by the end of September; submitting a bill on division of property and successor rights to the Federal Assembly by October; passage by the two republic national councils of bills making possible the non interruption of economic and social ties between the republics after independence, and cleaning up open issues in December. A sensitive issue between both sides was the dismantling of the Federal Security Service (FBIS). A Slovak director, Dr. Pavol Slovak, was named with a limited mandate to dismantle the agency and transfer its functions to the two republics.

The dissolution process did not take place without some tense moments. When the Slovak side tried to introduce a motion in the Federal Assembly calling for the creation of a Czech-Slovak "union," the Czechs felt they had been betrayed, as they had insisted that the only option was for the establishment of two fully independent states with their own institutions. An effort on October 1 to pass a law on dissolving the federation failed to win the required three-fifths majority. However, by October 6, the two sides were back on track, with the Slovaks realizing that no union would continue to join the two republics after independence, but both sides approved a number of agreements to govern specific aspects of the post-independence Czech-Slovak relationship. On October 26, when the venue shifted to the Slovak resort town of Javorina, agreements were reached on a customs union, open borders, and a law on the dissolution of the federation. At a subsequent meeting on November 9 in the southern Moravian town of Židlochovice, the two parties agreed on such measures as common tax reforms, a draft umbrella treaty of good neighborliness, free movement, prevention of double taxation, and cooperation in such areas as agriculture, food processing, forestry, and water management.

On November 25, by a small margin, and only with the help of opposition parties, the Federal Assembly passed the law dissolving the Federation, and effectively, itself, as of January 1. The law transferred all remaining federal property to the republics, put an end to all federal organs, including military and police forces, transferred legislative authority to a new legislative body formed of federal deputies elected in June 1992 as well as deputies of the republic councils, forbade either republic from using symbols of Czechoslovakia, and authorized the two national councils to pass laws relating to the exercise of republic authority. As things turned out, the Czechs decided in the end to keep the national flag as their own, despite Slovak opposition. Also, deputies elected to the Federal Assembly were effectively deprived of their mandates as no procedure could be worked out to incorporate them in a "transitional" body. By December, some twenty-five separate treaties and agreements were passed, mostly ratified by the respective national councils. These accords governed the post-independence relationship of the two republics, and included such areas as a customs union, monetary arrangement, demarcation of the border and border cooperation, abolition of visa requirements, a common approach on the stay of foreigners in both republics, environmental protection, social security, a free labor market, and legal assistance. The border issue was an example of the "devil being in the details": before January 1, 1993, the border was for administrative purposes only. Some towns and many economic activities straddled the border. Movement and activities would all have to be regulated. When I passed the border for the last time on December 30, 1992, returning from a trip to the embassy in Prague, I knew things would never be the same again.

12

HUMAN RIGHTS IN SLOVAKIA

There were always at least two sides to our human rights concerns in Slovakia. On the one hand, the United States hoped that the spirit of toleration and acceptance of political pluralism—generally the hallmark of Western democracy—would take root in the post-Communist states of the former Soviet bloc. On the other hand, human rights questions addressed by the outside world lent themselves to the political agendas of individual parties and politicians, although not always in the way we would have hoped.

Throughout my time in Slovakia, controversy over human rights issues was concentrated on two subjects: treatment of minorities, and freedom of the press. In the case of the former, the issue invariably concerned the Hungarian population, or secondly, the small Jewish minority, both of which I have covered elsewhere. The issue of freedom of the press usually revolved around attempts by Mečiar's associates to carry out policies which would restrict the possibility of others to criticize his administration. Closely related to this subject was the issue of Radio Free Europe.

Each year, under a law approved by Congress in the 1970s, our embassies are required to submit a report on human rights practices in the countries to which they are attached. These reports have a standardized format, to provide easy means of comparison. They include such traditional areas as freedom of speech, press, religion, and minority rights, as well as worker rights, women's rights, and the issue of political killings and disappearances. Consistent with the fact that Czechoslovakia was a single state until January 1, 1993, our reports on Slovakia were included in the Czechoslovak reports through 1992; that year, we started drafting separate paragraphs for Slovakia in each relevant category. Because the 1992 report was issued in 1993, the Prague embassy continued to have overall responsibility for its drafting. Unfortunately, there were a number of references to Slovakia that had not been checked with me that were simply incorrect. I tried to get some language rewritten but was only partially successful, as the entire series of reports covering all countries had by then gone to press. However, in the last analysis, the Slovaks did not focus on any factual errors but only on the fact that they had been found lacking in some human rights areas.

Depending on the local circumstances, such reports may become the subject of national debate. Such was the case in Slovakia, although events unfolded in a way I had not anticipated. On February 10, 1992, I was called into the office of Ján Klepáč, who invited me in his capacity as deputy speaker of the SNR in charge of foreign relations. I was not given any inkling of what Klepáč wanted to discuss. I soon understood his game. Klepáč had asked me to receive his "protest" against the "U.S. human rights report on Slovakia (for 1991)." He had before him a summary of the report—still on all of Czechoslovakia, of course—sent by the correspondent of *Rude Právo*, the organ of the Czech Communists, from Washington. I found it odd that Klepáč, who had already built his reputation as a leader of the nationalist wing of the KDH (he would soon split off and form his own party), would rely on Czech sources, and Communist ones at that. That night, without consulting me, he issued a press release to the effect that he had called me in to express his views and to protest the "inaccuracies" in the report. Our meeting was big news on television that night, and Klepáč continued the attack with interviews in the media.

When I unearthed more background on the affair, it became obvious that Klepáč had decided to use the United States in a most unseemly way, in an attempt to promote his own political ends. He had met with Slovak Minister of Foreign Relations Pavol Demeš the previous week and had asked Demeš to protest the report but was rebuffed. Particularly disturbing was the fact that Klepáč never even bothered to obtain a copy of the whole report before making his "protest." He followed up with a number of interviews that totally distorted the content of the document and included negative references that he invented out of thin air. The report was, on the whole, quite favorable to Slovakia, although it did refer to desecration of Jewish graves and increasing incidents of anti-Semitism perpetrated by some extremists. I wanted to make a forceful public rebuttal to Klepáč, who had lied in order to win a few cheap political points at our expense, but higher authority at our embassy decided the best reaction was to say nothing. Because Demeš and other government spokesmen came out with their own strong arguments against Klepáč, additional comments from our end were considered superfluous, even though it was our own report that was being maligned. Laszlo Nagy, who himself was responsible for human rights issues in the SNR, was upset that Klepáč had transgressed on an area that was his own portfolio. Nagy was quite pleased with the report, although he did note that some Hungarians felt the lack of higher education in their own language limited their ability to produce teachers at Hungarian secondary schools. Prime Minister Čarnogurský called the report "objective, positive, and balanced." As it turned out, Klepáč's tactics backfired; his party polled only 3 percent of the vote that June and was voted out of Parliament. There was some speculation early in 1993 that President Kováč would give Klepáč the post of foreign affairs advisor; Kováč wisely decided to offer it to Demeš instead. In 2001, Klepáč resurrected his public service career when he was named head of the Office of the President by Rudolf Schuster, Slovakia's second president.

The Klepáč episode did, however, afford us some lessons on how to conduct a dialogue on human rights in Slovakia. The problem was that self-righteous nationalism as epitomized by Klepáč was a typical response of those who saw Slovakia as always being "ill-treated" in the foreign media, or who sought to bolster their local position by protesting Slovakia's "innocence" of any wrongdoing. We also saw that individual and group prejudices, rather than governmental human rights violations, were the real culprits in Slovakia. The idea was to encourage a dialogue that would lead to better enforcement of existing human rights protections, but also encourage programs which attack existing prejudices and foster dialogue among groups where tensions might exist.

The question of freedom of the press has dogged Slovakia since long before independence. The period of repression after the post-1968 "normalization," while less severe than in the Czech Republic, still condemned a generation of journalists to either collaboration or silence. The principle that a journalist exists to propagate the party line was deeply entrenched in Czechoslovakia, as well as in all the other "socialist" countries. Even so, a few courageous individuals tried to carve some independent space, often using space in the crusading weeklies of the respective writers' unions. In Slovakia, the liberal *Kultúrny Život* was closed down after the 1968 invasion, although it was resurrected for a few months under another name before being permanently shut. Beginning in 1988, another weekly, *Literárny týždenník* (Literary Weekly), was allowed to publish as the weekly of the Union of Slovak Writers (Zväz slovenských spisovateľov). After November

1989, *Kultúrny Život* resumed its old place as a crusader for Western liberal ideas. The former Communist-controlled press became "independent," at least in name, while a number of new publications sprouted up. The switch was quite sudden, and some journalists, rather than becoming overnight liberals, exchanged their Communist credentials for those of Slovak nationalists.

The issue of press freedom was also wrapped up in a larger question that became part of a national obsession: treatment of Slovakia by the outside media. Most foreign journalists covered Slovakia from Prague, where the "action" was and creature comforts were greater. As Western journalists are prone to find and accent the negative in what they cover, it was inevitable that Slovakia's warts would find their way into the Western media. Some journalists simply stayed in Prague and filed their reports from there. Others would take trips to Slovakia, and occasionally would come to visit, looking for "insights." Except on rare occasions, I declined their request for a briefing. My position was an exceptionally sensitive one, and I did not want to be put in the position of being "blamed" for the views put forward in some article. I also felt that journalists should make up their own minds and not rely on me for any precooked conclusions. As things turned out, many journalists found their natural soulmates in the pro-federalist wing of the VPN (later ODÚ). While many of their interlocutors were articulate and educated people, the ODÚ gradually grew to reflect the views of a diminishing number of people. (After a visit to ODÚ headquarters, some U.S. congressional staffers, who had been briefed earlier by Mečiar's associates and the Nationalists, came out of their meeting quite satisfied, saying "now we finally heard the truth!") More likely, these visitors heard what they wanted to hear, which was not the same message that the majority of Slovaks were internalizing.

It was dismaying to find that an otherwise reputable journalist even from such a respected paper as the *New York Times* would approach me with the question, "Where are the problems? I'm looking for the problems." While many Slovaks convinced themselves that Prague-based journalists (and probably diplomats as well) simply reflected Czech prejudices about them, those journalists who decided to make Bratislava their home found officials to be just as suspicious of them.

The larger problem was the persistence of past practices from the Communist era, or their reemergence in a new guise. Journalists had no tradition of independent writing, but were expected to be propagandists for those who paid their salaries. Added to this "tradition" was sensationalism that developed in the new era of competition. I soon learned firsthand how low the standards of journalistic ethics were. In late 1992, I was visited by the editor-in-chief of the publication *Plus 7 dní* (Seven Days More), a biweekly that was a combination of news and analysis, but also included the crime story and sexual tip of the week. It was independent and at least on the analysis side had attracted some competent persons. The editor was interested in getting a grant from a U.S. government-supported program for independent journalism in Eastern Europe. While his application was pending, I was surprised to read that I had become the subject for the paper's weekly gossip column. It went something like this: "It is whispered that the U.S. government has for some time been dissatisfied with the quality of the reporting on Slovakia sent by its consul general, Dr. Paul Hacker. Some even go so far as to suggest that the microphone affair [see chapter 15 for details] was invented by the CIA to discredit the consul general. We wouldn't go so far, since the Americans are an honorable people. But with the CIA, one never knows."

I was taken aback when I found myself the subject of an obviously false and quite naive attempt to create a sensational news item out of whole cloth. There was no problem with my reporting in Washington, so one would have to question how the paper's editors would know anything about either the reporting or the reaction to it. I immediately wrote a letter to the editor demanding a retraction of the story. He replied in a personal letter to me, but declined to disavow his error publicly in print, probably because it was a highly embarrassing example of his irresponsibility. He claimed that, of course, it was inconceivable that his paper would publish any scurrilous remarks against the U.S. consul at a time when it was trying to win a grant from the U.S. government. While I did not succeed in getting the paper to issue a formal apology, I explained the background of the story to the person responsible for administering media grants at the U.S. Information Agency (now part of the Department of State), and he agreed with me that under such circumstances, it would be inappropriate for us to assist that publication.

Unfortunately, the canard that our embassy was misinforming Washington about events in Slovakia also appeared in the pro-government *Republika*, which emerged as a successor to the defunct and unlamented *Koridor*. This time, the paper predicted in an April 1993 commentary that Mr. Mečiar would face a chilly welcome in the United States because of unfavorable reporting by the U.S. Embassy. I protested to the publisher of *Republika*. Other journalists told me that the writer of the article had distinguished himself by being on the payroll of the secret police while working in the 1970s in Germany. I even drafted a letter to the editor, wondering how the journalist in question was so well informed about the content of classified and supposedly inviolate diplomatic correspondence. But in the end, I took the sage advice Louis Nizer gave to his clients itching to sue for libel—to "let the mud dry" rather than try to scrub it out (let the matter pass and it will be forgotten and unnoticed). Sad to say, though, while even the worst Communist tyrants never questioned the right of foreign diplomats to send reports back home to their host governments, Slovak officials under Mečiar did not hesitate to do so.

The most politically sensitive medium in Slovakia is television. Before the 1992 elections, Slovaks sympathetic to Mečiar or to the nationalists grew increasingly vocal over what they saw as the manipulation of federal television by the Czechs. But after the election, the government was determined to insure that Slovak Television as well acted in accordance with the "results of the election." Ivan Mjartan, then deputy minister of culture responsible for the mass media, explained that despite the victory of the HZDS in the elections, Slovak Television was allowing too many people representing or with connections to the former government to appear on the screen. Television, in their view, is not a forum for a full exchange of views or one that will naturally be opposed to whomever is in power, but more of a mouthpiece of the current government. Thus, the curtain rose on the "drama of Slovak Television."

On September 29, 1992, Minister of Culture Dušan Slobodník and his deputy Mjartan addressed an appeal to the Cultural Committee of the SNR asking for the dismissal of Slovak Television director Marián Kleis on the grounds of incompetence. The appeal noted that, whereas the SNR had recently passed a law which would change the makeup of the Slovak Television Council, which had the sole right to appoint or dismiss the Slovak Television director, it would take some time for this process to be implemented, and the political and economic situation in Slovakia was "much too serious" to allow such an important media institution to be controlled by a person "without proper ability." That same day, the committee passed a resolution recommending that the SNR's Presidium take up the matter. The following day, the Presidium itself passed a resolution dismissing Kleis and replacing him with Peter Malec, television program director. While in the end Malec himself proved as independent as Kleis, and was himself ousted, we found it instructive to note that the government had felt the need to go outside the framework of its own law which was meant to regulate the appointment of a television chief. The day before Slobodník's and Mjartan's appeal came to the SNR, a meeting of the liberal group HUMAN was held in Bratislava to discuss press freedom. Slobodník declined to attend and Mjartan represented the government instead. Mjartan refused to answer several questions, including why the government was so opposed to Radio Free Europe.

He criticized the foreign media, as usual plugging for more correspondents to be based in Slovakia. He also suggested that more Slovak correspondents should be sent abroad to give a "true picture" of their country. Asked his view of the role of the press in a democracy, Mjartan stated that the government had a responsibility to regulate the press, and that a democracy had "legal and ethical borders" which the government was sworn to protect. Of course, the question of who should determine those "borders" was one which remained unanswered.

There were other problems as well. In Košice, opposition to Mečiar was spearheaded by *Slovenský Východ*, a daily that gave no quarter to Mečiar and got none from him either. A few weeks after Mečiar returned to power, the paper was unceremoniously told by the person who owned the premises where it was published that it would "have to move." A new paper, loyal to Mečiar's government, started publishing in the very same place. Although *Slovenský Východ* found alternate premises and continued to maintain its popularity, the episode raised issues about harassment—issues that were not to go away after Slovakia became independent.

Problems with the media also spilled over into our own relations with Slovakia in the form of Radio Free Europe. RFE faithfully reflected American policy of supporting the territorial integrity of Czechoslovakia, but it was seen by Slovak nationalists as increasingly becoming a tool of those who wanted to maintain the status quo of the federal system. Already in 1991, I began to receive loud objections to RFE's reporting, with the notion that it was too "Pragocentric" and "anti-Slovak." Singer Ivan Hoffman wound up migrating to the Czech Republic because of threats made against him by those who could not tolerate his commentaries broadcast by RFE.

One comment I heard was that RFE had "outlived its usefulness" and that its continued existence was only helping to provide jobs for journalists of mediocre quality and whose existential interests demanded that they preach the continuing need for their services. RFE also leased time on the federal television station, and used its programming to promote views at odds with those of Slovak nationalists. I explained that RFE's statute required that it not broadcast a political line which would be at odds with U.S. policy, although it was not required to closely adhere either. I offered to send any specific criticisms to Munich if critics could note the program or particular views that troubled them.

There may have been some rationale behind the views of RFE's critics, but it was difficult indeed to accept the contradiction in their assertion that, on the one hand, the station had no influence or was not trusted by a majority of Slovaks and on the other hand, it should be shut down entirely because it was broadcasting "dangerous" views. Those who worked in RFE's Czechoslovak Service were both dedicated to the cause of a united country and were usually strong opponents of Vladimír Mečiar. On the other hand, RFE's efforts to put some balance in its broadcasts were thwarted by Mečiar's hostility (his unwillingness to appear on the air), and the difficulty of getting any HZDS officials to step before its microphones. The appearance of Roman Zelenay[1] and Rudolf Filkus at an RFE-organized post-election roundup in 1992 was a rare exception.

The station saw little in Mečiar's behavior or policies that was positive, and found much to criticize. For Mečiar, RFE was the "enemy" and that was the end of it. In one conversation in October 1992, he asked, "why does RFE hate me?" Mečiar was particularly incensed by a *New York Times* editorial that had just appeared, which argued in essence that "because of people like Mečiar, RFE broadcasts must continue." One reason why RFE took the tone that it did was because its editors felt that the station's listeners were expecting them to maintain an "oppositional" stance, especially after Mečiar's 1992 victory. In trying to delineate its role, the station conceived its primary purpose to be that of offering an alternative to Mečiar, in keeping with their own notion of what balance means in a democratic polity, and perhaps also given their own fears that Mečiar would manipulate the home-based media.

In October 1992, a delegation headed by then Principal Deputy Assistant Secretary of State for European Affairs Ralph Johnson[2] arrived in Slovakia for talks with Slovak officials on the subject of RFE. The delegation's mission was to consider the future role of the Radio—continue, transform, or shut it down. Its members were struck by the fact that, of all the places they visited, only in Slovakia did officials argue that RFE should be abolished. In a discussion with the delegation, Deputy Minister of Culture Ivan Mjartan argued that RFE had outlived its usefulness and that the middle wave radio frequency it had in Slovakia could be better used by new private radio stations. The delegation countered that RFE had made a contract for the frequencies and that the United States expected the contract to be observed. It was probably the vehemence with which Slovak officials reacted to the question of RFE's future that convinced the delegation that the station, at least as far as Slovakia was concerned, did play an important role in offering an alternative source of news and views to the people of Slovakia. At least for the moment, the government, as personified by Mjartan, understood that toying with the contracts under which RFE operated in Slovakia would invite a very strong U.S. reaction, and was therefore best avoided.

A few months after independence, I was to hear more about RFE. This time, I received a letter from a very irritated Roman Hofbauer, now minister of communications, to the effect that he was insulted by RFE's temerity in criticizing him. Since the U.S. government controlled the station, and radios controlled by one government do not criticize officials of another friendly state, he demanded we ensure that RFE cease and desist. I replied to Hofbauer that RFE is governed by its own statute, and otherwise determines its own editorial policy. Since RFE was replying to remarks Hofbauer had made in public, he could not expect they would be immune from criticism. I told him that RFE would have to broadcast any refutation he had of its commentary, but also added that, frankly, his views about criticism sounded suspiciously like those we used to hear from his pre-1989 predecessors. Hofbauer replied to my letter, even more agitated, suggesting that I had failed in my duty as chargé d'affaires. The episode clearly showed that some elements of the Slovak government had indeed adopted views about criticism which were entirely at odds with standard practices in Western democracies. They would not tolerate the right of others to refute their remarks, and rather than engaging in a civilized dialogue, their initial reaction was to seek out and use administrative methods to deal with their critics. In 1993, Hofbauer made the demonization of RFE and its forced removal from the airwaves one of his top priorities. In the end, not only did he not succeed, but he left an unnecessarily bitter and hostile legacy. Needless to say, we declined to play his game.[3]

13

* * * * * * *

THE SLOVAK STATE AND THE JEWISH QUESTION

Of all the skeletons that came back to haunt Slovaks from the past, none was more sensitive than their treatment of their Jewish fellow citizens during World War II. Under intense German pressure, Slovakia declared its independence on March 14, 1939, and until liberated by Soviet troops in 1945, became a puppet state under German tutelage. Slovakia's prime minister, Father Jozef Tiso, became the first and only president of the Slovak state. Under his administration, between 1939 and 1942, Slovakia's 100,000 Jews were gradually deprived of their livelihood and their civil rights. In 1942, more than two-thirds of them were deported to the death camps in Auschwitz; most of the rest were murdered during the Slovak Uprising in 1944. Only a handful survived. The deportation order was actually instigated by the Slovak government itself, which paid Germany in gold Reichsmarks for the "service" of removing its Jewish population. In this way, Slovakia attained the dubious distinction of being the only unoccupied country in Europe to deport its Jewish population during World War II.[1]

Although Tiso was executed as a war criminal on April 18, 1947, some Slovaks regarded him as a martyr to Communism and chose to forget his complicity in wartime events. The fact that he authorized about a thousand "exemptions" to deportation for a small number of privileged people and was finally forced to halt the forced exodus in the fall of 1942 after loud protests from many sources, including the Vatican, led some to believe that he was more a victim of circumstances than an accessory to mass murder.

Curiously, when I first met Ján Chryzostom Korec, the bishop of Nitra, who was later to be named Slovakia's first home-grown cardinal (a second Slovak, Ján Cardinal Tomko, is based in Rome), Korec devoted the bulk of our conversation to the Tiso interlude. We met at a hotel in Rosslyn, Virginia, while he was visiting the United States shortly before I departed for his country in September 1990. I had wanted to meet him and admired him for the role he played in leading Slovakia's underground Church during the height of Communist dictatorship, as well as for the suffering he endured under that regime, including imprisonment from 1960 until his release during the short-lived liberalization of 1968. In July 1990, shortly before his departure for the United States, Korec had participated in a ceremony unveiling a commemorative plaque at a school founded by Father Tiso in the 1930s in the town of Bánovce. The ceremony brought howls of protest from outside Slovakia, because the idea of rehabilitating a convicted war criminal was considered unacceptable. Korec insisted that he had not known what he was getting into, and had he realized the implications, he would not have participated in the ceremony. This explanation notwithstanding, Slovak Jews whom I met later scoffed at the idea that Korec did not know the nature of the ceremony he was being asked to bless.[2]

It is true that Korec, along with two dozen other Slovak dissidents, signed a public declaration in 1987 asking forgiveness for the persecution of Slovak Jews during World War II. While endorsing such a declaration was not considered an act of direct defiance against the Communist regime, as an independent political gesture in a country that frowned on such things, and as the first attempt to come to terms with the wartime past, it represented a courageous gesture on the part of its signers.

However, it was also clear from our conversation that Korec himself did not accept the view prevalent in the West that Tiso deserved his fate. The cardinal referred to a story often cited in Tiso's defense to the effect that three rabbis visited him in 1941 and beseeched him not to resign as president, in order to save the Jewish community. Jewish sources, however, considered the story apocryphal; in truth, the only thing the rabbis wanted from Tiso was help in stopping the deportations of their brethren.

According to public opinion polls, some 20 percent of all Slovaks shared Korec's view that Tiso was a positive figure for Slovakia. About a third held a generally positive view of the wartime Slovak state, balanced equally by those with a negative opinion and those with no view at all. Polls also showed clearly the persistence of anti-Semitism in Slovakia, although the phenomenon should be seen against the background of the opinion climate in other central European countries. While it is highest in Poland and lower in the Czech Republic, anti-Semitism in Slovakia is generally on par with values measured in neighboring Austria.

While anti-Semitic acts that gained world attention during our stay in Slovakia were mostly limited to desecration of graves, and despite the fact that most Slovaks would have to honestly say that they did not personally know a single Jew, instances of anti-Semitism still occurred, as revealed by individuals whom one would have expected to show more tolerance. During my initial call on Archbishop Ján Sokol, I had the opportunity to ask his reaction to assertions made in a recently published autobiography of Fedor Gál blaming the Church for intervention in the 1990 election campaign. Rather than give a matter-of-fact answer to the question, Sokol chose to reply, "What do you expect from that Israelite?" Asked to explain, he made it clear that "his people don't wish us well." However, Sokol vented his spleen on others as well, suggesting that the cultural level of eastern Slovakia was depressed because of the number of Gypsies. At this point, he caught himself and assured me that "of course, they're all God's children."[3]

Few things could raise Slovak ire as much as accusations that Slovaks are anti-Semitic. True, most Slovaks have never had direct contact with even a single one of their Jewish fellow citizens, given that the Jewish community now numbers around 6,000. When desecrations of Jewish cemeteries took place in 1991, the first reaction of Slovak officials was not that there were rowdies in their midst who needed to be cleaned out, but rather, that outside "provocateurs" must have been sent in to "blacken" the Slovak reputation. When the late Rita Klimová, a former Communist who happened to be Jewish herself, made a remark during an interview published in November 1991 alleging there is "inborn anti-Semitism" in Slovakia, some of my interlocutors who would have been ranked among the more moderate political factions became apoplectic. They even argued that Klimová had outlived her usefulness as Czechoslovakia's ambassador to the United States. Klimová, who at that time was battling the cancer that would eventually take her life, was spared for the moment by President Havel. She resigned her post in mid-1992 to make way for Havel's spokesman, Michal Žantovský, who also happens to be a Czech Jew.

The continuing sensitivity over the wartime treatment of Slovakia's Jewish population was evidenced in Nitra, which I visited on October 21, 1992, to join a delegation headed by Prime Minister Mečiar and Parliament Speaker Gašparovič to commemorate the fiftieth anniversary of the deportation of the Jews of that city to the death camps in Poland. Fewer than 10 percent of the six thousand Jews from Nitra herded into the cattle cars survived the war. While the Nitra commemoration was the last of a series of remembrances of the fiftieth anniversary of the deportations—all of which took place in 1942—it had some incongruous elements. Most strikingly, Slovak Minister of Culture Dušan Slobodník was absent, represented by his deputy, Ivan Mjartan. Slobodník's presence was vehemently resisted by members of the remnants of Slovakia's Jewish community because of his activities at the end of the war as an eighteen-year-old who admittedly took training offered by the SS to "resist" the Red Army. While Slobodník, who later spent several years in the Gulag for this episode, loudly protested that he joined the group only after receiving a notice to report, and that he feared for his life if he did not, the Jewish community felt his protestations were ludicrous, given the fact that there was no doubt, by the time Slobodník reported for "duty," that the end of the war was just weeks away. Slobodník sued the writer Ľubomír Feldek for slander when Feldek wrote that Slovakia should not have a minister "with a fascist past." Feldek won in the first round, but Slobodník won on appeal, at which time Feldek took the case to the European Court of Human Rights, which finally ruled in his favor in 2001. Slobodník died several months after that decision.[4]

Gašparovič read a declaration at the ceremony unveiling a plaque commemorating the victims of the Holocaust. The declaration said more about Slovak national aspirations, which were only now about to be fulfilled, than it voiced regret over the murder of Slovak citizens. Ignoring the role played by the Tiso regime in the persecution and deportation of the Jews, the declaration asserted that "Slovaks were never the initiators of aggression and violence," and that they therefore "rose up against fascism." Later on, in a private meeting with officials, the mayor of Nitra asked Israeli Ambassador Yoel Sher whether he had detected any anti-Semitism in Slovakia. Somewhat flustered by the question, the ambassador replied diplomatically that every country has anti-Semites, but studies have shown that too many Slovaks (about 50 percent) give the wrong answer when asked if they would like to have a Jew as a neighbor. Mečiar, quite typically, brushed the whole thing off with a joke: "If you asked Slovaks if they want Mečiar for a neighbor, probably 90 percent would vote no." Thus, the results of that day were mixed: the message about the government's condemnation of anti-Semitism and racism did get through, even if accompanied by much nationalist baggage. One also had to give Mečiar and his government credit for understanding that paying attention to the concerns of their small Jewish community is part of the price (though a rather small one) to be paid for acceptance into the larger democratic community.

14

TRNAVA UNIVERSITY:
ASSAULT ON ACADEMIC FREEDOM
OR DIALOGUE OF THE DEAF?

While as a rule of thumb we try to stay out of the domestic turmoil of countries to which we are accredited, sometimes U.S. diplomats are placed in the midst of a controversy, where they cannot come out without damaging their relations with one side or another, and where they must then govern their behavior by considering how their actions will best defend our own value system.

Such was the dilemma I faced when I received an invitation to the inauguration of Trnava University on November 8, 1992. Normally, the opening of an institution of higher learning is a time for celebration. The stormy circumstances surrounding the founding of Trnava University, however, opened up the sensitive issue of whether academic freedom was under attack in Slovakia just two months before the country was to become independent.

Trnava is the seat of the archbishopric of Slovakia, an ancient town about thirty miles north of Bratislava, some forty-five minutes away by one of Slovakia's few expressways. The town originally established a university in 1635, which was moved to Budapest in 1777. Shortly before he resigned as president of Czechoslovakia, Václav Havel approved the reestablishment of a university in Trnava. He named Anton Hajduk, an astronomer, as the university's first rector. There were two sets of issues, however, which called the whole project into doubt. First, legally speaking, Hajduk's appointment was subject to challenge because he did not have the university title of docent or professor required by law, nor was he approved by the university senate.

Second, the town of Trnava and Hajduk himself were closely associated with the KDH, which became an opposition movement after Mečiar's victory.

After Mečiar returned to power, three local politicians, including the head of the Trnava organization of the HZDS, demanded that Hajduk be recalled on the grounds that his appointment was in contravention of the 1990 federal law concerning the universities. Professor Julius Kováč, one of the signatories to the complaint, demanded that he himself be appointed as acting rector. In August, acting Minister of Education Dušan Slobodník called on Hajduk to give up his post after consulting with Ján Straský, who was then federal prime minister and acting president in the wake of Havel's July 20 resignation. Straský conceded that Hajduk's nomination had not been in keeping with the law on universities, but he also declined to dismiss Hajduk. Straský likewise refused to name Kováč to the post, since he had not been approved by the academic senate.

The problem was a bit more complicated than the confines of the law allowed. First of all, the law was designed to deal with already existing universities, not newly established ones. Hajduk could not have been appointed with the consent of a senate because no such body existed. A member of the anti-Communist political opposition, Hajduk was a participant in the "flying universities" in the 1980s—academic seminars that "flew" from one private apartment to another to avoid police surveillance but which took up topics that could not be touched in the Communist-controlled educational system. His lack of an academic title was due to political discrimination during the Communist years.

What now followed was an unnecessarily bitter, but not atypical, Slovak struggle. Hajduk steadfastly refused to give up his position, while Slobodník became increasingly bellicose. Head of the Institute of World Literature before being named minister of culture (and acting minister of education), Slobodník had strong nationalist credentials. He also had detractors, who felt that Slobodník's previously mentioned participation in an SS training course in the closing days of World War II made his appointment to a ministerial position in Slovakia an unseemly blot on the republic's reputation.

When Hajduk refused to resign, Slobodník attempted to starve the school into submission by cutting off funds. When that attack failed, he came personally to the school with a locksmith as well as television cameras and demonstratively changed the lock to Hajduk's office (although he left another lock untouched on a separate entrance). While the government charged that the university was in the hands of academically unqualified faculty, most of whom were visiting, rather than full-time lecturers, it was also clear that the university would not be able to attract a full-time staff until it could pay them by having its funds unfrozen.

During this period, Mečiar politicized the issue by suggesting that the real crux was an opposition plot to find a haven for academicians opposed to his government. Some of the better-known names included Miroslav Kusý, former head of the Office of the President in Bratislava, Soňa Somolányi, a sociologist strongly opposed to Mečiar, and Martin Bútora, an author and sociologist who had been a member of Havel's staff in Prague and who would serve as Slovakia's ambassador to the United States from 1999 to 2003. Each side believed the law supported them and that the other party was acting illegally. In mid-September, Matuš Kučera, a fifty-nine-year-old professor specializing in ancient history, was named to take over the education portfolio from Slobodník. While no one could compete with Slobodník when it came to fiery rhetoric, more than a few intellectuals voiced suspicion of Kučera, whose career had clearly benefited from the post-1969 Communist "normalization" period. But while he was initially expected to take a more moderate stand than Slobodník on the Trnava University issue, Kučera in reality set out to complete what his predecessor had been unable to accomplish—the full destruction of the institution while it was still in its bud stage. He intended to carry out this task by presenting the government with a bill to close down Trnava University. Mečiar strongly supported him, arguing for his part that the university had become a dumping ground for castoffs from the previous government, all of whom were now his political enemies. The logic of Mečiar's position was that, once his enemies had been hounded from the political scene, so too must they be "neutralized" in any other places where they might find a platform for their views.

In early November, I received an invitation card signed by Hajduk inviting me to the official opening of the university on November 8. The opening was well timed, because it preceded parliamentary consideration of Kučera's bill to close down the university; had such a bill been passed, the opening would have been illegal. I had already heard that organizations such as the Committee for International Academic Freedom in New York had expressed concern over the intentions of the Slovak government on the Trnava issue. While I had not received any inquiries myself, from long experience, I knew it was only a matter of time before questions would start coming. I was aware that a diplomat could compromise his effectiveness through any actions that were perceived as interference in his host country's internal affairs. I also felt that the Slovaks would soil their own reputation for academic freedom if they went ahead with plans to close

Trnava University. The government would have a tough time convincing outsiders that it was only concerned with the quality of instruction for Slovak youth. After consulting with John Evans in Prague, I resolved that my best course of action would be to attend the opening, but to try to do so as inconspicuously as possible. I avoided the High Mass that preceded the opening and tried to stay in the background. My Hungarian colleague, Jenö Boros, who was considering whether to attend, asked me what I planned to do. He finally decided to stay away, feeling that his presence could add to the already considerable tension between Hungary and Slovakia. The only other diplomat who did attend was the Polish consul general, Jerzy Koroc, who reminded me that, since he was a university professor, he considered it entirely natural that he attend the opening of a new university.

I avoided "exposure" until after the unveiling of a bust in the university was over. Several journalists recognized me and asked me for my comments. I had to politely turn them away. Some of them tried a classic ploy and asked me for my "personal" view of the controversy. When their microphones were off, I repeated Ambassador Black's cautionary words, "in this business, we have no personal opinions." I also decided to decline an invitation by the head of the Faculty Senate to make a few impromptu remarks to the gathering.

Fatefully, however, the cameras focused on me and my name was prominently mentioned in the evening news broadcasts. In attendance were a number of distinguished academic guests, but most Slovak academicians stayed away. Some claimed that Kučera had threatened retribution against any Slovak academicians who attended. It was quite clear, though, that both the faculty and students felt themselves under siege, and Hajduk received a standing ovation when he spoke. Later that day, I met him in his now-liberated office. I wanted not only to hear his side of the story, but also to remind him that the United States was not a party to the dispute, and that my presence should not be construed as an official intention to insert ourselves. I expressed the hope that a peaceful resolution would be found. Hajduk told me that he would receive his candidate's title within the next few days and that the Academic Senate would reconfirm him, thus destroying any pretext the government had to force his resignation. While most of the politicians attending the opening were from the KDH, it happened that SNS leader Černák had sent one of his parliamentary deputies, Vladimír Miškovský, to represent him. Černák later confessed, with a certain pride, to the fact that he had voted against Kučera's bill when it came up for discussion in the government.

Two days later, Kučera was asked about the opening when he met journalists after a trip to Parliament. He then uttered a remark he would soon regret—stating that "international guests must have been well paid" for attending. I heard the news while returning to Bratislava from Prague that evening and was both amused and astounded. The next day was the Armistice Day holiday, but I was in the office at work as usual. The phone rang, and the first of several journalists asked for my reaction to Kučera's remark. In such a situation, one has to be extremely careful: dwelling on the question of whether I was paid off for attending or whether my attendance was appropriate would deflect attention from what was the real issue—whether the government's handling of the case raised valid concerns over academic freedom. Accordingly, I limited myself to saying that I would wait for the minister to clarify his remarks before replying. This way, I got myself off the hook, avoiding polemics, and allowing Kučera himself to step away from the brink. The journalists assured me that they had his exact remarks on tape, and he could not deny that he made them.

When I went on leave a few days later, John Evans came down from Prague to represent the United States at the funeral of Alexander Dubček, who had died from complications stemming from an automobile accident several months earlier. There, he met Kučera, who promised to send me an apology. The apology was sent, but it turned out to be something quite different from what was promised. As it turned out, Kučera did not regret anything he said, but instead apologized for the "sensation-seeking journalists" who twisted his words. When I saw Mečiar just prior to my departure, I waited for the proper opening to ask him about Kučera's remarks. Mečiar replied that Kučera should not have said what he did, but added that I should not have attended the opening either, as I had lent "moral support" to the university administration. I tried to downplay the fact that my presence was a political gesture—it would only make Mečiar even more hostile. Instead, I pointed to expressions of concern in the United States over academic freedom, and my desire to see things with my own eyes ("You could at least have sent your assistant," he protested). Gašparovič, whom I was directed to meet on the microphone incident (see chapter 15), was more emotional, saying that I had participated in an illegal gathering. I asked him how he, a lawyer, could make such a judgment before a court could rule on the question of legality. His reply was not unexpected for someone whose legal education came under the Communist system: the matter was "so obvious" that the courts had "nothing to say." There was, however, a glimmer of hope in Gašparovič's position. Unlike Kučera, it was clear that he was looking for a way out of the crisis that would address the government's concerns about the quality of instruction but do so without causing the university to close.

Weeks later, some Slovak friends voiced the view that my presence in Trnava had saved the university. My presence, they felt, had shown quite visibly that the United States had an interest in what was happening in Trnava. While I realized that they exaggerated, my small hope in attending helped to make the point that there was international interest in the survival of the university and that failure to take account of that interest would be detrimental to Slovakia's human rights reputation abroad. A diplomat's role in a controversial setting is never easy. Before this episode, some oppositionists associated with the old VPN had condemned me for being "too close" to the government. Perhaps I had now redeemed myself in their eyes, although my bit part in the Trnava drama was not intended to be a balancing act. When I was invited back to Trnava to participate in a pre-Christmas bazaar whose prize event was the auctioning off of Slobodník's now-infamous lock, I politely declined. I had made my point and didn't wish to drive in the nail. At the same time, the humor of the event was not lost on me. I resolved that our future relationship with Trnava University would be to draw it into our academic exchanges, such as the Fulbright program.

One of the sad memories of this episode, however, is that it brought out the worst, not the best, in Slovakia. The urge to destroy one's opponent seemed to be the ultimate objective of those managing the government's strategy. The notion that a university cannot contain members of a political opposition is a throwback to the purges that followed the Communist coup of 1948 and the "normalization" after the 1968 invasion. Indeed, I could not help recalling the words of Gustav Husák on his return from Moscow in October 1969 (when I happened to be in Prague), that he would not allow the academic sector to be a "reservation" for "rightists." Had only academic issues been at stake, they could have been settled quietly by academic institutions. Unfortunately, the political crossfire caused needless and damaging friction.

Kučera lasted another half year. After he had survived one attempt to recall him (he had by that time become exceedingly unpopular in Slovak universities), his colleagues in the HZDS themselves threw in the towel and voted to return him to his position as professor of ancient history.[1] In 2000, he was named director general of the Slovak National Museum (since retired), and in what must have been a spirit of forgive and forget, he was awarded the "Order of Ľudovít Štúr First Class" on September 1, 2005.

15

THE MICROPHONE EPISODE

While on leave in Washington in November 1992, I was shown a report that had more implications than I could then imagine. It told of the discovery on the eighteenth of the month of more than a dozen microphones on several floors of our consulate during a routine check by a technical security team that was preparing the building for transformation into an embassy. Since the intention was that an embassy would be sending and receiving classified traffic, the building had to be more secure than was the case for our heretofore unclassified operation. The devices were found on several floors, including in the corridor right outside my office. Although we had suspected that microphones had been planted by the secret police before 1989, we had been assured that all such devices had been deactivated and the wires cut since that time. We were taken aback to find that not only were the microphones still in the walls, but they were very much alive and working.

A simple electrical resistance test allowed us to pinpoint the adjacent building as the source of devices that were using the microphones. Shortly after the tests were initiated, however, further testing then showed that the wires had just been cut. Whoever was monitoring the microphones became aware that he had been discovered and quickly folded up operations. Other strange things happened the night we discovered the microphones. Our team tried to call Frankfurt for assistance and found its access to an outside telephone line suddenly blocked. A threatening phone call was received promising to "get you for this." Policemen who were supposed to be on patrol outside the building were suddenly withdrawn.

At this time, the federation was still in existence, and our diplomatic relations were still exclusively with the Czech and Slovak Federal Republic (ČSFR), the name under which the country had been known since a bitter Czech-Slovak struggle over the issue in early 1990, so it was decided to issue a formal protest to Michal Žantovský, then the ambassador of the ČSFR in Washington. Perhaps the idea that something would come out of the protest was a bit misplaced, but our State Department continued along the normal course in this case. Our primary objective was to determine responsibility for the penetration of our building, and to ensure that such episodes would not be repeated.

When I returned to Bratislava in early December, I was informed that our protest had been leaked to the Czech media in Prague, which had spread it over the front pages that same morning when I landed.[1] In short order, the microphone episode would become a cause célèbre that ultimately led nowhere but which gave our relations some unwanted drama just when the Czechs and Slovaks were about to go their separate ways. Before I returned, Ambassador Basora, under instructions, had journeyed to Bratislava to talk to Mečiar about the matter. Mečiar assured the ambassador that the Slovaks had nothing to do with the episode but that he would appoint Gašparovič to head an investigating commission.

During December, I was called to weekly meetings in Prague to deal with the episode. The fact that the matter had been leaked made our efforts that much more difficult. The Czechs and Slovaks quickly reverted to their customary pose of mutual finger-pointing. The Czechs assured us that, yes, even though security was a federal responsibility, they had by that time lost de facto control over Slovakia's security apparatus—which was not officially established in any case for several more months. The Slovaks, for their part, insisted that they had no capabilities in this field, which belonged to the federal government. Not long after, the Slovaks also reverted to a plot mentality; first, the whole episode was a "Czech plot" because, after all, it was the Czechs who publicized the protest, obviously to "discredit" the Slovaks on the eve of independence. Later on, the plot scenario suggested the United States was somehow to blame; after all, why had we waited until the eve of independence to suddenly find that our building had someone else's live microphones working in it? One Slovak contact told me in mid-December that at the Slovak government's December 8 meeting he had heard that the theory was brought up that the United States had "timed" the discovery of the devices in order to be in position to "exert pressure" on Slovakia. The "pressure" we had hoped to exert, and the results we allegedly wanted to achieve from that pressure, were never indicated. Of course, American logic did not dovetail with Slovak logic in this case.

When the ambassador came down to Bratislava for a final call on Mečiar December 21, he was shown some pictures of what were purported to be cut wires at the point in the wall where the operation had allegedly taken place. Mečiar asserted that, from the state of rust on the wires and the plaster on the walls, it was impossible for the wires to have been cut as recently as we said they were. He insisted that the room had been boarded up and all activities ended in early 1990 just as was supposed to be the case. In effect, he expected us to disbelieve our own incontrovertible evidence to the effect that an operation was being conducted against us as late as November 18. The ambassador was disappointed that this was as much as we would get from Mečiar, but the realist in him said there was no point in harping on the matter. He judged that Mečiar considered the "evidence" he showed closed the case and that any attempt on our part to press the matter would only inflame our relations without getting us closer to the truth. This view was also predominant in Washington. At the same time, we had been promised a final report of the investigation, which was now in the hands of the Slovaks, and I was instructed to keep pressing for it.

After independence, the responsibility for cleaning up the aftermath fell on my shoulders. In the meantime, there was silence. On March 9, the prosecutor general's office announced that an investigation conducted by the military prosecutor general (and deputy to the state prosecutor general) had made its final report, which was along the lines of what Mečiar had told us. I was given a summary of findings through the Foreign Ministry, and was invited to follow up directly with the prosecutor general. We had a number of meetings afterwards, including several with his staff, and I eventually received an expurgated version of his original report, which was classified "top secret" because it included interviews with a number of former secret police agents. As soon as I received the report, I had to dash over to Vienna, translate it myself, and send it quickly to Washington.

The prosecutor general insisted that his staff had done a credible job, qualifying his statement with the words "on the basis of evidence available to us." I explained to him that our own evidence contradicted his findings. At his request, I was able to get an expurgated version of our own report on the matter, giving him some indication of the technical readings our people had made, and what we were able to conclude from them. We had initially not supplied Slovak investigators with any of our own findings because we felt the facts were so obvious something was going on that they should be able to uncover it on their own. Once the prosecutor general obtained our information, he asked if we wanted to request that his investigation be reopened. Our instructions were to say that we would not request a reopening ourselves, but would leave it up to him to decide how to proceed; he himself later decided to reopen the case.

I originally went back to the Slovak government because I had received a number of inquiries from journalists as to whether we had obtained the promised report. It was embarrassing to have to state that we had not, but I did not want to leave the impression that we were somehow cooperating with Slovak authorities to cover up the facts.

Before this episode passed, I had to weather one other storm. Our vice consul, Richard Polka, had gone to Košice in eastern Slovakia with the very laudable program of interviewing visa applicants who would otherwise have had to travel to Bratislava, as well as to keep up our ties with eastern Slovak notables. Without my knowledge, he paid a visit to the opposition daily *Slovenský Východ*. While there, he had gone beyond his brief and made some remarks on the microphone issue which the newspaper then published as an interview. While our issued "press guidance" restricted us to remarking that the matter was being discussed in diplomatic channels and that we stood by the embassy's earlier statements on the issue (especially that we had incontrovertible evidence proving that the microphones were live), he wound up discussing the issue with a paper which was Mečiar's sworn enemy and would have loved nothing more than to "expose" the prime minister. Although the interview essentially said nothing new, it had the very negative effect of renewing media interest and speculation. I had more than enough work in limiting the damage, starting with trying to turn off the journalists who were hounding me with calls demanding an explanation. Although no one in Washington specifically blamed me for this lapse, I know that the question in their minds must have been "How could he have allowed this?" When I met Mečiar several weeks later, he was still fuming about the episode, accusing the United States of wanting to remove him from power, and presumably assuming the interview was our way of getting at him through his political enemies. While I tried to explain that it was unauthorized, and that the person involved had been reprimanded, I knew that he would never take my explanation seriously. However, in the longer run, we also believed that there were other interests in the field of security that would join the United States and Slovakia, especially our common efforts against drug smuggling and terrorism, and that our ties would best be served by positively engaging them rather than continuing a fruitless debate on why the microphones were still working.

16

★ ★ ★ ★ ★ ★ ★

VLADIMÍR MEČIAR

Vladimír Mečiar is one of those personalities whom one usually winds up either hating or loving, but who will never leave you unmoved. More than any other individual, he has been the dominant figure of post-revolutionary Slovakia. For better or worse, he left his own stamp on Slovak politics, and came to be the Slovak face outsiders saw and generalized about while trying to understand the Slovaks and their mentality. He was and still is Slovakia's politician par excellence, never at a loss for words, and a master of tactics who has dominated the political scene whether in or out of power. Mečiar's legendary memory has allowed him to challenge colleagues or opponents on the smallest detail. While often referred to in the West as a former boxer—he certainly conjures the image of a Slovak "Rocky" in his voice and mannerisms—he would surely prefer to be remembered as the person who engineered Slovak "emancipation" in 1993—the culmination of Slovakia's development as a nation.

According to Mečiar's official biography, he was born on July 26, 1942, in Zvolen in central Slovakia. After finishing his military service, he served in various functions in the Czechoslovak Youth League (Československý Zväz Mládeže or ČZM) and was chairman of the ČZM district committee in 1967–68. He had entered the Communist Party (KSČ) in 1962, but was expelled in the wake of the Soviet-led invasion in 1970, a year after he lost his functions in the Youth League. He later claimed that he was disciplined because some anti-Soviet leaflets had "found their way" to his desk. Following his removal, he became an assistant smelter worker in the ZTS Dubnica

Steel Works. In 1977, he completed studies as a correspondence student of the law and was granted the degree of Doctor of Jurisprudence at the Faculty of Law of Comenius University. In the first half of 1990 he was minister of interior and environment in the first post-Communist government. He was elected to the Federal Assembly in June 1990, but rarely attended sessions, as he also became the prime minister of Slovakia at that time. He held the post until he was ousted on April 23, 1991. His wife Margita is a pediatrician; he has four children.

Owing to the demands of protocol—I could not meet Mečiar until Ambassador Black had called on him—I waited until January 21, 1991, the day she returned to Prague, to make my introduction. Mečiar was subdued and uncharacteristically humble at our first meeting. He recalled the close ties between the United States and Slovakia, cemented by the emigration of hundreds of thousands of his brethren to our shores. Responding to my question on his relations with the Slovak diaspora, he replied that it should first get its own act together before coming to him with specific demands.

Mečiar's basic problem was his unstable nature. One was either a friend or an enemy, and could easily slip from the first column to the second without warning. Mečiar came to my office, then still in the Devin Hotel, one day before I hosted our first Fourth of July reception since the consulate was closed in 1950. He explained he would not be joining us the following day, but wanted to affirm that he had no argument with the United States. He still felt bitterness toward those former government colleagues who had engineered his removal from power two months earlier and refused to be placed in the position of having to shake hands with them when he felt repulsed by the idea. He had a special venom toward Ján Čarnogurský and his brother Ivan. One of the nicer things he would say about the prime minister, mocking Ján's hobby of skydiving, was that his policies were like parachute-jumping: "600 meters down and two kilometers of drifting."

Mečiar also had a tendency to try to be all things to all people, and got himself tangled up in the ensuing contradictions. For example, he once told us he wanted U.S. investment in Slovakia and was prepared to offer American investors preferential treatment because the United States was needed as a "counterweight to German influence." However, on a later occasion, he gave the Germans a diametrically opposite message, and wound up reversing an earlier decision to invite General Motors to set up an Opel assembly plant, giving the nod to Volkswagen instead. The GM executives who had negotiated with him were considerably frustrated by the experience, and one told me he thoroughly distrusted the prime minister. Mečiar also felt he could cultivate ties with the United States by appearing a strong bulwark against Communism. When I met him just after his June 1992 victory, he exulted that, had it not been for the HZDS, the "Communists" would have taken over the country. He returned from a visit to the United States in May 1993 with the statement that unnamed congressmen had warned him about the dangers of making any deals with the "Communists," which for him was political shorthand for the SDĽ. However, given the fact that all but two members of his government were former Communist Party members, his statement was less than convincing. I did not argue with him, but reminded him of a conversation I had had the previous week with one SDĽ official in eastern Slovakia. My interlocutor recalled that in 1989, 450,000 Slovaks were members of the Communist Party (KSS). The SDĽ had 50,000 members (many of whom were new recruits); where did the others go?

Mečiar could be extraordinarily kind when he felt it to be in his own interest. In July 1992, I received an urgent request to meet him because our new ambassador, Adrian Basora, wished to call on him as soon as possible after presenting his credentials to President Havel. The president had already decided to resign, but had scheduled the credentials ceremony before the effective date of his resignation. While I requested only a five-minute meeting with Mečiar, we continued to chat, and he then invited me to an adjoining room for lunch. To my amazement, the whole Slovak government was there already. I had not met most of its members, and the last thing I needed was a story to the effect that the U.S. consul general was acting as a kind of proconsul in Slovakia. During our discussion, Mečiar used a tactic he would try several times over the years: he would offer some views to me, judge my reaction, and then publicly come out with the same views a few days later. In this instance, he announced he had received some information about a "secret" Czech plan, devised by then Prime Minister Petr Pithart, to pressure Slovakia in the event of a split. Some aspects of the plan allegedly included forced return of Slovak Romanies living in the Czech Republic back to Slovakia. Two days later he went public with these charges. While he caused the Czechs some consternation, they refused to be baited and replied in a matter-of-fact fashion, and in a few days the issue was forgotten.

While some of Mečiar's associates were certainly exhilarated by the possibility of working with him, others who were not willing to proffer the unquestioning loyalty he demanded gradually soured in their relationship. People like Kňažko or Filkus, who proved too independent-minded, found themselves out of a job. In Filkus's case, he was eased out of his job to become ambassador to Austria, but he soon lost that position because of statements he was said to have made that were at odds with government policy. Mečiar surrounded himself with people whom he trusted and felt comfortable with, such as Ivan Lexa, chief of the secretariat of the HZDS, and later chief of the prime minister's office and from 1995, the head of the notorious Slovak Information Service (SIS—the Slovak security service).

Anna Nagyová was another close associate. Inherited from Mečiar's predecessor Milan Čič in 1990, she stayed with the "boss" through thick and thin, both in and out of government. Kňažko tried unsuccessfully to remove her from her position as head of Mečiar's office where, as his private secretary, controlling access to the prime minister gave her a great deal of influence. Securing an appointment through her with the "boss" was like being granted a special dispensation. When I first met her in July 1991 at the Koliba Expo restaurant on a hill overlooking the city, there were no BMW limousines in attendance. Mečiar had just been deposed, and Mrs. Nagyová drove him to our meeting site in a very proletarian Škoda 136. When we sat down to eat, I realized she was missing. Mečiar had sent her to another table. I asked her to join us, and that was the end of her "exile." Mrs. Nagyová knew when to intrude and when not to, as far as Mečiar was concerned. After her boss's return to power, for a while Mrs. Nagyová was elevated to the position of head of the Office of the Prime Minister.

Sometimes, though, her insistence on being the boss's alter ego forced one to do some delicate side-stepping. Shortly before former President Jimmy Carter arrived for a visit to Slovakia in June 1993, we met Mrs. Nagyová to go over some administrative details. On this occasion, a group of Carter's fellow Georgians, who happened to be part of his Secret Service contingent, accompanied us. Mečiar was determined to go all out for Carter, treating him with the honors due a visiting head of state, and making sure his every waking moment was occupied. Carter, however, was traveling with his wife, daughter, and eldest grandchild, on what was essentially a pleasure trip. After attending a UN conference in Vienna, the Carter party went first to Budapest in a rented Volkswagen microbus, and then headed for Slovakia. Mrs. Nagyová informed us that Mečiar himself would meet Carter at the border and Carter would then be transported in Mečiar's BMW limousine (the Škodas were history at this point) into Bratislava.

I suggested that Carter, a very unpretentious person, would be content to travel in his rented van and would not wish to be separated from his family. However, it was evident that Mrs. Nagyová was not willing to hear my recommendations. But then the two Secret Service agents, quietly and diplomatically, explained that "President Carter likes to travel with his family." Mrs. Nagyová finally had to back down, and agreed that Carter could get to Bratislava under his own power. When Carter arrived at the Bôrik Hotel where he would be staying for several nights, the first question he asked me was "How do I get rid of this guy?"—referring to Mečiar's desire to squeeze every minute he could from Carter's presence. But the former president and his family did enjoy themselves, and they were given free run of a shop that made folk art objects and treated to dinner with dancing at a suburban "traditional" restaurant.

On other occasions, we saw indications that the desire of Mečiar's staff to "shield the boss" could be carried too far. In August 1992, we tried to arrange a call by an important U.S. Senate delegation headed by George Mitchell of Maine, the majority leader, and including Foreign Relations Committee Chairman Claiborne Pell. We were first told that Mečiar would be out of town, and then suddenly, he was back in town. By the time we received the go-ahead, it was too late. We were a bit incredulous when we were asked why we had not tried to arrange a meeting, and then to find Mečiar himself telling us he "knew nothing" about the delegation visit.

Despite his image as a very public "man of the people," Mečiar also has a very private, even secretive side. He would go to great lengths to ensure that information that could negatively impact him or his movement would not leak. Accordingly, when he had his first dinner meeting with Ambassador Basora, in order to make him more comfortable, but also to make the point that Americans could communicate with the Slovaks in their own language, I volunteered to interpret between the two. Interpreting for five hours straight in both directions is physically as well as mentally grueling, and on future occasions, Eva Salnerová or one of Mečiar's staff members assisted us. Before the HZDS held its first congress, I asked a number of his close associates about the possibility of inviting the Bratislava consular corps as guests. I recalled that when I served in Finland, it had been the practice of major political parties to invite accredited diplomats of the member countries of the Conference for Security and Cooperation in Europe (CSCE; the organization was succeeded by the Organization for Security and Cooperation in Europe, OSCE) to their congresses. Close relations developed as a result. In Slovakia, the VPN, KDH, and Hungarian parties had routinely extended invitations to local consulates to send observers to their congresses. I was told that the HZDS congress would be divided into open and closed portions. As it turned out, we were invited to neither.

Mečiar also showed an extraordinary desire to dominate and be in charge. During his polemics with the prime minister, Kňažko charged that Mečiar treated the cabinet like a schoolmaster treats his schoolchildren. One story that circulated in 1992 was that Mečiar had decided to send Michal Kováč to Prague as chairman of the National Assembly. Kováč did not want to go because he knew the job would be short-lived. In the end, he did as he was told. After assuming the presidency, Kováč proved less tractable. Another minister told us the issue is not that he was a dictator, but that Mečiar always wanted to be in charge. We confirmed this for ourselves when we offered to send some documents on trade and investment through the relevant ministry. Mečiar demurred, saying he wanted us to send the information directly to him. We also noted that, when gently reminded that some of his domestic policies and statements did not register well abroad, Mečiar's first reaction was a knee-jerk defense, rather than an attempt to understand foreigners' reactions.

In his relations with the United States, Mečiar sometimes tried to come across as "the best friend you will ever have," while at other times he played the jilted lover. He was genuinely concerned about his image in the United States, fearing that being depicted as the devil would derail his political effectiveness at home. Like many other Slovaks, he expressed reservations as to whether our Prague embassy was adequately transmitting Slovak viewpoints to Washington. But in thinking that he could simply pass himself off as a staunch anti-Communist and thus gain a blank check from the United States to support whatever policies he undertook, he badly misunderstood the crux of American concerns.

In February 1993, when our East European Deputy Director Tom Gerth visited Bratislava, Mečiar eagerly invited him to lunch as the first official from Washington to arrive after independence. However, it was clear that Mečiar had his own agenda. Most importantly, he complained that the United States had not responded to his overtures for assistance made the previous year to Ambassador Basora. He was particular incensed over the 1992 Human Rights Report, which he characterized as being authored by "someone who either has never been to Slovakia or someone who hates us." He would not go into specifics as to what aspects of the report were most bothersome, and did not calm down when Gerth explained that a human rights report that calls attention to possible problems is not necessarily meant to be condemnatory.

After I was unsuccessful in getting a grant for Mečiar under the International Visitor Program, he then toyed with the idea of visiting the western United States as the guest of Leo Danihels, a California-based Slovak American businessman who later became president of the Slovak World Congress. In early 1992, Mečiar came to our consulate to get a visa, but his trip never materialized. He explained he had received information that the Slovak police would try to arrest him before the 1992 elections in order to discredit him. Others suggested the real explanation lay in his falling-out with Kňažko. On our part, we always felt that any move to arrest him would backfire and cause the downfall of any government that tried to carry out such a move. Under the conditions existing at the time, it would have led to a surge in his popularity.

During his periodic meetings with Mečiar, Ambassador Basora tried to be frank without taking a mentoring tone. At times, he expressed concern over Slovakia's image abroad. But he also tried to get Mečiar to understand how the Western mentality operates, and how Mečiar himself could take steps to improve his image. He noted how the Bosnian experience had affected Western thinking—to wit, the poisonous effect of interethnic hatred—and suggested how Mečiar might avoid repeating with Hungary the same mistakes that had been so pernicious during the Yugoslav crisis. It was clear that Mečiar was carefully noting down what he heard. During their last conversation, after relations had already been strained over the microphone incident, Mečiar still paid the ambassador the great compliment of noting that he considered him to be a "logical man."

17

OTHER SLOVAK PERSONALITIES

Michal Kováč

Michal Kováč had a background in banking that landed him in such diverse places as London and Havana. In London, he was working for the branch office of the Czechoslovak Trade Bank (1967–69) and had been in Cuba from 1965–66. From 1978 to 1989, he was a researcher at the Research Institute for Finance and Credit, and was later attached to the Central Institute of National Economic Research. Back in Prague in the first 1989 post-Communist government, he was minister of finance, and was carried over into Mečiar's first cabinet. When Mečiar was recalled in April 1991, Kováč was asked to remain in his position, but he soon resigned as an "act of solidarity" with the HZDS leader. Soon after the HZDS was organized in April 1991, Kováč became one of its deputy chairmen. The fact that Kováč, along with Minister of Economy Rudolf Filkus, would have been welcome to remain in government, suggests that he enjoyed support over a wide political spectrum. However, during the 1992 campaign, he did not resist the temptation to engage in name calling, using epithets such as "neocolonialists" to refer to the Czechs during a rally in Bratislava. Although he had no real interest in running for federal office in 1992, he dutifully took up the proffered post of speaker of the Federal Assembly, with a mandate to find a smooth way to dissolve the federation and ensure that Slovakia got its proper share in the succession.

To some, Kováč was a more likely candidate for a provincial party post in the old days. His eastern Slovak accent certainly did nothing to enhance his charisma. Nor could he get rid of the old lexicon. In his inauguration speech on March 2, 1993, he included the exhortation to engage in *poctivá práca* (honest labor)—a phrase that was one of the favorites of Communist agitprop. At the same time, after discussing current politics with him, it was clear that he was a very adept insider who carefully thought through every action he would take. He was a person who eschewed frontal collisions, but this trait did not make him a weakling. Those who joined his staff after he was elected president did so still fearing that he might not be a truly independent figure. Some were pleasantly surprised to see that Kováč was determined to be his own man, and to maximize the use of the powers granted to him under the Slovak Constitution.

While I had met Kováč briefly several times before, my first opportunity for an extended chat came in the closing days of 1992. We met in the speaker's office in the Bratislava Castle, just one floor below the president's office, that had been arranged for Václav Havel but was now empty, except for the presence of some middle-level officials looking for something to do. With a smile, looking at the ceiling, I asked Kováč whether he intended to "move upstairs," both literally and figuratively. He explained where the nomination process stood, noting that his namesake, then Deputy Prime Minister Roman Kováč, had a few more committed votes than he did. However, when prodded a little further, Kováč warmed to the idea that a president should act independently and be a counterweight to the prime minister. He made it clear that he considered himself to have more of an independent base in the HZDS than did his colleague Roman. Indeed, when the voting took place, support turned to Michal Kováč precisely because of the view that he would be more independent as president. However, in politics nothing is permanent. Roman Kováč wound up resigning his post as deputy prime minister in Mečiar's cabinet and joined the ranks of the opposition.

In early 1993, when Mečiar was being bombarded by accusations of authoritarian behavior, Kováč privately defended the prime minister as someone who had a right to his job because he had been put into power by democratic means. He noted, however, that Mečiar's tenure was not indefinite and would depend on the degree to which he retained public support. To avoid a crisis early in his tenure, he also gave in to Mečiar's demand that he fire Milan Kňažko. As time went on, however, Kováč became more and more willing to assert his political prerogatives, first by declining to support Mečiar's nomination of Ivan Lexa as head of the SIS (and later as minister of privatization), and in 1994, by taking public issue with Mečiar and suggesting it was time for him to step down. I could not help but feel a certain sympathy for Kováč—we were both heading institutions that had no road maps to guide them, and whose predecessors had functioned several decades earlier under very different historical circumstances.

Kováč had a very strong feeling about his role as Slovakia's image-maker and ambassador of good will. In his inaugural remarks, he took pains to disassociate himself from those Slovaks who called him "Slovakia's second president" and thus conferred legitimacy on the rule of Father Tiso. He was keenly aware that by embracing the Tiso regime he would besmirch his own reputation abroad, and therefore he carefully chose a formula that condemned the crimes of Tiso and his regime while recognizing that the Slovak people had made some positive accomplishments during that period.

Ján Čarnogurský

I first met Čarnogurský in May 1990 at the Czechoslovak Embassy in Washington, when he was visiting as deputy prime minister of the federal government. Čarnogurský had a solid reputation in Washington as a lawyer who had defended persecuted dissidents and had himself become a victim of Communist repression. He had been arrested by the Communist regime with a number of other prominent dissidents at the beginning of the November revolution in 1989. All were freed within a few days. Yet Čarnogurský's background was much more complex than his work as a human rights lawyer. His father, Pavol, had been a leading official of the Tiso regime, and as newspaper articles pointed out in the early 1990s, had issued decrees for confiscating properties of Jews and Czechs who fled Slovakia soon after its Nazi-sponsored "independence." The elder Čarnogurský created an uproar with some remarks in 1990 that appeared to whitewash the Tiso regime.

Čarnogurský's own politics were also complicated. His attempt to straddle the two incompatible poles in Slovak political thinking—opting for a common state with the Czechs or for independence disguised as "confederation"—did not win him friends in either camp. He first came out first for a confederation and later for a confederation with federal elements or a federation with confederational elements. In one interview, he plugged Slovak entrance into the European Community with "our own star on the European table," thus intimating that Slovakia would be an independent member of the EC (EU or European Union after 1994) despite continuing in a common state with the Czechs.[1] One of Čarnogurský's close associates suggested that his verbal meanderings were tactical—designed to soak up sentiment for an independent identity while maintaining the dialogue with the Czechs in a way that would continue the common state. Unfortunately, these verbal sleights of hand confused rather than clarified the issue, leading many Czechs to assume that he was pro-independence but a bit more sophisticated in his approach than were the Slovak nationalists.

A deeply religious man, Čarnogurský tried to make his Christian Democratic Movement (KDH) into a viable competitor for the good will of Slovakia's four million believers. However, the KDH took that support too much for granted and saw its vote reduced by half between the 1990 and 1992 elections. A basically decent person, Čarnogurský identified his movement so closely with the Catholic Church and its teachings that he became vulnerable to accusations that he was ushering in "black totalitarianism" or Church dictatorship. He had some other political eccentricities, including a morbid fear of "freemasonry." When invited to the inauguration of the first postwar lodge of the international Jewish service agency B'nai Brith in Bratislava, he first demurred until assured that despite the fact that B'nai Brith is organized in lodges, it has nothing to do with the Freemasons. Čarnogurský also included an attack on "freemasonry" in a speech he was to deliver in New York, but the reference was deleted by a British advisor at the last minute. However, he attacked "liberalism" in the same speech, and the reference remained in place. Years later, the KDH would return to the theme that it was a bulwark against liberalism in Slovakia. He claimed that even Czechoslovakia's first president, Tomáš Masaryk, in his conversations with the Czech writer Karel Čapek, had also condemned liberal ideology. In so doing, Čarnogurský alienated a number of Americans who otherwise admired him; after all, who were Čarnogurský's foreign supporters, if not liberals themselves? Other advisors despaired that, while Čarnogurský had a good mind for the law, he was weak on economics—a matter of greatest concern to his constituents.

As prime minister, Čarnogurský suffered because of the belief among many Slovaks that his government was somehow illegitimate—that it had usurped power from Mečiar on the sly while he was out of the country, in a "political coup." Čarnogurský also had the bad fortune to preside over a government that was implementing an economic reform program that bore a "made in Prague" label, and which resulted in a rapid increase in Slovak, but not so much Czech, unemployment.

18

U.S. POLICY AND CZECHOSLOVAKIA

From Single State to Peaceful Split

In considering the relationship between our policy toward Czechoslovakia and the outcome of events—most important, the breakup of the country—one is struck by the fact that our policy had such marginal relevance for the outcome. While the U.S. preference remained the preservation of a single state, the forces that were tearing the country in two were not subject to U.S. influence, and policy options were soon reduced to opposing or accepting a process that was beyond our control. The United States favored a united Czechoslovakia principally because we believed that it was not in the interest of East Europeans to break up into fragmented mini-states, but additionally because we did not wish to undercut efforts by President Havel and the people associated with him to maintain a single country.

Of all the successor leaders of Eastern Europe, it is safe to say that Havel probably made more of an impression on the American body politic than any other politician. When Havel spoke before the U.S. Congress in February 1990 about the legacy of Thomas Jefferson, he could do so without arousing the slightest feeling that he was merely being polite to his hosts. Havel, to Americans who knew him, embodied the continuing relevance of the ideals of the American Revolution more than two centuries later. His moral stock was boosted by the fact that he had a long record of struggle against dictatorship in his own country, and that he had paid the price for his convictions by years of imprisonment. At the same time, his lack of political skills hampered him in dealing with touchy Slovak sensitivities.

When Havel visited the United States for the second time as president in October 1991, the Department of State was looking for ways in which to boost his efforts to keep the country together. One idea that was approved was to upgrade our consulate to the status of consulate general. The former term is used to refer to smaller representative offices outside of a country's capital, while the latter term is used for larger offices in major cities. Although our offices in Slovakia were originally established (1948–50) at the consulate general level, the decision made in 1990 was to start off as just a consulate. There was no intention to deprecate the importance of Slovakia in the general scheme of things, but the original idea was to set up a minimal office with one American whose functions would include reporting on developments as well as taking care of the welfare of American citizens. In fact, though, this decision put the level of U.S. representation below that of every other country then or subsequently represented in Slovakia, since ours was the only consulate, all the others being consulates general. But if the upgrade to a consulate general was intended to show the Slovaks that the United States was singling them out for special recognition, that effort was lost in the bureaucratic shuffle. We heard about the upgrade from news reports, but we never received any official notification from Washington. Even after Havel returned home (directly to Bratislava) on October 28, 1991, we still had no official word. I asked John Evans to find out what was going on, and he subsequently learned that a decision memorandum had been approved by the undersecretary for management the day before Havel's arrival. Later, we received notification. However, rather than underscoring that the move reflected the increasing importance of Slovakia, it merely reminded us that the upgrade to consulate general was to be accomplished "without additional expenditures." Indeed, the only expenditure entailed was $160 for new signs outside the building and on my residence.

If our secret desire was still to see the country stay together, by the summer of 1991 we had a distinctive shift in emphasis. When I met Mečiar on July 3, I explained to him that our policy toward Yugoslavia was now premised on accepting any outcome, so long as it expressed the will of the people, and was decided by democratic means. This course of action also held true for Czechoslovakia. When Bob Hutchings of the National Security Council (NSC) subsequently visited Bratislava and had lunch with Mečiar, he reiterated this guiding principle. I felt a bit relieved, because Slovaks had become increasingly critical of U.S. dedication to their country's "territorial integrity" as missing the point. Mečiar registered the point very carefully. While he was scrupulously careful about using for his own purposes any information he received privately from us, in subsequent polemics with pro-federalist Slovaks, he could not resist the jab that the United States no longer supported their position. Of course, there was a subtle difference: the United States would accept any outcome that reflected the expression of democratic will of the people, even if our own private hope was that the country would remain intact.

When I arrived in Washington for consultations in January 1992, the question on everyone's lips was "will they separate?" There had been considerable splitting of bureaucratic hairs over the answer to that question. In the State Department, where the wish may have been father to the thought, the expectation was strong that the country would remain undivided. People in the intelligence community, however, were strongly convinced that the country could not remain together. In the end, they were proved right. When I met some colleagues in our European Bureau, they were a bit taken aback by a cable sent a few months earlier from Prague titled "If Czechoslovakia Splits." The embassy had been doing its job of analyzing trends, and its report was based on the thesis that we could no longer take the future of the country for granted, and needed to start to consider scenarios under which a split would take place. My own conclusion at the time was a bit of bureaucratic fence-sitting. On the one hand, I told my colleagues, the Mečiar and Klaus programs for the future of the country were quite incompatible. If no one flinched on either side, the inevitable result could only be a split. On the other hand, I felt there was a certain amount of political posturing in the rhetoric on both sides, and that one could not then exclude flexibility before getting to their bottom-line positions. At that moment, the Czech and Slovak national councils were still meeting to forge a political agreement—one which was initialed in early February, but which ultimately collapsed when the Slovaks proved unable to ratify it.

The U.S. Aid Program

One of the most important instruments of U.S. policy in post-1989 Czechoslovakia was the aid program. One of the many bones of contention between Czechs and Slovaks was the feeling held by the latter that they were not getting their fair share of international assistance. While this feeling spilled over into relations with the United States, in actuality, the United States did make special efforts to ensure that the Slovaks received their fair share of assistance. Not only did we set up in January 1992 the only office of the United States Agency for International Development (USAID) existing outside a national capital, but we also gave Slovaks more aid than their one-third proportion of the population would have warranted. This was due to the recognition that the Slovaks had more genuine need for assistance than did the Czechs, but also served the political purpose of showing that the United States cared and was responsive to Slovak requests.

The U.S. assistance program in Slovakia, as in the rest of the region, was conducted primarily under the 1989 SEED (Support for East European Democracy) Act, which, together with other U.S. programs and initiatives, was designed to strengthen the new democracies of Eastern Europe, to ensure that they met internationally recognized human rights standards, continued the transition to a market economy, and were anchored to the Western economic and political community. The realization of these objectives involved a number of initiatives that included removing legal and bureaucratic restraints to entrepreneurship, advancement of privatization and enterprise restructuring, and capital and technical assistance to new entrepreneurs. In helping advance democracy, it included support for national parliaments, local governments, independent media, and technical assistance and training to support improved public administration and tax reform. The third aspect of the program addressed quality of life issues, focusing on cost-efficient health care and housing, measures to deal with unemployment, and assistance for responsible environmental management.[1]

One of the aid programs that received the most attention from the media and the public was the Czech and Slovak American Enterprise Fund (CSAEF), whose Bratislava office was headed by Leighton Klevana, an American lawyer born in Slovakia just before World War II. The CSAEF program provided for a total funding of $60 million spread over several years, with the understanding that profits would be plowed back into operations, and that the program would eventually become self-sustaining. Klevana also worked to gain additional funding from partner agencies in Japan. Under the "first come, first served" principle, the CSAEF wound up with a mix of about two-thirds of all projects approved for Slovakia. These included the manufacture of fire extinguishers, orthopedic devices, motorcycles, cement roof tiles, and gaskets. As each new factory opened, Klevana arranged for a gala ceremony, and I always tried to make time on my schedule to lend support. Klevana's operation was also invaluable in the sense that, until 1993, we did not have a functioning commercial office, and his many contacts throughout Slovakia helped us find partners for American businessmen interested in joint ventures.

USAID also funded a number of other significant initiatives that brought Americans down to the grass roots to work with their counterparts. The International Executive Service Corps (IESC) established an office in Bratislava. Its function is to place expert advisors, usually retired American businessmen, with individual firms to provide assistance in such areas as management, marketing, and quality control. Three of the thirty-two advisors sent in 1992 were assigned to the ZTS Martin firm, an armaments manufacturer. Few problems were more sensitive for post-Communist Slovak governments than the need to restructure the armaments industry. Slovakia had prospered during the old days when tank and other heavy armaments factories were built on its territory. With the market all but dried up, there was an urgent need to put productive capacities to new uses. The Slovaks had already begun the process, looking toward construction equipment as the most promising substitute. However, the profits from tank production were enormous; Demeš once showed a chart noting that it took eighty-three tractors to equal the profits from one tank. Mečiar at times toyed with the idea of maintaining some military production, using the most advanced U.S. technology. Ambassador Basora, after consultations in Washington, convinced him that such an option would not be viable.

Through Price Waterhouse, USAID financed a $1.7 million privatization program in Slovakia, working with four firms to make recommendations for restructuring, and using modern accounting principles. Deloitte and Touche was awarded contracts to privatize the rubber chemical sector and to assist the Slovak Ministry of Privatization. The U.S. Department of Justice and the Federal Trade Commission sent two-person teams for six-month periods to advise the Slovak Anti-Monopoly Office on enforcing competition laws and to advocate market-oriented solutions to economic problems. They also provided internships to Slovak officials to expose them to U.S. competition policies and law enforcement techniques.

The Treasury Department provided advisors to the General Credit Bank and to the finance minister. A program to train Slovak bankers was initiated in 1993. Similarly, the Securities and Exchange Commission (SEC), in cooperation with the Financial Services Volunteer Corps, provided advice on issues related to trading investment company shares and shares of publicly held companies. An advisor from the SEC also helped in the process of establishing a stock exchange in Bratislava.

Another sought-after agency was the Trade and Development Agency (TDA), which provided funding for feasibility studies where there was the likelihood of a significant input of U.S. technology and equipment. Minister of Industry (in the first Mečiar and subsequently Čarnogurský governments) Ján Holčik was a great fan of the TDA, and once prevailed upon

Ambassador Black to come down from Prague to ceremoniously sign one agreement. In addition to projects in such areas as municipal waste management, the TDA also carried out studies in all of what was then Czechoslovakia for recommendations regarding new legal and regulatory telecommunications structures in preparation for privatization.

In the area of energy efficiency, various projects included low-cost energy efficiency improvements, increasing efficiency of operations at the giant Slovnaft plant, and an assessment of U.S. trade and investment potential. The Southern Electric Company was given a contract to assist the Slovak Electric Power (SEP) company with management and finance, and the Nuclear Regulatory Agency helped upgrade safety at Slovak nuclear power installations. In agriculture, the Volunteers in Overseas Cooperative Assistance (VOCA), much as did their counterparts in the IESC, advised on the organization and operation of agricultural cooperatives, privatization of state farms and state food processing industries, and promotion of farm tourism. A number of other programs were launched to help Slovak agriculture, including a major effort run by Iowa State University to help restructure agriculture and provide technical assistance to the emerging private agribusiness sector. The U.S. Department of Agriculture, for its part, offered fellowships for Slovak farmers to visit the United States and helped fund research on crop outlooks.

The USAID program on quality of life issues involved the environment, health, and housing. In the environmental field, programs concentrated on supporting legal, regulatory, and policy reform, improving the efficiency of private sector environmental investments, and helping the private sector play a larger role in environmental management. Much of this work involved providing advisors to help draft new regulations or work on specific projects, training, or initiation of various studies on practical issues.

In the health field, USAID supported the activities of Project Hope, which opened its European office in the Slovak capital. Project Hope has been oriented to such projects as nursing practices, cancer screening in women, and resuscitation skills for health care personnel. Other areas of concentration included the establishment of a high quality pediatric cardiology and cardiatric surgery capability in a $2.4 million project conducted jointly with Children's Hospital Boston, and $1 million in emergency medical supplies to Czechoslovakia to combat shortages. In the area of housing, USAID programs aimed at privatizing the housing market, helping in construction management, and developing a financing system for urban infrastructure projects.

In the area of democratic initiatives, some plans included management training in a program organized by the University of Pittsburgh for Czechs and Slovaks, assistance on criminal justice through the auspices of an assistant U.S. Attorney assigned for six months, support to the Slovak National Council to strengthen its research and reference capabilities, and the International Media Fund, whose objective is to strengthen independent media in Eastern Europe.

One should not fail to mention other, privately funded initiatives that brought Americans to Slovakia. One of the most successful of these, Education for Democracy, allowed some two hundred Americans—mainly in their 20s, but including some of retirement age—to come to Slovakia (and for a time, the Czech Republic as well) in order to work in educational and business installations to train Slovaks in English and to bring part of their American culture and American values with them. Even in the most remote parts of Slovakia, when I visited various institutions, I would always be introduced to "our Americans" from Education for Democracy. Like so many citizen initiatives, the idea came from an American in Alabama whom Dr. Demeš had met during his period of study just before the 1989 revolution. Under Demeš's auspices at the Ministry of Education, and later at the Ministry of International Relations, the program was continued. Other useful activities included the Fulbright program, which was reinstituted in 1990 for all of Czechoslovakia, and the Sabre Foundation program, which facilitated the sending of 16,000 medical and children's books to Slovakia.

While these initiatives were wide ranging and imaginative, one should also note that they were designed to have a longer term impact on the country, and consequently, except in limited cases, were not easily recognized by the average Slovak as an instrument that caused an improvement in his or her daily life. Consequently, we sometimes met with the complaint that the United States was not doing enough in Slovakia, or that the effects of U.S. assistance were not clearly evident. For this reason, we realized that we needed to pay increasing attention to the public relations dimension of our activities.

At the same time, the message we delivered was that, while it was easy to ask for assistance, it was harder to use it effectively. While the Slovaks were concerned with getting their fair share of aid funding, they were told that it was the quality of economic reform programs, not politically motivated quotas, that determined further aid. The future of any aid program would be dependent on its usefulness and effectiveness. Cultural differences also limited the effectiveness of advisers in some programs. For example, one private banker lamented in early 1993 that Americans do not understand the psychology of Slovaks; few advisors had a sufficient command of the Slovak language, and Americans failed to understand that Slovaks needed significant help in acquiring skills that would allow them to negotiate and write business plans. Outsiders, including the IMF, he complained, failed to realize the effect that decades of a command economy had on Slovaks, who would always have a "mixed economic model," perhaps "on the Austrian line."

Prior to the 1992 elections, there was at times a strange symbiotic quality to this aid-driven relationship. For the Čarnogurský government, every U.S. project directed to Slovakia was proof that the Slovak administration was doing its part for its people. However, it was quite clear to us that U.S. aid was sought to bolster the dwindling political fortunes of Čarnogurský and his allies. While on the one hand, it was natural that we deal with whatever government was democratically elected to power, on the other hand, U.S. aid was relied on as a political crutch that ran the risk of opening us to accusations that we were politicizing the aid program. In December 1991, for instance, I journeyed to the town of Rimavská Sobota with most of the Slovak government to attend an open meeting. Presided over by the deputy prime minister for economic affairs, the regional session aimed at showing people in the provinces, and their local officials, what the Slovak government was doing to advance their interests. In Rimavská Sobota, I was also expected to make a few remarks about U.S. aid programs that would be of special interest to inhabitants of an economically depressed area such as that one. As the idea was to ensure that as many Slovaks as possible were aware of our programs and how, for example, aid to small enterprises could be helpful to their economy, we felt our participation was in order.

High-Level Visits

On August 21, 1992, we hosted the highest-level U.S. Senate delegation ever to come to Slovakia on a lightning visit that lasted for five hours, but which was unfortunately accompanied by record heat that reached 106 degrees. The delegation was led by Majority Leader George Mitchell and included Foreign Relations Committee Chairman Claiborne Pell, three other Senators, and several staff members. The highlight of the visit was a call on Slovak National Council Speaker Ivan Gašparovič, who pointedly said he would welcome their advice if it would be "beneficial" to Slovakia. Mitchell, who would soon journey to Croatia to open the U.S. Embassy there, stressed the peaceful nature of the process taking place in Czechoslovakia, and sharply contrasted it with the bloody events in the former Yugoslavia. Gašparovič, when asked whether the Czech-Slovak split was now inevitable, answered in his own way, reciting a litany of Slovak complaints about the Czechs, and pointing to a "new system of collaboration" between the two republics. But he avoided directly using the word "yes." However, he confirmed that Slovakia would henceforth have its own relations with other states and international bodies. While Gašparovič, along with Minister of Privatization Augustin Marián Huska, attempted to assure his audience that the split would not lead to undue economic difficulties, Senator Warren Rudman of New Hampshire demurred, arguing that a divided country would be deprived of the economies of scale, and that its dissolution would mean the end of an existing small-scale economic bloc. Not surprisingly, his Slovak interlocutors refused to accept this reasoning. The delegation also met with Kňažko and had lunch at my residence—made only slightly less sweltering by our attempt to train every available fan on our guests. By this time, the Slovaks had honed their approach to foreigners; the dreaded "I" (independence) word was stricken from their vocabulary, and, as Kňažko smoothly put it, the goal was to "restructure" relations with the Czechs. The Slovaks oversold their case; Foreign Relations Committee Chairman Ivan Laluha, for one, seemed genuinely surprised that the only subject visitors ever seem to be concerned about was "human rights."

When Ambassador Adrian Basora came to Slovakia in the summer of 1992 and discussed the issue of eventual Slovak membership in NATO, Mečiar politely demurred. Basora was not one to press the point, and noted that the United States has a perfectly acceptable relationship with Austria, a neutral country, but the fact that Austria is not a military ally places certain limitations on the relationship. But after independence, political pragmatism made Mečiar gravitate to the idea that Slovakia required an anchor, and that anchor must be with the Western alliance. He was quite adamant in stressing this view when he visited Brussels and NATO headquarters in early 1993. He also supported the continuation of an American role in Europe. While one can speculate about his motivations—Mečiar is if nothing else the quintessential political tactician—we welcomed his readiness to cooperate, as well as his professed commitment to Western values.[2]

In the fall of 1992, the United States picked up some small political capital among the Slovaks for our "understanding" response to the process by which the federation would dissolve. While the United States stressed that the process should be by democratic means and preserve constitutional democracy, a market economy, and the international commitments undertaken by the federation, some European states, the Slovaks complained, had tried to issue "ultimata" to the effect that a referendum had to be held before they would agree to continue to support the successor states. In the end, though, the process was accepted by all parties concerned.

19

INDEPENDENCE AND ITS AFTERMATH:
THE DOMESTIC ANGLE

The Square of the Slovak National Uprising was the place to be at midnight, January 1, 1993. The site of so many spectacles associated with Slovakia's post-1989 history, it was now filled with merrymakers, many of whom were fortified with bottles of champagne or even stronger beverages. Vladimír Mečiar, surrounded by politicians from other pro-independence parties, attempted to address the crowd at five minutes past twelve to inform them that the millennial yearning of Slovaks to live in their own state had finally been achieved. But few in the crowd seemed to focus on his words. Mečiar called the demise of the ČSFR part of the geopolitical changes occurring all over the world, a result of the divergent paths of development in both republics after 1989, as well as the "mistakes" made at that time. The Slovaks should be happy not only to have achieved their own state, he said, but also over the new possibility of directly participating in European and world-wide integrative processes. Three days later, he told the budding Slovak military that a Slovak armed force would be necessary because, although the country had no enemies, "we have no allies either." Mečiar characterized relations with the United States as important, and in an implicit reference to the bugging incident, claimed that someone tried to "embitter" those ties toward the end of 1992. He pledged that Slovakia would respect the inviolability of all diplomatic offices and all obligations arising from international conventions. He also voiced positive expectations for relations with neighboring states: the Russians, Ukrainians, Czechs ("the most voluminous of relations"), Hungarians ("non-interference in internal affairs and inviolability of borders"), and Austrians ("our only border with a market economy and advanced democracy").

At midnight, the Czechoslovak tricolor was hauled down and the new Slovak flag raised, and border posts with the old national emblem were painted over. Slovaks who had been performing border controls for the federal government now did so in the name of the Slovak Republic. Necessity, however, made a lot of transitional arrangements imperative. Within a few days, border controls were enforced with the Czech Republic, although in some cases, citizens living in towns that straddled the new border could go back and forth without difficulty. On independence day, Slovaks lined up for first-day issues of their new postage stamps, although the former Czechoslovak stamps continued to be legal tender. The currency was yet to be split, and Slovaks continued to travel abroad on Czechoslovak passports. Despite considerable lobbying by the American Banknote Company, the Canadians wound up with most of the lucrative contract for printing Slovak passports (and later currency). That morning, I trooped with my fellow diplomats to the Parliament building to watch the NRSR approve a declaration announcing that Slovakia was one of two successor states to the ČSFR; it also made the assurance that the country would adhere to its international legal commitments and be governed by the rules of a pluralistic democracy.

The stroke of midnight on New Year's Day 1993 also elevated our consulate general to an embassy. To be sure, we were the same persons, and had the same operational capabilities we did on the last day of December 1992. But our responsibilities quickly multiplied. The first sign of change was the fact that we began to get rather urgent calls for overflight clearances for U.S. military flights that passed over Slovak territory. Until independence, this task was handled routinely by our Defense Attaché's Office in Prague. Now, because the Prague embassy no longer had any writ in Slovakia, we had to do these things ourselves. My sorely tried assistant, Eva Salnerová, soon became our "overflights officer." She had to quickly master the intricacies of entry-exit corridors, coordinates, and drafting diplomatic notes. While the Slovak Foreign Ministry sent us routine messages by diplomatic note before independence, we had scrupulously avoided reciprocating because of the fact that notes are sent to countries with which we have diplomatic relations, and at that time, such was not the case with Slovakia.

The problem, though, was that many requests for flight clearance came in as classified messages. One of the unwanted "fringe benefits" of the microphone affair was to raise the view among our security people that our facilities were especially susceptible to penetration. Thus, any possibility of giving us the capability to send, receive, or store classified information got lost in the security bureaucracy. We started getting urgent messages from assorted U.S. Air Force personnel asking why we had not replied to a pressing clearance request. In fact, the request had fallen through the cracks and remained in the mailbox at our embassy in Vienna. As time wore on, the Air Force learned to live with our limitations; it excised the names of high-ranking individuals on specific flights out of the messages and thus was able to send the requests through our unclassified fax.

The next responsibility placed on us was notification of troop movements under the CFE (Conventional Forces in Europe) Treaty. Every time there was a significant movement of our forces in Europe, we were treaty bound to inform the Slovaks. This requirement existed despite the fact that few of our Slovak interlocutors knew (or probably cared) about such movements. As Eva was busy with overflight clearances, and as CFE notifications had to be hand delivered to the host government, I took the logical step of designating my driver Jozef Moronga as the official "CFE officer," having him draft the notifications and deliver them as well. One of my initiatives wasn't received well in Vienna. Because of the need to send out cables from Vienna, I once tried to draft a message in Bratislava, seal it in a double envelope, and give it to Jozef to take to Vienna. The message was "sensitive but unclassified," and our Foreign Service National employees are permitted to handle such materials. However, the next time I came to Vienna, the Regional Security Officer presented me with a pink slip—notice of security violation—as a thank you for my innovation. But, he assured me, since the document wasn't classified, the violation would "not be sent on to Washington."

Independence also brought a handover of administrative support from Prague to Vienna. Almost every day, it seemed that a car from Vienna would be at our doorstep, bringing an administrative or personnel officer. The help was immensely useful, as we still lacked a permanent American administrative officer, but we also realized it was a stopgap. In early February, we realized just how little we were the masters of our own fate when we were suddenly informed that our employees could not be paid until further notice because our central payroll office in Paris had heard that the Slovak crown was being devalued by 10 percent against the Czech crown. Just after the effective date of the separation of the two republics' currencies, an employee of the Paris office read an article that carried the story of the devaluation, and accepted it as fact, without bothering to check with us. (The devaluation actually came on July 10—three days after my departure.) What really happened was that the temporary currency of each republic (in fact, Czecho-slovak banknotes marked either "Slovakia" or "Czech Republic") started to trade at a discount in banks in the other republic. Thus, a Slovak trading in 100 Slovak crowns at a Czech bank would get only 90 Czech crowns for them. However, the same thing was true for Czechs needing Slovak crowns. Officially, however, the two currencies retained parity. The new system also brought in vastly increased contributions for social security, with decreased take-home pay. Our employees were upset about that, but a similar setup simultaneously went into effect in the Czech Republic.

Dissonance in the HZDS

Probably the major political development in the spring of 1993 was the denouement of Mečiar's relationship with Kňažko. It had already become clear the previous November that tension was building between the two. Mečiar had sent Lexa to "investigate" possible lapses in the Ministry of Foreign Affairs (MFA). Kňažko rejected Mečiar's demand that he resign. President Kováč, recently installed in office, was also not about to agree automatically to Mečiar's demand, and asked the newly established Constitutional Court to make a decision as to whether the new Slovak Constitution required that the president dismiss a minister if the prime minister so recommended. While the court eventually ruled that the president did have the power to decline the prime minister's demand, Kováč's hands were tied by the fact that Mečiar himself threatened to resign, and bring the whole government down with him, if Kováč failed to approve Kňažko's dismissal. Mečiar also vowed he would not accept a request to form a new government if such an eventuality came to pass. Thus, Kováč signed on to Mečiar's demand, as he told a television interviewer, to avoid the political instability that would surely erupt so soon after independence, and on March 19 summoned Kňažko to the palace to tell him that his dismissal was the "lesser of two evils." Within two hours, Kňažko was replaced by Jozef Moravčik, who had been federal foreign minister during the last six months before the breakup. Ten days later, on March 28, Kňažko was replaced by Roman Zelenay, his one-time deputy in the MFA in the first Mečiar cabinet, as HZDS deputy chairman for international affairs. Kňažko promptly bolted the HZDS and took seven other deputies with him.

I had first met Moravčik when he was dean of the Faculty of Law at Comenius University. Despite the fact that Kňažko resented Moravčik for taking his job from him, Moravčik declined to play Mečiar's game of criticizing Kňažko's stewardship of the MFA, and instead recalled in an interview that Kňažko had been his close friend since their student days. Unequivocally, Moravčik said he would place emphasis on joining the EC and trans-Atlantic security structures. His reaction to other questions was sober and typically low-key.

A day before Kňažko's ouster, his cabinet colleague Ľudovít Černák resigned, but in this instance, on his own volition. The ostensible reason for his leaving the government was Mečiar's decision to nominate General Imrich Andrejčák as Slovakia's first minister of defense. Černák felt that the job should be handled by a civilian, and he also objected to Andrejčák's close ties to the former Communist regime. But, as the Slovak saying goes, this was only the "drop that caused the glass to overflow" (or the straw that broke the camel's back).

While Černák had wrestled for months with the question of whether or not he could do more good outside the government than inside, he finally came to the conclusion that he could no longer remain on Mečiar's team. He recounted that some of his policy objections included the high-handed attempts by the minister of education to close down Trnava University (see chapter 14), the behavior of Minister of Culture Dušan Slobodník, the absence of macroeconomic viewpoints in the government, inefficient taxation measures, and excessive burdens on entrepreneurs. Černák criticized Mečiar for indifference to cooperation with other political parties, for his unwillingness to consider a broader political coalition or recruitment of opposition figures in strategic posts, such as head of the Security Service or Office of Supreme Control.

Several months later, in early June, Černák came to call at our embassy. He was expecting to go to the United States to attend an international conference on minorities, and asked our assistance in making some contacts in Washington. The trip never materialized, because Černák's party was involved in negotiations over a possible coalition agreement with the HZDS that would allow the nationalists to take control over education, labor and social affairs, health, and telecommunications, and also receive the deputy premiership for economic affairs—a post that would have gone to Černák. He was ambivalent as to his options: would a delay of several months cause the economy to falter and his own party's fortunes to prosper? When asked "what should I do?" I carefully sidestepped the question, knowing that it was hardly the role of a foreign diplomat to be advising a politician in his host country as to the political steps he should take. I suggested that Černák consider the degree of influence he would have over economic and social policy, the resources he would have available for health and education, and the degree of power over economic affairs he would have as deputy prime minister. What was of interest, however, was Černák's desire to play the "Washington card." In the early months of Slovak independence, Slovakia's political leaders, ranging from its president and prime minister, and now to several opposition leaders, including the SDĽ's Weiss, all felt that shoring up their relations with U.S. officials would be to their benefit. We were naturally happy to oblige as far as circumstances would permit.[1]

Several other ministers also left the cabinet for reasons other than their own volition. On June 13, the controversial minister of education, Matuš Kučera, was finally recalled, this time not due to a move by the opposition, but because of a vote of no confidence within his own HZDS (see chapter 14). Two days later, the embattled Ľubomír Dolgoš, increasingly at odds with Mečiar over privatization policy and regarded as less than competent by some of his party-mates, resigned from office. When I ran into him a few months later, he was in Washington, D.C., spending a year's sabbatical on a scholarship.

The Winter of Our Discontent: The Economic Angle

When the bonfires stopped burning and the last firecrackers were popped, Slovaks began to face the new reality ushered in by independence. Discontent arose from a number of issues that came together in the immediate post-independence period: first, sharp rises in the cost of living (8.9 percent in January alone, nearly equal to the rise for all of 1992), stifling legislation that placed new burdens on businessmen, withholding of social payments to families, and shortages of essential medicines. On February 12, thousands of businessmen gathered in the eastern Slovak town of Lučenec to protest high taxes and social insurance payments that amounted to 38 percent of the employee's income. They were particularly incensed that these payments were required only from the private sector. Some businessmen estimated that payments and taxes raised the basic cost of salaries by as much as 90 percent, and they predicted that many of their associates would simply end their entrepreneurial activities and end up on state welfare rolls. True to his role as dissident within the government, Minister of Economy Černák was the only minister who actually showed up, and he told the protesters that many of their complaints were justified. They exempted him from their demand that the government resign; as it turned out, however, Černák himself subsequently chose to resign. At that stage in Slovakia's development, entrepreneurs did not make up a political and economic force strong enough to make credible their threat of a general strike.

Nor were Slovaks heartened by the way in which the government botched up the system for dispensing child support payments—an income supplement depended upon by many families to balance their budgets. The previous system of basing payments on the number of children was scrapped for one in which payments were made regardless of how many children were in a family. However, a means test was indicated, and payments were suspended by many agencies as the government attempted to find a formula that would allow families to prove that their income was below the legal maximum and still qualify for support payments. Pensioners were removed from eligibility lists for any state-sponsored income supplements; teenagers who were unemployed were no longer eligible for compensation, and newly married couples could no longer receive state-subsidized loans. Contributing to the agony was the imposition of a value-added tax of 23 percent on most goods (5 percent on food and books) that resulted in price rises often exceeding the nominal amount of the tax.

Trade unionists, whose constituents were hard hit by the new measures, were up in arms. In early February, as a form of protest, trade union representatives left the tripartite (government, union, employer) Council for Economic and Social Accord, a body that tried to informally work out guidelines on social policies and benefits, because the government regarded the unions only as "firemen who need to put out the flames of social unrest" after defective policies were followed.

One of the ministers who came in for especially sharp criticism was Minister of Health Viliam Soboňa. Soboňa had ignited controversy after the HZDS took over the reins of government by becoming in effect the "dismissal king," through his wholesale dismissals of hospital directors and other officials. He was unable to establish a viable national insurance scheme, and was accused of presiding over a dangerous drawdown in stocks of essential drugs. While Soboňa was insisting that there was a sufficient stock of insulin, others, such as the diabetic writer Ján Šimonovič, were threatening to initiate a resolution recalling Soboňa "even from the nether world" if the demise of diabetics was caused by their inability to find insulin. Because of the general insolvency in the health care sector, many potential suppliers were reluctant to sell drugs to medical institutions, fearing that they would never be paid. While Soboňa hoped to alleviate the financial crunch in health care by encouraging hospitals to go into profit-making activities, the hospitals felt they could not increase their charges for such items as laundry and catering sufficiently to make a difference.

At the same time, there was little inclination to fan the fires of social unrest in newly independent Slovakia. The feeling that "we're on our own" had brought with it a sense of restraint and social responsibility despite the tensions that those recently enacted inequities caused. Mečiar, the "great communicator," was also in a stronger position to contain the discontent than his predecessors had been.

Despite the fact that initial plans called for maintaining the monetary union of both republics for six months, this idea quickly proved untenable. When I met with Czech and Slovak bankers in mid-January, they expressed the view that a monetary union was unstable and the sooner it was ended, the better it would be for all. I was told by one leading Slovak banker that about a billion crowns (some $35 million) had been deposited in Czech banks since the first of the year by Slovaks who were concerned that their currency would become worthless after a monetary exchange. Finance Minister Tóth had already contributed to this feeling by making assurances that bank deposits would remain inviolable; raising the issue even as a denial contributed to public anxiety. Another symptom of instability was the strong demand for a maximum limit on foreign currency (about $140 per six months), as people sought to put their limited assets into something more stable.

As the second largest party, and the pariah of Slovak politics until it joined a coalition after Mečiar lost a vote of confidence in the spring of 1994, the SDĽ represented one of the basic question marks of Slovak politics. When I met Weiss at the end of May, he was clearly distressed by Mečiar's assertions that the United States would not like to see the SDĽ in a Slovak government. While this question was definitively answered the following year, in the spring of 1993 there was still a cloud of uncertainty. Mečiar had stated on returning from a trip to the United States in May 1993 that influential members of Congress had told him of their opposition to bringing the SDĽ into a coalition, and that therefore, that option was "out." I felt it was best to simply ignore that statement, rather than, as Weiss suggested, publicly take issue with Mečiar. Obviously, the United States was not in a position to tell the Slovaks who should or should not be included in a government. As mentioned above, ex-Communists found their way into every major political party, including Mečiar's HZDS (SDĽ members did, indeed, participate in coalition governments later in the decade). While an individual congressman might have expressed himself in the way Mečiar described, the views attributed to us by Mečiar certainly did not reflect the official policy of the U.S. government. What Mečiar clearly did grasp was our view that Slovakia could count on our continued support if it developed a free market economy, preserved human rights, and practiced democratic procedures. I told Weiss that the very idea that leading American officials should try to prevent a major Slovak political party from participating in a future coalition was surprising, since such a matter was clearly an internal

Slovak one to decide. At the same time, I felt it would be inopportune to follow Weiss's suggestion that I issue a statement to that effect, especially when no one had asked us to comment. Weiss was particularly concerned that the United States might seek to repeat Soviet mistakes of the past forty years by dictating to the small states in the region. I assured him that nothing could be further from our policy, and that we refrained from playing favorites among specific political subjects.

While the press at the time focused on the issue of whether the SDĽ would prove worthy of being invited into a government, for Weiss, the issue had its other side—the SDĽ had to weigh its own options and decide when the timing would be most auspicious. Meanwhile, although the external image of the SDĽ at that time had become that of a fence-sitter, Weiss had developed some very cogent strategies about how to play his own hand. In late spring 1993, the opposition was unable to bring down the HZDS government because it could offer no viable alternative. Secondly, to move against the HZDS would be to risk destabilizing the country on the eve of its planned entry to the Council of Europe, although by that time the COE had already overwhelmingly recommended Slovakia's admission. Also, many in the SDĽ thought it could do a better job of controlling the government from outside than as a weak partner on the inside. Finally, the HZDS was itself deeply divided over whether to make overtures to the SDĽ.

At the SDĽ's conference May 23, the party took the giant step to favor Slovak membership in NATO and enhance relations in the meantime. Pavol Kanis, the party's deputy chairman, fought hard to insure that such a plank would be included in the SDĽ program. He stated quite bluntly that "in competition for a share of power," the party would not be "boxed into a corner" and silenced by its competitors as an "unreliable political subject." Quite clearly, the SDĽ was concerned about being tainted by Mečiar, and its ever-pragmatic leadership found the way out. What was striking was not only the degree to which the SDĽ was willing to recognize that a pro-NATO stance was part of the essential consensus of Slovak politics, but also the fact that Weiss was openly considering the possibility of a visit to Washington to burnish his own political credentials back home.

Hardly was the ink dry on the Slovak declaration of independence than strange things began to happen at *Smena*. The paper was the organ of the Communist Youth League (ZSM) before 1989, and its assets had been taken over by the government. In late 1992, it followed a policy of what could be described as restrained opposition to the HZDS. That fall, it looked more and more likely that there would be a collision between the government and the paper's editors, with Slobodník hinting that he had found various irregularities in the paper's administration. Finally, shortly after independence, it was announced that the government agency overseeing *Smena* had decided to dismiss the paper's editor-in-chief and one of his deputies for alleged poor management. The move had been widely expected and the editor-in-chief, along with forty-nine staff members, simply quit their jobs and started a new newspaper whose title was a take-off on the original (*SME NA*, meaning We on [followed by the individual day of the week]). Eventually, *SME NA* (soon shortened to *SME*, or We) was awarded a grant by a U.S. government–funded foundation designed to promote independent media in the former Communist bloc. When I asked the editor-in-chief whether he felt his dismissal should be qualified as a human rights violation, he answered in the negative: "If the government stops us from publishing a new paper, then it would be a violation." As it turned out, *SME NA* became immediately popular, and even the old *Smena* did not become the government mouthpiece as some had feared.

Other acts taken under Slobodník's leadership aroused questions about the government's commitment to a plurality of views. Early in 1993, his ministry announced it would remove subsidies from a number of publications whose readership was "marginal." In reality, this was a thinly disguised way to crush several intellectual outlets whose views did not conform to those of the HZDS leadership.

20

INDEPENDENCE AND ITS AFTERMATH:
THE FOREIGN ANGLE

After leaving the podium on the SNP Square, Mečiar's first act as prime minister and acting president of the independent Slovak Republic was to receive the act of recognition from chiefs of foreign missions. We had not been invited to any ceremony, and, as I mentioned at the outset, the fact that no one was answering the phone at the Foreign Ministry made it impossible for us to arrange an exchange of notes until later that day. Recognition was an act of supreme importance to the Slovaks, as it established their legitimacy on an equal footing with the Czechs and provided entrance to various international bodies for which independence and recognition were a prerequisite.

I caught up with Kňažko later that morning after the Slovak Parliament issued its formal declaration of independence; at the ceremony, I noticed that several Slovak Americans had returned to their homeland to be present at the historic event. Kňažko suggested that we meet after his afternoon press conference to formally exchange notes. So that afternoon, along with scores of foreign correspondents, I watched Kňažko's first press conference as foreign minister of an independent state, held in the Hotel Forum. Kňažko's message was that Slovakia would be a good European citizen; it wanted to participate in the process of European integration, would be involved as one of the Visegrad Four (also including the Czech Republic, Poland, and Hungary), would not export arms to risk areas, and would seek to coordinate its policies on this score with the United States and other states. He rejected the notion of a restored "Little Entente" against Hungarian expansionism. Journalists attempted to engage him in a semantic debate over how his foreign policy conception differed from Mečiar's. One noted that, in his remarks earlier that day, Mečiar had placed relations with the United States first, whereas Kňažko had said relations with neighboring states, most especially the Czechs, would be of foremost priority.

When it was all over, Kňažko and I retired next door, and before the cameras, we exchanged notes of recognition. My note was addressed to Mečiar, and Kňažko's note was from Mečiar to President Bush. His was the signed original; mine was hastily typed the previous evening after I received telegraphed instructions in Vienna which had been sent from Washington. When the deed was done, I went back to the office to inform our Operations Center that the exchange of notes had taken place, and that we had formally established diplomatic relations. I used the opportunity to formally invite the foreign minister to our embassy the following Monday to participate in our ceremony to commemorate the upgrading of our relations.

While Kňažko was too diplomatic at that stage of his dispute with Mečiar to get into details about his own differences with the prime minister on foreign policy, had he been completely open, he would probably have stressed that he wanted to make it clear that Slovakia was part of the West and wished to join Western institutions, whereas Mečiar still harbored illusions about Slovakia playing off East and West. The difference between the two men was probably more tactical than substantive. True, the previous summer, when we had raised the issue of Slovakia's future orientation with Mečiar, he had opted for a neutral stance. Now, with independence, he felt it was necessary to make sure there were no doubts about Slovakia's desire to be part of the West, although his remarks about "turning east if rejected by the West" still haunted him.

I caught up with Kňažko again on February 25, the only diplomat willing to accept an invitation to attend his press conference. At that point, Kňažko was hopeful that he could play the "Kováč card" in preventing his ouster from the Foreign Ministry. He said that Kováč had pronounced himself "satisfied" with the way the MFA was working (Kováč the previous day told journalists that he was "delighted" to hear that the Ministry was working on a strategic document whose goal was to list major foreign policy priorities).

Kňažko then announced he was holding a meeting, which took place March 4–6, with Slovaks from the diaspora to discuss their relations with their mother country, now that it was independent. He also announced plans for establishment of a permanent conference on foreign policy which each month would draw together representatives of political parties and educational, social, and religious organizations to consider foreign policy issues.

While the immediate idea was to develop his own personal constituency, the larger concept was a sound one.

Kňažko took issue with Mečiar as well on such sensitive issues as relations with Hungary. In contrast to Mečiar's assertions about threats from Hungary, especially those associated with military modernization, Kňažko retorted that the upgrading of its military was an internal affair for Hungary and did not threaten Slovakia. He said the two states were "condemned" to have good-neighborly relations, and called "short-sighted" Hungarian attempts to sidetrack Slovak entry into the Council of Europe over alleged maltreatment of the Hungarian minority. On other issues, such as the basis of the dispute over the Gabčikovo-Nagymaros project, he dismissed Hungarian assertions, but did so discreetly.

Because Kňažko ignored Mečiar's invitation to resign his post, Mečiar started to bypass him on such important matters as a visit to Brussels that took place February 23–24. Not only did Mečiar force Kňažko to abandon his own trip to the European capital on the pretext that it was "too commercial," but he made his own arrangements to visit without going through Kňažko's ministry. Kňažko was humiliated, but also furious, stating publicly that the action was unprecedented and that it threatened Slovak credibility, as well as the country's ability to speak with one voice. Mečiar's tendency to act on his own, however, continued after Kňažko was dismissed.

The big event in Washington in the spring of 1993 was the opening of the Holocaust Museum, which would come to be acclaimed for the thoroughness of its approach to a subject whose essence can never be fully captured. The Museum's opening was the first occasion for many European heads of state to travel to Washington, where everyone, of course, wanted to have a meeting with President Bill Clinton. As it happened, though, because of the limitations on the president's time, only President Lech Wałęsa of Poland and President Václav Havel of the Czech Republic were scheduled to have a full audience.

Kováč looked forward to making the journey and had sent Pavol Demeš to Washington beforehand to work out his program. The visit had the potential of being a major public relations coup for both Kováč personally and Slovakia. Since his inauguration, Kováč had made it quite clear that he was not a successor to Father Tiso and that he condemned the crimes carried out by Tiso's cabal. A major objective of the visit was to establish a cordial relationship with American Jewish organizations, all of which knew only too well about the Slovak wartime record, and of the attempts made in subsequent years to whitewash the Tiso regime.

A few days before he was to depart, I received an urgent instruction to inform the president that his request for a separate call on President Clinton could not be granted. Our colleagues in Washington had worked diligently to carry out this request, knowing the importance of avoiding any step that would suggest that, in this early stage of their existence, the United States was tilting toward one of the successor states in Czechoslovakia. My instructions did not offer any other advice. I found President Kováč that night at the Hotel Kiev, where many notables had been invited for the "politician of the year" sweepstakes organized by the weekly *Slobodný Piatok*. I was invited to join him at a table where he was sitting with Mečiar and some other high officials. When I gave him the news, his immediate reaction was to ask whether there was any point in going at all, since Havel was scheduled to have a meeting with President Clinton. I urged him not to cancel his plans, and told him that even if he did not have a separate meeting with President Clinton, the trip would be very valuable for him and for our bilateral relations.

As it turned out, everyone was a winner. We were able to squeeze in fifteen minutes for a private meeting between the two presidents, after convincing people who had just taken over in the White House about how important it was to put relations with Czechs and Slovaks on an even keel. Kováč's straightforward and unassuming approach also made friends for him in the United States. When he spoke about his Jewish classmates who disappeared from school one day in 1942 and never came back, he did so from the heart and with deep emotion.

As President Kováč was preparing to embark for the United States, we received word that Mečiar might also have travel plans of his own. Typically, this news reached us through back channels, rather than from Mečiar's office. I informed the State Department on May 5 that Mečiar was likely to travel to the United States within the following two weeks, but was hamstrung by not getting official word directly from Mečiar's people. It had been Mečiar's deeply held conviction that a distorted and prejudiced view of Slovakia existed in official quarters in the United States, and that such a view could be corrected only by his personal intervention. Although he knew better than to say so openly, Mečiar intimated on several occasions that much culpability lay in the reporting sent by our own consulate/embassy. Of course, to say so directly would have meant that he had access to our diplomatic correspondence, and that his assurances that no one was "reading the mail" from Bratislava were suspect and not believable.

I finally got to see Mečiar on the eve of his departure. He decided that our intervention might, in the end, actually be of some assistance in getting appointments in Washington. While our colleagues in Washington recognized the usefulness of facilitating contacts for the prime minister, they also felt a bit taken aback by his habit of acting on his own and then coming in with requests at the very last minute. But if Mečiar had been moody and tense before departing for Washington, he was confident and relaxed on his return from a four-day visit that included everyone on his wish list except for President Clinton. While there was a certain bravura in his claim that "I turned everything around," Mečiar felt he had made tangible progress in a number of areas. He had been upset by reports issued by the International Monetary Fund (IMF) that Slovakia's economic prospects as an independent entity were poor. He claimed that, as a result of discussions with the IMF, officials admitted that they were using a flawed database and working-level experts were then directed to use the latest economic data when making a prognosis about Slovakia. Mečiar claimed that Slovakia's economic achievements were "admired" by the IMF and that his country would be at the head of the list of former Communist countries to be considered for credits by the Fund.

Others who accompanied Mečiar to Washington had a more modest appraisal of his visit. Ivan Horský, for one, writing in the respected daily *Národná Obroda*, remarked that the $90 million currency stabilization loan expected from the IMF paled in comparison with the $400 million for neighboring Hungary or $1.25 billion for Pakistan. While Horský noted that some in the U.S. Congress applauded (although, as time would tell, they did not follow up) Mečiar's call for a "Marshall Plan–type" aid program for Eastern Europe, he also recalled that Mečiar's idea of a fivefold increase in armaments production to help finance military conversion projects was met with incredulity. The correspondent of the Slovak Broadcasting Corporation noted in a commentary from Washington that Mečiar's trip was somewhat ill-timed, coming as it did only a month after Kováč's visit, and at a time when the U.S. administration had other preoccupations. Mečiar was, in the last analysis, only one of the many foreign leaders who came and went that year to Washington. He did, however, make some useful contacts in the Democratic Party, and arranged for former president Jimmy Carter to visit Slovakia the next month, following Carter's attendance at the Vienna Conference on Human Rights. One learning experience came unexpectedly to the Slovak prime minister. From the questions he got in Washington, it was clear that his interlocutors were well informed about Slovakia; indeed, one of them surprised him with a question about a statement made by a Slovak opposition leader just a few hours earlier.

Military Contacts

One area where we might have smoothed the transition by retaining our ties to Prague was in the area of contacts between our defense establishments. Our Office of the Defense Attaché in Prague had maintained cordial contacts with both its Czech and Slovak counterparts during the time of federation. Many of our attachés were on a first-name basis with leading Slovak generals. I had argued for maintaining these contacts via Prague on a transitional basis for practical reasons, but the policy line decided upon in Washington was, for political reasons, to end all responsibilities our Prague embassy had for Slovakia, and to transfer to our colleagues in nearby Vienna those that could not be immediately taken over by our new Bratislava embassy.

It was less than three weeks after independence when I received a visit from General Thomas Lennon, who was based at EUCOM (European Command) in Vaihingen, Germany, and was responsible for the Military-to-Military Contact Program in the Plans and Policy Directorate. The program he administered was a brainchild of General Colin Powell, then chairman of the Joint Chiefs of Staff and who also visited us in Bratislava. It was designed to improve contacts with the militaries of the states of Eastern Europe and the newly independent states of the former USSR. The agenda had several facets, including setting up a joint contact team that would be established directly in the military headquarters of the receiving state, and providing various short-term training activities. Overall, the concept was designed to influence the military establishments of these states to take their place as an instrument of a democratic society, as well as to help build confidence vis-à-vis the militaries of neighboring states.

On March 11, 1993, a small bit of history was written when General Lennon, accompanied by Major Steve Hoog, became the first U.S. military official to engage in official contacts with the budding Slovak defense establishment. Lennon was received by Igor Urban, the state secretary or deputy minister for defense, and Imrich Andrejčák, until recently the federal minister of defense, and soon to be named Slovakia's first defense minister. Andrejčák was pleased at the attention, and saw Lennon's visit as an indication of American confidence in the viability of Slovakia, as well as a way of giving a boost to the prestige of the fledgling Slovak military. Before the end of my tour, the first Slovak military officials were received in the United States. This was truly a sea change from the situation existing just a few short years earlier, when the United States was regarded as the enemy and treated with deep suspicion.

Relations with the Czechs

It became clear rather quickly that the East European penchant for bureau-cratizing the essentials of life was in full bloom at the new Czech-Slovak border. Independence came before the Czechs and Slovaks could develop a system for working out the details of their economic relations as two inde-pendent states in the least disruptive manner. In one case reported in late January, one businesswoman recounted her trials in trying to fill out and get the proper stamps for a five-page "unified customs declaration" that was now mandatory for her shipments to the Czech Republic. Czech cus-toms officers told her that the instructions on filling out the form that she received from their Slovak counterparts were invalid. While the agreement to divide the country provided for a customs union between the two repub-lics, it did not provide for effortless transit of goods, since with indepen-dence, both republics had now imposed a 23 percent value-added tax (VAT). Documentation was needed to insure that goods passing over the border paid the necessary taxes at the destination. There was also a requirement to prepay the VAT and to deposit the money at the proper post office. Drivers recounted tales of spending as much as two days at the border and having to borrow money for their overnight accommodations. The mentality that it was more important to have drivers wait for two days to clear customs than to allow a single carton of untaxed cigarettes across the border failed to see the larger costs involved but was, unfortunately, very much in evidence.

In a January 23 editorial, the trade union daily *Práca* detailed the disor-der that was already apparent: chaos at customs offices, inadequate legisla-tion personnel and technology, as well as contradictory information. Heads of major firms wrote to the prime ministers of both republics urging that something be done to avoid interrupted production, shutdowns, and unem-ployment. The five-page customs form, which also serves as a tax declara-tion, together with regulations on deposit of monies for VAT prepayments made some exporters wonder whether it was all worth the trouble. Until regulations were eased, initial trade figures showed a considerable drop in the first month of independence.

There were many other indications that the "velvet divorce" with the Czechs was not without frictions. While the Slovaks were now running their own show, there were residual questions that caused emotions to soar. When I met Slovak Minister of Economy Jaroslav Kubečka on June 30, one of the topics we discussed was an announcement that the Czechs were planning to produce a modernized version of the T-72 tank. The usually mild mannered technocrat reacted sharply. He was especially scornful of

Václav Havel, who he said would have to "give back his [Nobel] Peace Prize" for approving Czech plans to resume heavy armaments production at the Plzen Škoda works. In 1990, as federal president, Havel had decided that Czechoslovakia should stop producing tanks for "moral reasons." The tanks were produced in Slovakia, and as Kubečka put it, Havel in effect "took the bread out of the mouths of sixty thousand families." The Czechs had "misled world opinion" and caused unnecessary economic damage in Slovakia.

To set matters straight, I recalled an earlier conversation I had with officials at the Dubnica armaments factory to the effect that it was not "Prago-centralists" but simply economic realities that were forcing the Slovaks to cut production. Markets were drying up and the Russians could undercut Slovak prices by half on T-72s. Kubečka backtracked somewhat, admitting that the markets would never return to the peak of the 1980s, but complained that the cutoff was too swift. He suggested that production would continue, but in the hundreds, rather than the thousands annually.

Kubečka's woes did not end with the Czechs. The EC (now the EU) had its own way of shutting out the East Europeans. In recent months, an epidemic of hoof-and-mouth disease had been "discovered" and was used as an excuse to bar meat products from Eastern Europe. Miraculously, after Easter, it was determined that there was no threat of epidemic at all. This decision came too late for the Slovak meat industry, which was relying on pre-Easter lamb sales to Western Europe. Whenever the Slovaks or their eastern counterparts showed ability to compete in the West (e.g., on steel products), they found themselves squeezed out of the markets by protectionist measures. Most recently, the Austrians had found ways to bar Slovak chemical imports because they displaced local producers. Kubečka said such practices were not only disappointing, they were "downright distasteful," and that if this was the introduction his country was getting to a market economy from the West, it would rather decline the invitation.

The Gabčikovo controversy was not solved by the unilateral Slovak decision to complete the major part of the project on the Slovak side of the border, allowing the canal to open in November 1992. However, the Hungarians had boxed themselves into a corner, where they had little effective leverage on the Slovaks, and could not, in any case, push the Slovaks into any solution which would mean forgoing the benefits of production of electricity at Gabčikovo. The Hungarians stuck to the line that the old river bed was drying up and that irreparable damage was being done to both Slovak and Hungarian drinking supplies, but the Slovaks were mostly unimpressed. In early 1993, negotiations were pending on a temporary water regime that would permit a certain minimal water supply through the old river bed, while allowing enough into the new canal to turn the turbines that were generating electricity—and thus, cold cash—for Slovakia. I could sympathize with our colleagues in Washington who were reading reports from our embassy in Budapest quoting Hungarian predictions that an ecological disaster was on the horizon, and then reading my own reports, in which Slovak officials refuted these contentions point by point. I suggested in one dispatch that the Hungarians could have improved their own credibility by simply cooperating with the Slovaks in making water quality measurements. That they did not suggested that they might have something to hide. The United States, which usually sends out démarches to many countries seeking support on all sorts of issues, now found itself besieged by the Hungarians and Slovaks (the latter sent Binder and other experts to hold seminars to argue their case) trying to get the United States to side with their position. However, the U.S. allergy to getting involved in disputes among friends was just as strong as ever, and we remained on the sidelines.

21

★ ★ ★ ★ ★ ★ ★

DO VIDENIA, SLOVENSKO

As my three-year tenure in Slovakia would come to an end in early July, it was time to prepare for the transition and make ready for the time when I would have to say *Do videnia, Slovensko* (goodbye, Slovakia). July 2 was the time for farewell calls on Slovakia's top officials, including President Kováč, Prime Minister Mečiar, and Speaker Gašparovič. At the same time, I used the occasion to introduce my successor, Ellie Sutter. I was struck by the president's statement that he hoped I would be a "good spokesman for the Slovak cause" in my future work. While a diplomat must be the spokesman for his own country's cause, I assured him that I would leave with fond memories. A diplomat should report honestly about conditions in and the views of the country to which he or she is accredited in all their variety and permutations, but in the last analysis, he is responsible to those who have sent him in the first place. What some people in Slovakia could not understand was that uncritical advocacy of the views of the country where a diplomat is based could only lower his own credibility at home.

Our session with Mečiar was more substantive. Mečiar had just received a delegation of the IMF, which he said had pressed him to institute a 20 percent import surcharge on finished products. When I replied that this might have an adverse effect on foreign investors based in the Czech Republic who had expected a unified market of fifteen million persons to remain after the split, he assured that exemptions could be granted in specific cases, and recalled that larger firms should be able to withstand the impact. As things

turned out, only eight days later, on July 10, Slovakia announced a 10 percent devaluation of its currency. Mečiar was concerned at the lack of interest shown by American investors, but he also recognized that government
facilities to assist investors were lacking.

Our meeting with Gašparovič mostly concerned the process of revamp-
ing the Slovak government. At that moment, just having returned from
Strasbourg, where he shepherded Slovak entry into the Council of Europe,
Gašparovič was optimistic about the future. He was also sure that the HZDS
government would last for its full electoral mandate, and that it would be
augmented with supporters of ousted Foreign Minister Kňažko. As events
over the next months were to show, his predictions were overly optimistic.

July 4, 1993, was our opportunity to say farewell to hundreds of Slovaks with whom we had worked closely over three years, and whose fate
had become in some ways intertwined with our own. Mečiar arrived at the
embassy residence with Zbigniew Brzezinski, who eighteen years earlier
had been one of my advisors when I was writing my Ph.D. dissertation on
the country where I was now serving. Brzezinski diplomatically assured his
hosts that mine was "an excellent work," although I suspect the details had
faded from his memory in the intervening years. Two days later, on July
6, I drafted my final message, noting that the "keys to the mansion" were
being turned over to my very able successor. As is the privilege of an outgoing chief of mission, I also penned a few words about the country where I
had spent three years of my life, and whose fate I had closely watched as it
struggled to leave behind the legacy of the past, and finally to find its own
identity as an independent nation. I was well aware that there were many
question marks and doubts in Washington about where Slovakia was going.
I also knew that some colleagues had warned that the split would marginal-
ize Slovakia as far as Washington decision makers were concerned.

In one positive sense, Slovakia was on the way to becoming marginal-
ized. It had its problems, to be sure, but they were not of the caliber that
would catch the attention of policy makers in the way that events in former
Yugoslavia were gripping public attention. What I did argue for was more,
rather than less, U.S. attention to the country in the future. I felt that the
continued expression of U.S. concern over the country's future, enunciated
in such ways as high-level contacts with its leaders, continuation of a strong
aid program, and measures to bring Slovakia into closer interaction with
its European neighbors, most especially with Western institutions, was an
important policy for us to follow. I was also aware that too many reports of
holdups in privatization, chauvinistic remarks or actions against minorities,

or manipulation of the press, could easily cause Slovakia to be placed in a tacit classification in Washington that characterized it as "least likely to succeed." While I never found out what kind of reception my final words had, I was pleasantly surprised to hear from an Air Force major whom I shared breakfast with at the Residence Inn in Montgomery, Alabama, a few weeks later that he had not only read the cable, but remembered it well!

POSTSCRIPT: SIXTEEN YEARS OF INDEPENDENCE

Much has happened since I left Slovakia—then a young nation with uncertain prospects—more than sixteen years ago. In the year 2004, Slovakia came of age in two important aspects: the country was admitted to membership in the North Atlantic Treaty Organization on March 29 and joined the European Union on May 1. Acceptance as a full member of both institutions was an expression of confidence in the policies Slovakia has followed, as well as a manifestation of optimism with regard to the country's future course. Certainly, in the physical sense as well, Slovakia is becoming more like a typical European country, with modern hypermarkets now greeting visitors to Bratislava and other major urban centers. Bratislava is served by express trains that whisk passengers to Vienna from a new terminal built in the southern suburb of Petržalka, even though they still take nearly an hour to make the forty-mile journey. Border formalities are being simplified. The spread of the Internet has vastly improved communications and the flow of information.

Our embassy has greatly expanded since the heady days of early 1993. Our original consulate building has been remodeled and the structure next to it—from where the infamous eavesdropping operation was mounted—is now part of the embassy itself. Comparing our operations then and now is like comparing a mom-and-pop store with a supermarket. The USAID office, which in its early days eclipsed the rest of the embassy in the number of personnel and scope of its operations, has been shut down—a tribute to its success. However, some of its programs promoting democracy and economic reform have remained in place and are administered from a regional office in Budapest. The total budget for these activities has exceeded $200 million. The dowdy Carlton Hotel that housed Claiborne Pell and his wife in the late 1940s has been completely remodeled and was reopened in 2001 as a five-star member of the Radisson SAS chain. In addition, whereas in 1990 we had to compete with local vehicles for the right to park in front of our offices, today the street in front of our embassy building has been blocked off to traffic, and a security zone has been put in place in recognition of the dangers posed in this age of terrorism.

Slovakia's path in more than a decade since independence has been tortuous to say the least. Vladimír Mečiar was the dominating figure of the first decade as a sovereign state, whether in or out of power. Despite the collapse of his coalition governments and the many questionable acts of his administrations, he remained until recent years the most formidable politician in Slovakia, defeated only when the opposition combined forces in an "anyone but Mečiar" coalition. In the 2004 presidential election, Mečiar actually came out ahead in the first round, and even when the opposition rallied behind his former close associate Ivan Gašparovič, he was still able to garner the support of 40 percent of the electorate.[1] In addition, his HZDS movement, which was rebaptized in 2003 as a political party, up until 2002 consistently maintained its position as the top vote-getter in every election held in the country, despite its many splits and defections, as well as the isolation its policies cost the country under Mečiar's rule (the party was outvoted by the socialist SMER, the Hungarian MK, and the Liberal SKDU in 2006). The history of Slovakia's party politics since independence has been one of constant fractionalization, as old parties split, new ones are founded, and minor parties get swept away or amalgamated with stronger partners. In this final chapter, I will review some of the highlights of Slovakia's first sixteen years as an independent state.

Mečiar's First Swan Song

While Kováč carefully avoided getting into a confrontation with Mečiar during my tenure, it was clear that he had his misgivings about Mečiar's behavior—doubts that were measurably strengthened by the influence of members of his staff. When the split between the two became public, Mečiar was forced to resign his post as prime minister in 1994 after suffering a loss of confidence in Parliament and hanging on for several months heading a government with minority support. Several splinter members of his HZDS movement had formed a new organization called the Democratic Union (DÚ), and divisions in the Slovak National Party (SNS) deprived his coalition of its ruling majority. On March 11, 1994, just before he was forced out of office, Mečiar delivered what might have been considered his political swan song. Addressing the Slovak National Council, he acknowledged that he had made his own mistakes and admitted that he had his own imperfections. He accused Václav Havel of giving him headaches as Czechoslovak president and complained that Michal Kováč had now taken on this role. Most significantly, in reflecting on his own position, he declared: "I know this state inside out. I know every element in its mechanism, everything we fixed, failed to fix or resolve. I know where it is heading. I know its potential."

Human Rights and the Mečiar Years

If Mečiar already showed his capacity for vengeance in the period following his 1992 election victory, this character trait took a much more sinister turn in the period after his return to power in October 1994. He, or people under his close command, set in motion a series of steps whose legality and constitutionality were questionable and which caused great harm not only to the people of his own country but also to Slovakia's image abroad. After winning a decisive victory in the October 1994 elections, he joined with the Slovak National Party (SNS) and the newly formed Association of Slovak Workers (ZRS, a splinter group from the reformist post-Communist SDĽ) to form a new coalition.[2] Some of his more vindictive acts included the following:

1. Soon after resuming power in 1994, in what was later dubbed the infamous "Night of the Long Knives," Mečiar and his coalition partners canceled about fifty privatization decisions in order to bring privatized companies under the control of their associates; steps were taken to ensure that the opposition was shut out of chairmanships of all parliamentary committees and that only faithful followers of Mečiar were installed in strategic positions in the mass media, the office of the prosecutor general, and the security services. In a bid to overturn the mandates of HZDS defectors who founded the opposition Democratic Union (DÚ), Mečiar claimed that the ten thousand signatures on their nominating petitions were forged and that, therefore, their parliamentary mandates should be annulled.

2. The most serious abuse of power was the attempt to neutralize and intimidate President Kováč, who tried unsuccessfully to block Mečiar's appointment of Ivan Lexa, first as minister of privatization and later as chief of the Slovak Information Service (SIS), which Mečiar was turning into a menacing tool of intimidation against his own political enemies. In a bizarre incident, on August 31, 1995, Kováč's thirty-one-year-old son Michal Jr. was abducted and tortured by a gang of what was widely believed to be SIS personnel operating under Lexa's command. A warrant had been issued by Interpol because the younger Kováč was wanted in Germany for questioning on possible fraud and conspiracy charges, but it could not be executed in Slovakia. He was stopped by a group of armed men in Bratislava and, after being physically abused and forced to drink several bottles of liquor, he was thrown into the trunk of a car and dumped outside a police station across the border in neighboring Hainburg, Austria.[3] When he was found by Austrian police, he was at first held in custody pending possible extradition to Germany, but after the circumstances of the case came to light, was allowed to return to Slovakia. The following year, an investigation into the episode turned deadly when Robert Remiáš, a policeman working on the case, was blown up when a bomb exploded as he attempted to start his car. No one has ever been tried for his murder, although Lexa, under suspicion, had his parliamentary immunity lifted and was for a time placed in custody. He fled to South Africa after being released on bail but was extradited to Slovakia in 2002.[4] The same Jaroslav Svěchota who had once briefed Americans during the Gulf War and later became deputy chief of the Slovak Information Service was heavily involved in the Kováč kidnapping and other crimes. In a 1999 interview published in the Slovak weekly *Plus 7 dní*, he argued that Mečiar himself had ordered the kidnapping, in the hope of discrediting President Kováč and consequently ensuring that Slovakia would not be invited to join any Western institutions. Svěchota himself was convicted by a Bratislava court in June 2004 for embezzlement during his tenure in the SIS (he was never tried for the kidnapping). He received a conditional sentence because of his poor health.[5]

3. The SIS engaged in a provocation against Rudolf Baláž, head of the Slovak Bishops Conference and a consistent opponent of Mečiar's authoritarian rule. Bishop Baláž was offered $200,000 for a triptych painting in his possession called *Adoration of the Three Kings,* whose real value was much less than the price that was paid for the purchase. When police were sent to search his residence, he was accused of illegally selling an item which was part of the country's cultural heritage to a foreign

buyer. In reality, however, he had the right to sell the painting, as it was not one of Slovakia's protected cultural objects. It turned out that the "Swiss" businessman who completed the transaction (and subsequently disappeared) was actually an SIS agent, and the affair was part of a scam to discredit and silence the regime's critics.[6]

4. In 1997, President Kováč decided to add to an already planned referendum on whether Slovakia should join NATO[7] a proposal to change the system of electing the president from a vote by Parliament to a popular election (already necessitated by the collection of the requisite number of signatures). The NATO referendum involved answering three separate questions. His move was prompted by fear that Mečiar would take over presidential powers in the event that, as provided for in the original 1992 Constitution, Parliament could not muster a three-fifths majority (90 votes) to elect his successor. Indeed, when Kováč's term of office ended in March 1998, such a deadlock did take place, and Mečiar used his temporary powers as president to issue an amnesty to all officials involved in the kidnapping incident—although the amnesties were subsequently annulled by the Dzurinda government that took over from Mečiar in October 1998. On April 22, 1997, a month after the president proposed the additional question, Mečiar and his cabinet announced they would not distribute ballots that included the proposal on direct elections. The Central Referendum Commission (CRC) declared that the cabinet's decision was illegal, but Interior Minister Gustav Krajči refused to accept the Commission's view and ordered the referendum ballot to deal with the NATO issue alone. The Constitutional Court ruled that the question of direct elections could be on the ballot but was not automatically binding. When the referendum was held—with only the three questions dealing with NATO on the ballot—it was chaotic, and only 10 percent of eligible voters participated. When the voting was over, the CRC declared it to be invalid, not because of the extremely low turnout, but due to the fact that the fourth question was not on the ballot distributed by Krajči's ministry. The scandal over the referendum issue caused great harm to the country's international standing and assured that Slovakia would not be included in the first group of countries invited to join an expanded NATO.[8] It also caused the resignation of Slovakia's minister of foreign affairs, Pavol Hamžik, who said that he was unable to fulfill his duties in the wake of the referendum fiasco.[9]

5. František Gaulieder, a deputy in the HZDS, defected from the movement in 1996 after a falling out with Mečiar. Soon afterwards, a letter surfaced in which he purportedly resigned his post as a member of

Parliament. The document was used to cancel his mandate and award it to another person in the HZDS, although Gaulieder claimed he had never written it and it was a forgery. Subsequently, a bomb exploded outside his home as a warning. He fought the issue in the courts, but it had still not been decided by the time all mandates were up for review by the voters in the 1998 elections. His case was interpreted as yet another indication of shortcomings in the country's democratic process.

6. Attempts were made to control the universities and cultural life. An act that placed strict limits on university autonomy was passed over President Kováč's veto in October 1996. It was strongly opposed by educators. New universities would be established and older ones, especially where political opposition to the government was rampant, had their funding cut. The Ministry of Education was given control over the appointment of professors. Various officials who protested the increasing domination of cultural life by state authorities were dismissed by Ivan Hudec, who was then the minister of culture.[10]

From Mečiar to Dzurinda

Elections held in September 1998 finally brought an end to Mečiar's four-year rule. Actually, his HZDS still came out as the top vote-getter, with 27 percent of the votes, winning 43 seats in the 150-member Parliament, compared with 61 seats in 1994. But the opposition had mobilized in four parties: the Slovak Democratic Coalition (SDK), which had been put together by Mikuláš Dzurinda of the KDH, the Party of the Democratic Left (SDĽ), the Party of the Hungarian Coalition (SMK), and the Party of Civic Understanding (SOP). Together, they polled 58 percent of the votes. The HZDS tried to use various means to thwart its political enemies, including changing the election law to mandate that each party in an electoral coalition win a minimum of 5 percent of the votes in order to qualify for electing members of Parliament. It also appealed to the Supreme Court in an unsuccessful bid to invalidate the SDK's registration. The SDK, which received 26.3 percent of the vote, was originally founded as a coalition of the conservative Christian Democratic Movement (KDH), the liberal Democratic Union (DÚ), the conservative-liberal Democratic Party (DS), the Social Democratic Party of Slovakia (SDSS), and the Green Party in Slovakia (SZS). In order to meet the criteria laid down by Mečiar's stringent electoral law, the SDK was registered as a party, rather than as a coalition.[11] Along with biased coverage of the campaign by state-controlled media (Slovak Television devoted only 16 percent of its election news to the opposition), officials likewise harassed media not under their direct control.[12] The Nationalists were returned to Parliament with 11 percent of the vote (in the subsequent 2002 elections they did not reach the 5 percent threshold). In the end, Dzurinda's allies returned a total of 93 members to the 150-member body. The opposition was supported by city dwellers, those with higher education, businessmen, professionals, and students. On the other hand, Mečiar's HZDS and the SNS became the political vehicles of the less educated, older, and more rural elements of the population.[13] After the elections, Mečiar resigned his parliamentary mandate in favor of Ivan Lexa, with the intent of giving Lexa immunity from prosecution, now as a member of Parliament. Mečiar announced his retirement from politics—a retirement that was short lived, because he returned as a presidential candidate in 1999 and 2004, and was reelected to Parliament in 2002. His move was of no help to Lexa, whose parliamentary immunity was lifted by the NRSR on April 9, 1999. However, he has never been convicted of a crime for his activities as SIS chief.[14]

Once in office, Dzurinda's government moved to return Slovakia to the path of economic reform and to reverse some of the human rights violations that had taken place under the previous administration. The government appointed a new chief of the Slovak Information Service and pledged to ensure that its intelligence apparatus would no longer be used as a means of political struggle against the opposition. Controls on universities were lifted, and private mass media were encouraged. Some officials in the state media who had been appointed by the previous government using political criteria were removed. A new post of deputy prime minister for human rights and minorities was created, and a member of the Hungarian Coalition, Pál Csáky, was appointed. While he was very attentive to the needs of the Hungarian minority, however, representatives of the Romanies criticized him for lack of sensitivity to their special problems, including continuing physical attacks on some of their members by skinheads or occasional allegations of police brutality. These problems have continued to the present day.[15] A new language law was promulgated, returning to minorities the right to use their language in official dealings with state authorities wherever those minorities constituted 20 percent or more of the population of a particular district or locality. The government, in contrast to its predecessors, offered a number of committee chairmanships to the opposition. In the economic field, privatization was resumed, and important reforms of the health care sector and the tax system were initiated. These measures helped improve Slovakia's profile as a reform-minded country in the West, but they also contributed to a fall in public support for the coalition parties, due to fear that these actions would increase unemployment. Corruption continues to be a problem, especially in the awarding of government contracts and in the judiciary. In 1999, after a constitutional amendment was successfully approved, Rudolf Schuster became the country's first popularly elected president, defeating Mečiar in his attempt at a political comeback by a margin of 57 to 43 percent.

In 2002, Slovaks returned Dzurinda and his allies to power. His SKDÚ party received 15 percent of the votes, and won 28 seats in the 150-member Parliament. While the HZDS again received the largest number of votes (19.5 percent, with 36 seats), the parties in Dzurinda's coalition (including the KDH, the right-wing Alliance of the New Citizen or ANO, and the Party of the Hungarian Coalition or SMK) in total elected 78 deputies to the NRSR. For the first time in post-Communist history, the SNS or Slovak National Party did not receive sufficient votes to return to Parliament. The post-Communist SDĽ also received less than the minimum 5 percent of votes needed to remain in Parliament. But the reborn Communist Party of Slovakia (KSS) was able to capture the protest vote—mainly because of dissatisfaction stemming from hardship caused by economic reform—and garnering for the first time since 1989 sufficient support to return deputies to the NRSR (11 in all, with six percent of the votes). The results of the 2002 elections allowed the formation of a center-right reformist government that was different from the "rainbow coalition" that took over in 1998, and allowed the realization of significant economic reforms. According to the analyst Oľga Gyárfašová, the reforms, while unpopular, are nevertheless unchallenged.[16]

U.S. and NATO Pressures Against Mečiar in the 2002 Parliamentary Elections

Because the stakes in Slovakia were regarded as so high, by the time the country was preparing for the September 2002 elections, U.S. officials were blunt in warning Slovaks of the consequences of voting for the wrong party. U.S. Ambassador to NATO (and later Under Secretary of State) Nicholas Burns, both during a visit to Bratislava in the run-up to the election, and in media interviews there, made it plain that "we do not trust people who were in the previous government; we do not believe they have changed." In an interview with the Vienna daily *Die Presse,* Burns warned, "If his party were to return to power in Bratislava, that would be a fundamental obstacle to

Slovakia's entry into NATO."[17] U.S. Ambassador to Slovakia Ronald Weiser, for his part, made it quite clear that year that the wrong electoral choice in Slovakia would shut the country out of NATO membership. Typically, in a Bratislava radio interview, Ambassador Weiser remarked, "The only other obstacle that would face you is the outcome of your elections and whether your new government will share the values of the NATO alliance." This point was vigorously repeated in many of the ambassador's public remarks before the election. Although the HZDS polled more votes than any other political organization, because of Mečiar's continuing dominance, it was persona non grata as a coalition partner for any other potential political partner. In the end, President Rudolf Schuster asked Dzurinda to form a new government, avoiding the possibility that Slovakia would suffer further international isolation had Mečiar returned to power. In November 2002, at the Prague NATO Summit, Slovakia was formally invited to become a member of NATO. In a May 2003 referendum, Slovaks approved joining the European Union. Significantly, the vote in favor was 92.5 percent—the highest among all the states joining with Slovakia—but the rate of participation was only 52.5 percent—the lowest in the group, and just over the 50 percent minimum for the referendum to be valid.[18] One of the high points in Slovakia's emergent role under Dzurinda was the summit between Presidents George W. Bush and Vladimir Putin held in Bratislava on February 24, 2005. This was the first visit of a sitting American president to Slovakia.[19]

Slovak-Hungarian Relations

Under the Mečiar government, relations with Hungary were often tense. In November 1995, the government passed a new law on minority languages that effectively repealed most of the guarantees granted in the earlier 1990 law, including the provision for using languages other than Slovak when the population of a community exceeded 20 percent of the total. It made proficiency in Slovak a condition for employment in any state-run institution, including education. All official documents were required to be written in Slovak. Local government meetings were required to be conducted in Slovak, even if all the participants were Hungarians or of other nationalities. There were limited allowances made for oral communication in health care and for church services to be conducted in a minority language. But bilingual report cards were prohibited and all school records had to be kept in Slovak.[20]

In addition to adjustments in the language law, Mečiar's administration carried out a reshuffling of the country's regional structure in 1996. Eight regions were established, and most of them stretched in a north-south direction. While this did not end Hungarian control of local districts where they were a majority, it thwarted any possibility that they would be in control of one of the larger regional units. Earlier, on March 19, 1995, Slovakia and Hungary signed a treaty of friendship reiterating the inviolability of their common borders and stipulating protection of ethnic minorities. However, given the sharp limitations on the use of Hungarian spelled out later that year in the language law, many Hungarians in Slovakia felt the treaty had brought them nothing. In 1997, Mečiar proposed reducing the barriers for Slovaks and Hungarians living as minorities in each others' countries to emigrate to their respective motherlands—a step that some suggested was tantamount to calling for a population exchange.[21] In 1999, the Dzurinda government passed a new language law which effectively restored most of the rights that had been withdrawn in 1995.

The passage of the law was accelerated because protection for minority languages was one of the criteria established by the European Union for judging the qualifications of states aspiring to membership. However, several Hungarian MPs nonetheless protested that it did not go far enough in protecting their rights.[22] In general, one important achievement of Dzurinda was his inclusionary policy toward Slovakia's Hungarian population—a strategy which has helped reduce tensions within the country, as well as with Hungary itself. One measure of his success was the fact that, during the run-up to the 2002 election, a leader of the traditionally anti-Hungarian Slovak National Party (SNS), asked what the major issue for the SNS would be in the campaign, with no hesitation picked "unemployment" rather than the expected "national issue."[23]

The Gabčikovo-Nagymaros Dam Dispute

As mentioned in chapter 7, after the Slovaks unilaterally implemented their decision to complete the Danube canal on their territory, in April 1993, Hungary and Slovakia agreed to submit their case on the Danube dam dispute to the International Court of Justice (ICJ). Nearly four and a half years later, the ICJ handed down a ruling that found both parties in the wrong, for different reasons, but did not offer any clear way out of the impasse. The September 25, 1997 decision, among other things, stated:

Hungary's unilateral decision to suspend work on the project in 1989 was illegal, because the 1977 treaty described the project as "single and indivisible."
Likewise, using the same "single and indivisible" principle, Slovakia's proceeding with "Variant C" was also illegal.

The 1977 treaty was still in effect and the parties were instructed to negotiate a solution to the problem of implementing this ruling, as well as how
to accomplish the core aims of the original agreement.[24]

The decision brought considerable ferment in Hungary, where opinions
varied from going ahead with the original plan to complete the Hungarian
portion of the project in the lower Danube to demanding that more water
be diverted to the Danube. Resuming the dam project on the Hungarian
side, however, is still extremely risky, given the fact that opposition to the
undertaking is still high. As the Danube has historically been the largest
body of water flowing through Hungary, the diversion of most of its flow
through Slovakia also impinges on the Hungarians' own sense of national
identity. To date, there has been no final solution to the issue, although the
two sides did resume negotiations in April 2004.

Bilateral and Multilateral Relations Since 1998

As part of his drive to gain acceptance and legitimacy for Slovakia in the
West, Prime Minister Dzurinda has also sent his country's troops abroad to
participate in peacekeeping operations. There is a joint Czech-Slovak peacekeeping force in Kosovo, and the Slovaks have also contributed troops to
peacekeeping operations in Bosnia. Slovak military engineering brigades
operate in both Afghanistan and Iraq. But the context in which official support has been given is somewhat problematic. First of all, the desire to join
the West and Western institutions that was so prevalent as the country
emerged from Communist rule has somewhat changed focus. In recent
years, Slovakia has faced the reality of conflict between the United States
and some of its allies over the propriety of U.S. military intervention in
Iraq, or U.S. pressure to exempt American citizens from the jurisdiction of
the International Criminal Court. A large number of Slovaks favor a passive
role for their country in world affairs, and only half support the basic concept of NATO—going to war to defend an ally under attack. Slovaks tend
to define security issues as more narrowly focused on their own economic
security and less on external threats. In a recent poll, as many as 68 percent

of Slovaks said that strong U.S. leadership was either undesirable or very undesirable. After three Slovak soldiers were killed in Iraq, the opposition party SMER used its opposition to U.S. policies, both in Iraq and in general, to differentiate itself from the governing coalition, from which it took power in the 2006 elections.[25] These views were buttressed by a more or less passive political culture and a sense of Slovakia's proper world role that is still in the formative stage.[26] One area that until recently was highly vexing for bilateral relations was visa issuance. After years of bilateral discussions and the signing of a visa waiver agreement with the United States, Slovakia (along with the Czech Republic) became one of seven new states added to the visa waiver program on November 17, 2008. The program allows Slovaks to enter the United States for business, tourism, or transits without a visa for stays up to ninety days. However, under this new program, travelers must still present an application for authorization prior to leaving their home country. This application allows the U.S. Department of Homeland Security to perform a security check before the traveler departs for the United States. In case the application is rejected, the traveler must apply for a visa as before.[27]

In the June 13, 2004 elections for representatives to the European Parliament, the first in which the country participated, only 17 percent of eligible Slovaks went to the polls. This figure is far below the participation rate of more than 70 percent in the 2002 parliamentary elections or 84 percent in 1998, and is the lowest of any of the new EU member countries which took part in the poll, as well as of any EU member that ever participated in any Union-wide elections. While, on the one hand, the Slovak government tried hard to join Western political and economic institutions, on the other hand, there is a significant amount of passivity and skepticism among the electorate. Parties represented in the pre-2006 government coalition polled 51 percent of the votes and elected eight of the fourteen Euro MPs to which Slovakia is entitled.[28]

The 2006 Parliamentary Elections: A New "Direction"

In the parliamentary elections that were held on June 17, 2006, Slovak voters decided it was time for a change. The party SMER—Sociálna Demokracia (Direction—Social Democracy), headed by Robert Fico, a former leader of the post-Communist SDĽ, captured a plurality of votes and formed a coalition with Mečiar's HZDS, known since 2003 officially as LS-HZDS—Ľudová strana—Hnutie za demokratické Slovensko (People's Party—Movement for a Democratic Slovakia) and the Slovak National Party (Slovenská národná strana) headed by Ján Slota, the former mayor of Zilina. Slota is well known for his anti-Hungarian and anti-Romany statements.[29] The government includes eleven ministers from SMER, three from the SNS, and two from the HZDS. Fico's government has been taking a less pro-American stance than its predecessor. For example, he pulled 110 members of a Slovak engineering brigade out of Iraq, calling the war there "unbelievably unjust and wrong."[30] At a NATO meeting he hosted in Bratislava in October 2009, he claimed that the Iraq war was fought for oil and said Slovakia would not host any revamped U.S. missile shield on its territory.[31] But in contrast to his earlier statements, he also said his country could increase its contingent of engineering troops in Afghanistan. Domestically, Fico has sought to rein in the privatization policies of his predecessor, arguing that they were causing too much social pain through limitations on welfare benefits.[32]

Some Final Thoughts: Constancy and Change

In its second decade of independence, Slovakia exhibits the historical contradictions between the legacy of its past and the lure of its future. Most significantly, the country has turned away from the authoritarian and manipulative tendencies of the Mečiar years and has embraced political competition and economic reform. To an important extent, this progress has resulted from the growth of civil society and the proliferation of the NGO sector. NGOs, for example, took the lead in rallying citizens behind the cause of free and fair elections in 1998. They also helped rally popular support for NATO membership.[33] Their growth has been fostered by U.S. and European aid programs, and has been one of the great success stories of foreign assistance programs.[34] Yet, the road to long-term political stability remains beset by many complications. While Mečiar suffered a number of political defeats from 1998 to 2004, he continued to be a presence in Slovak politics, despite being discredited for his antidemocratic activities. The fact that he received the largest number of votes in the first round of the 2004 presidential elections showed that the governing coalition underestimated his ability to maintain a solid core of support. His HZDS, despite its metamorphosis into a center-right party, is still more of an extension of its leader than an organization with a coherent program and ideology. Down but not out, he remains a political pariah with little real chance of resuming power in his country. In any case, institutional changes since he left office, such as the establishment of a judicial council to vet candidates for the judiciary, and direct election of the president, will in the future make it more difficult for power to be so concentrated and misused.

On the other hand, the Dzurinda government was itself wracked by conflict and Dzurinda suffered a corresponding loss of popularity. His majority in Parliament collapsed in 2004 with the defection of seven deputies to the new Slobodné Fórum (SF or Free Forum). The deputies were led by Defense Minister Ivan Šimko, who himself resigned from the government after refusing to dismiss a security official as demanded by Dzurinda. More recently, however, Šimko, who missed by one vote being elected to head the SF, also resigned from that organization, which he had helped to create. Because the dissident deputies generally supported the government in specific votes on policy issues, the coalition lasted through the parliamentary elections which were held on June 17, 2006. Sharp disputes within the government also arose on issues such as abortion, causing the KDH to warn that it would bolt the coalition if laws were liberalized.[35] A treaty with the Vatican also calls for Slovak youth to take mandatory courses in religion from ages eight to sixteen, but allows students to choose to study ethics as an alternative. This provision took effect in September 2004.[36]

Slovakia's political and economic debate will take place from now on within the framework of the country's new membership in NATO and the EU. This international context will help ensure that Slovakia remains committed to Western values. However, the fracturing of the U.S.-European consensus in the wake of the Iraq war also means that Slovakia will be pulled in several directions as it sets its own policies. Indeed, even a personality such as Čarnogurský has come out against Slovakia's membership in NATO, arguing that the organization is still latently directed against Russia, and that membership will force Slovakia and other countries to get involved in conflicts, such as in Iraq, where they have no national interests.[37] The country's continuing high unemployment rate of 15 percent is also a wild card as far as economic stability is concerned.[38] The persistence of corruption in the country, and the pervasive feeling that the average citizen is not better off than he or she was in the past, also take their toll. Indeed, a poll taken in October 2004 on the fifteenth anniversary of the 1989 revolution found that only 20 percent of Slovak respondents viewed the current system as having clear advantages over the pre-1989 era, whereas 55 percent thought that advantages were greater in the past than in the present.[39] Slovakia's democracy is still young and fragile, but with each successful peaceful transfer of power, it is hoped that backsliding will become less and less likely.

Notwithstanding the positive prognostications made in this book, as Slovakia nears the end of the first decade of the twenty-first century, it would be remiss not to mention some of the trends prevailing in the latter part of 2009. One of these is the amendment to the Slovak Language Act (Zákon o štátnom jazyku, or "law on the state language"), which took effect on September 1, 2009. The amendment tightens requirements for use of Slovak in official settings including schools (even Hungarian language schools must conduct their administration in Slovak). The new law punishes those who break rules on the proper use of Slovak in public with fines of up to €5,000 (about $7,000). The only exceptions made are for those areas where minorities make up 20 percent or more of the population. Signs in Hungarian-populated districts can only be the Hungarian equivalent of the Slovak and not a different name. Hungarians in both Slovakia and Hungary have roundly criticized the new law as discriminatory.[40] The weekly *Economist* also published a sharply critical article on the law, using the Slovak language for its title.[41] It noted that the amendment comes as the culmination of a strongly negative attitude toward things Hungarian taken by the Fico government, including scrapping plans for a joint textbook commission with Hungary. A German Europarliamentarian, Michael Gehler, the vice chair of the European Parliament's foreign affairs committee, also wrote recently that the new law violates commonly accepted EU standards on the use of minority languages.[42]

Minister of Culture Marek Maďarič, for his part, strongly denied that the purpose of the amended law is to suppress the Hungarians or other minorities. He argued that the issue is allowing everyone access to information in the state language and ensuring that Slovak is the language of communication understood by all citizens. He also denied that private use of minority languages would be subject to legal sanctions.[43]

The new law represents a continuation of the struggles over the use of the Slovak or Hungarian languages referred to earlier in this book. It reflects, in the larger sense, continuing Slovak fears that somehow the unrestrained use of Hungarian in part of the country will be the prelude to a creeping annexation of southern Slovakia, and in its turn, it contributes to feeling among Hungarians that they are being discriminated against and being used as a political football. To be sure, the "pro-Slovak" attitude of Fico's government sits well with voters, despite criticism that it represents political pandering that deflects attention from other shortcomings in public life.

Another area worth watching is the government's attitude to criticism. The Institute for Public Affairs (IVO) conducts quarterly studies on the state of democracy in the country. Its report published in July 2009 noted a worsening in terms of rule of law and rights of independent media. Fico, for his part, rather than react to the specifics of the IVO report, accused the organization of being "in the opposition ideological headquarters."[44] Such accusations bring to mind the harsh words of Gustav Husák quoted earlier regarding his determination not to allow the academic arena to become a reservation for "opposition" forces or the tactics of Mečiar and his colleagues in the 1992 conflict over Trnava University. Given a situation where the media is facing increasing challenges from officials who are ready to sue for what are presumed to be slanderous statements or where the independence of the judiciary is being placed into question, one is left to ponder where these trends will go. Recent developments, in which government officials from Prime Minister Fico to Supreme Court President Štefan Harabin are able to sue journalists for libel and get large rewards in the process, do not bode well for freedom of the press. Harabin himself has collected over €180,000 from such lawsuits.[45] Perhaps the best words to end this book are those used by Beata Balogová in the English-language weekly *Slovak Spectator*, where she noted,

> This year, the country will remember the 20th anniversary of the Velvet Revolution, which will most probably force many people to weigh and assess the path this country has walked from November 17, 1989, until today. Yes, the path has been immeasurably tougher and more challenging than many students might have thought during those cold November evenings when they stood on public squares living the revolution. Among those grand principles then were freedom of the press, plurality of opinions and an independent judiciary. None of these is ever a permanent endowment and each needs to be continuously nourished, protected and even fought for.
>
> Citizens need to be watchful and alert whenever there are even the slightest signs of corrosion in these basic tenets of democracy because in the deafening noise of political declarations about progress and respect for the rules, these precious objects can be easily broken and it might then take many years and the loss of many people's faith to fix them again.[46]

GLOSSARY OF SLOVAK
POLITICAL ORGANIZATIONS

ANO (Aliancia Nového Občana) Alliance of the New Citizen (ANO means "yes" in Slovak): Liberal Party, member of the ruling coalition. Founded in 2001 by former minister of economics Pavol Rusko, former head of the Markiza television channel.

ČZM (Československý Zväz Mládeže) (Czech: ČSM or Československý Svaz Mládeže) Czechoslovak Youth League: The monopoly organization for Czech and Slovak youth, modeled on the Komsomol; set up after the 1948 Communist coup; collapsed in 1968, but replaced in 1970 by the ZSM, or Zväz Socialistickej Mládeže (Union of Socialist Youth).

DS (Demokratická strana) Democratic Party: Victor in the 1946 elections in Slovakia; destroyed by the Communists in 1948; renewed in 1989; junior partner in the 1990 coalition government. In 1998 joined other parties to form the SDK (Slovak Democratic Coalition). It merged with the SDKÚ in January 2006 to form the Slovak Democratic and Christian Union—Democratic Party (Slovenská demokratická a kresťanská únia—Demokratická strana, SDKÚ-DS).

DÚ (Demokratická únia) Democratic Union: Founded on April 23, 1994, as the merger of the Alliance of Democrats (chairman, Milán Kňažko) and the Democratic Union of Slovakia (chairman, Jozef Moravčík), both of them representing splinter factions of HZDS and then allied in the so-called Center Bloc. The DÚ joined other parties to form the SDK in 1998 and in July 2000 decided to merge into Prime Minister Dzurinda's new SDKÚ, thus ceasing to exist.

Egyutelles (Coexistence): Major political party encompassing the Hungarian minority in Slovakia (but nominally including other minorities as well); stressed Hungarians' national interests. The party was merged with the Hungarian Christian Democratic Movement and the Hungarian Civic Party into the Party of the Hungarian Coalition (Hungarian initials MPK) on June 27, 1998.

FBIS (Federálna bezpečnostná informačná služba) Federal Security Information Service: Was the post-Communist federal security service that was disbanded with the end of the Czech and Slovak Federal Republic in 1993.

HZD (Hnutie za demokraciu) Movement for Democracy: Founded in July 2002 by persons who splintered off from the HZDS. Founding chairman was Ivan Gašparovič, who became Slovakia's third president on June 15, 2004. Web site: http://www.hzd.sk.

HZDS (Hnutie za demokratické Slovensko): Movement for a Democratic Slovakia: Formed in March 1991 by Vladimír Mečiar and other Slovak politicians who split off from the VPN (Verejnosť proti Nasiliu). Formed the Slovak government in June 1992 and again in 1994. Renamed People's Party—Movement for a Democratic Slovakia on June 14, 2003 (LS-HZDS—Ľudová strana—Hnutie za demokratické Slovensko). Junior member of the coalition government formed in July 2006. Web site: http://www.hzds.sk.

KDH (Kresťanskodemokratické hnutie) Christian Democratic Movement: Formed in early 1990 by Ján Čarnogurský and others who had participated in the Christian resistance movement to the Communist Party; was an original partner of the SDK, but in 2000 refused to join Dzurinda's SDKÚ. Web site: http://www.kdh.sk.

KSČ (Komunistická strana Československa; Slovak initials KSČS) Communist Party of Czechoslovakia: The ruling party in the country from 1948 to 1989, after which time it was disbanded. Known as the KSS (Communist Party of Slovakia) in Slovakia, and since 1993 as the KSČM (Komunistická strana Čech a Moravy—Communist Party of the Czech Lands and Moravia) in the Czech Republic.

KSS (Komunistická strana Slovenska) Communist Party of Slovakia: Ruling party 1948 to 1989; disbanded 1990, reestablished 1992 by a group of dissidents who were dissatisfied with the social democratic orientation of the successor SDĽ. Elected eleven members to Parliament in 2002, none in 2006 (received 3.88 percent of the votes). Web site: http://www.kss.sk.

MKDH (Maďarské Kresťanskodemokratické hnutie) Hungarian Christian Democratic Movement: A political grouping of Hungarians in Slovakia, without formal ties to the KDH, merged on June 22, 1998 with Egyutelles (*see separate entry*) and the Hungarian Civic Party into the Party of the Hungarian Coalition (Hungarian initials MKP).

MNI (Maďarská nezavislá iniciatíva) Hungarian Independent Initiative: Smaller, liberal Hungarian party joined as a junior partner with the VPN in the government formed in 1990; became the Hungarian Civic Party in 1992, which itself was merged into the Party of the Hungarian Coalition (Hungarian initials MKP) on June 22, 1998.

MS (Matica Slovenská) Slovak Heritage Society: After 1989 became the hotbed of pro-independence and nationalist activists; it also opposed measures that would favor minorities (especially Hungarians) at the expense of Slovaks. Originally founded in 1863 to preserve Slovak language and culture. Web site: http://www.matica.sk.

NRSR (Národná rada Slovenskej republiky) National Council of the Slovak Republic (*see also* SNR).

ODS (Czech) (Občanská demokratická strana): Moderate right-wing Czech party founded in 1991 by Václav Klaus, former Czech prime minister and current Czech president. Web site: http://www.ods.cz.

ODÚ (Občianská demokratická únia) Civic Democratic Union: Founded in 1992 from the now-defunct VPN; went out of existence in November 1992.

SDA (Sociálnodemokratická alternativa) Social Democratic Alternative: Founded in 2002 by former officials of the SDĽ, such as Peter Weiss and Milan Ftáčnik, who wanted to emphasize their social democratic orientation. Merged with SMER in January 2005.

SDK (Slovenská demokratická koalicia) Slovak Democratic Coalition: Was founded on July 4, 1998, as a federation of five parties: DS, SDSS, SZS, DÚ, and KDH. Became defunct in 2001 after Chairman Mikuláš Dzurinda founded the SDKÚ.

SDKÚ (Slovenská demokratická a kresťanská únia) Slovak Democratic and Christian Union: Political party founded in 2000 by Mikuláš Dzurinda, Slovak prime minister from 1998 to 2006; largest party in the governing coalition ruling Slovakia until 2006. After merging with the Democratic Party (DS) in January 2006, it changed its official name to SDKÚ-DS (Slovenská demokratická a kresťanská únia—Demokratická strana). Web site: http://www.sdkuonline.sk.

SDĽ (Strana demokratickej ľavice) Party of the Democratic Left: Founded in 1990 as the successor to the Communist Party of Slovakia (KSS). Joined with SMER when it disbanded on December 31, 2004, but a new party of the same name was registered May 3, 2005; it received only 0.13 percent of all votes in the 2006 elections.

SDSS (Sociálnodemokratická strana Slovenska) Social Democratic Party of Slovakia: Forced to amalgamate with the Communist Party in 1948; reborn after 1989; headed for a short time by Alexander Dubček in 1992, merged with SMER January 1, 2005.

SF (Slobodné Fórum) Free Forum: Founded by former Defense Minister Ivan Šimko and several other members of the SDKÚ after Šimko was dismissed by Dzurinda; Šimko was defeated by Zuzana Martináková for the SF chairmanship by one vote, and he resigned from the SF in October 2004. Web site: http://www.slobodneforum.sk.

SIS (Slovenská informačná služba) Slovak Information Service, the Slovak state security service: Founded soon after the country became independent; during Mečiar's rule from 1994 to 1998, it was misused against political opponents. Today, its activities are supervised by a parliamentary committee. Web site: http://www.sis.gov.sk/index_sis.html.

SKDH (Slovenské Kresťanskodemokratické hnutie) Slovak Christian Democratic Movement: Breakaway party formed from the KDH in 1992 to promote the idea of an independent Slovakia. Renamed Christian Social Union (KSÚ or Kresťanská sociálna únia Slovenska); failed to win the 1992 or 1994 elections; now defunct (merged with the SNS in 1998).

SMER—Sociálna Demokracia (Direction—Social Democracy): Party founded in December 1999 by Robert Fico, a former member of the SDĽ. Moderate reformist; Fico was dissatisfied with the policies of the governing coalition; won 13.6 percent of the votes in 2002. In the 2006 elections, his party won 29 percent of the vote and he became Slovakia's prime minister in a governing coalition with the HZDS and the SNS (*see separate entries*). Web site: http://www.strana-smer.sk.

SMK (Strana Maďarskej Koalicie; Magyar Koalíció Pártja [MKP]) Party of the Hungarian Coalition: SMK was founded on June 21, 1998, from the merger of three Magyar parties: Hungarian Christian Democrat Movement (MKDM), Coexistence (E), and Hungarian Civil Party (MPP). Web site: http://www.smk.sk.

SNR (Slovenská národná rada): The Slovak National Council or Parliament; 150 members; official name changed in October 1992 to NRSR (National Council of the Slovak Republic or Národná rada Slovenskej Republiky). Web site: http://www.nrsr.sk.

SNS (Slovenská národná strana) Slovak National Party: Formed by pro-independence Slovak politicians who broke away from the VPN in early 1990; was a junior partner with the HZDS in the coalition formed after the 1992 and 1994 elections, and with SMER after the 2006 elections. Web site: http://www.sns.sk.

SOP (Strana občianskeho porozumenia) Party of Civic Understanding: Founded on April 5, 1998, by former President Rudolf Schuster and ceased to exist on April 1, 2003, when it merged into SMER. Web site: http://www.sop.sk.

SWC, Slovak World Congress: Umbrella organization of Slovaks living abroad, founded in 1971 and headquartered in Toronto; it has frequently sought to whitewash the 1939–45 puppet Slovak state.

SZ (Strana zelených) Slovak Green Party: Founded in 1990; elected four members to the NRSR as part of the SDK in 1998, but none in 2002; represented in some regional legislatures. Known as Strana zelených na Slovensku (Green Party in Slovakia) until 2006. Web site: http://www.stranazelenych.sk.

SZM (*see* ZSM)

VPN (Verejnosť proti násiliu) Public Against Violence: Formed in November 1989 as the first, all-encompassing Slovak political movement against the then ruling Communist Party. Renamed ODÚ (*see reference*) in 1992.

ZRS (Združenie Robotnikov Slovenska) Association of Slovak Workers: Founded as a splinter group of the SDĽ in 1994; became a member of Mečiar's coalition government that year. Received only 0.29 percent of the votes in the 2006 elections. Web site of Zvolen regional organization: http://www.zrs.zvolen.szm.sk.

ZSM (Zväz Socialistickej Mládeže) (Czech: SSM, Svaz Socialistické Mládeže) Union of Socialist Youth: Communist-controlled monopoly youth organization founded in 1970; disbanded in 1989. Was reconstituted in 1997 as an "independent, voluntary, leftist" youth organization but is closely tied to the KSS and its "anti-imperialist" political line, under the name Socialist Youth of Slovakia (Socialistický zväz mladých). Web site: http://www.szm.hng.sk.

GLOSSARY OF CZECH AND
SLOVAK PERSONALITIES

Belousovová, Anna (1959–) (née Malíková) First deputy chair of the Slovak National Party (SNS) and deputy speaker of the Slovak parliament. Married to a Russian, Belousovová strongly condemned the Estonians in 2007 for moving a statue of a Soviet soldier from a main square in Tallinn, calling it "an insult to the memory of those who fought against fascism."

Budaj, Ján (1952–) Environmentalist, one of the leading personalities of the November 1989 Velvet Revolution in Slovakia. Member of the Slovak National Council for the SDK 1998–2002.

Čalfa, Marián (1946–) A transitional figure, as a member of the KSČ he was the first Czechoslovak prime minister after the November 1989 revolution, holding that position until after the June 1992 elections. He joined the VPN in 1990 (and later its successor organization, the ODU-VPN). As a Slovak who made his career in Prague, he had two handicaps as far as Slovak nationalists were concerned: he was a "Czechoslovakist," whom they deemed closer to the Czechs than the Slovaks, and a former Communist official. He was deputy prime minister from 1988 to 1989.

Čarnogurský, Ján (1944–) Deputy prime minister of Czechoslovakia 1989–90, deputy prime minister of Slovakia 1990–91, prime minister of Slovakia 1991–92. Chairman of the Christian Democratic Movement (KDH) 1990–2000. Trained as a lawyer, Čarnogurský was active in the pre-1989 period as a defender of dissidents—a role that brought him into conflict with Communist authorities, and imprisonment for several months before the November 1989 revolution. He was Slovak minister of justice 1998–2002, after which he retired from active politics. His position on social issues is generally reflective of Catholic teachings, including strong opposition to abortion. His father, Pavol, was an official of the wartime Slovak government.

Černák, Ľudovít (1951–) Minister of the economy and industry and trade and tourism 1992–93 and again 1998–99; chairman of the SNS 1992–94, at which time he was recalled from his position and excluded from the party. He proved more moderate on many issues than his party colleagues. He became chairman of the board of directors of Sitno Holding in 2000.

Čič, Milan (1932–) First prime minister of Slovakia after the 1989 revolution, Čič was earlier (1988–89) minister of justice in Communist Slovakia. With a background as a member of the Faculty of Law of Comenius University, he was named to head the Slovak Constitutional Court in

1993, where he served until 2000. In 2004 he was named chief of the Office of the President of the Slovak Republic.

Csáky, Pál (1956–) Slovak Member of Parliament since 1990; deputy prime minister for European affairs, human rights and minorities 2002–6 and for human rights, minorities and regional development 1998–2002; chairman of the SMK (Hungarian Coalition Party) since 2007.

Demeš, Pavol (1956–) Slovak minister of foreign relations 1991–92; presidential advisor on foreign relations 1993–97; director, Slovak Academic Information Agency since 1997; currently head of the German Marshall Fund Office for Central and Eastern Europe. Trained as a biologist, Demeš brought his enthusiasm for education into the field of international exchanges and diplomacy even before Slovak independence. In recent years, he has been active in programs to promote democracy in such places as the former Yugoslavia, Ukraine, and Belarus.

Dienstbier, Jiří (1937–) Czechoslovak foreign minister 1989–92. Educated as a journalist and active in the 1968 reform movement. Dismissed from his posts after "normalization," Dienstbier worked mostly as a manual laborer until 1989. He was one of the original signatories of the Charter 77 Appeal, and served three years in prison for his opposition activities (1979–82). He divides his time between special diplomatic missions, writing, and lecturing.

Dubček, Alexander (1921–1992) Best known as the "Father of the Prague Spring," which followed his election as first secretary of the Communist Party of Czechoslovakia on January 4, 1968, and lasted until the Soviet-led invasion of August 21 that year. Employed in the Slovak State Forest Enterprise from 1970 to 1985, he returned to political life after the November 1989 "Velvet Revolution." He became chairman of the Czechoslovak Federal Parliament in 1989, and held the post until his death in November 1992, from complications of an auto accident that took place on the Prague-Bratislava highway two months earlier. Dubček was elected chairman of the Social Democratic Party in Slovakia in 1992.

Duray, Miklos (1945–) Hungarian political activist Duray was imprisoned in the early 1980s for his political activity. Since 1998 he has been a parliamentary deputy for the SMK.

Dzurinda, Mikuláš (1955–) Economic advisor to the KDH in the early 1990s. Slovak prime minister 1998–2006; chairman of the SDKÚ-DS (Slovak Democratic Christian Union). As prime minister after Mečiar, he sought to firmly anchor Slovakia to the United States, NATO, and the EU, and to relaunch economic reforms. However, because these reforms caused widespread unemployment, he gradually lost popularity with the electorate.

Feldek, Ľubomír (1936–) One of the founders of the VPN, before 1989 Feldek had a successful literary career that included poetry, short stories, and novels, but also some paeans to Leonid Brezhnev. In 1992, after writing about the fascist past of then Minister of Culture Dušan Slobodník, he was sued for slander in a case that was only decided by the European Court of Human Rights in Strasbourg in 2001 (against Slobodník).

Fico, Robert (1964–) Slovak prime minister since 2006, chairman of the SMER (Direction) party. Background in legal affairs. Former member of the post-Communist Party of the Socialist Left (SDĽ). More socialist and less pro-American than his predecessor, Mikuláš Dzurinda.

Gál, Fedor (1945–) A survivor of the Holocaust who was born in the Terezin concentration camp, Gál was a sociologist who founded an institute of social analysis in Bratislava after the 1989 revolution. He was head of the coordinating committee of the VPN until 1991, and after the victory of the HZDS in the 1992 elections, he moved to Prague. He is an advisor to the G-plus-G publishing house, and is involved in writing.

Gašparovič, Ivan (1941–) President of the Slovak Republic since 2004 (when he ran against Vladimír Mečiar), Gašparovič's career before 1989 was involved in the legal field as a teacher at the Faculty of Law of Comenius University (Bratislava). He was elected chairman of the Slovak National Council in 1992, and was put in charge of the U.S. Consulate "microphone incident" investigation by Mečiar. While initially a close confidant and collaborator with the prime minister, Gašparovič later went his own way and founded a new Movement for Democracy (HZD) in 2002, complaining about Mečiar's undemocratic methods.

Hamžik, Pavol (1954–) First head of the Slovak mission to the CSCE (later OSCE) in Vienna 1993. Minister of foreign affairs 1996–97, deputy prime minister 1998–2001. Worked in the federal ministry of foreign affairs 1984–85 and in the Czechoslovak Embassy in Copenhagen 1985–89. Chairman of SOP 1999–2003.

Havel, Václav (1936–) Ninth (and last) president of Czechoslovakia 1989–92, and first president of the Czech Republic 1993–2003. Havel, a gifted playwright, made a name for himself in Czech drama during the creative rebirth that preceded the 1968 "Prague Spring." Active in opposition circles during the post-invasion "normalization" period, Havel was one of the authors of the Charter 77 Manifesto, and was imprisoned on several occasions, lasting as long as four years, by Communist authorities. Havel has been a passionate spokesman for nonviolent resistance and democratic ideals. During the period prior to the split of the Czechs and Slovaks, Havel was regarded as hostile to Slovak aspirations by

Vladimír Mečiar, who was incensed by Havel's last-minute appeal before the June 1992 elections not to support parties that wanted to jettison the country's unity.

Hofbauer, Roman (1940–) Mayor of Bratislava July–September 1990. Founding member of HZDS. Minister of transportation and communications 1992–94. Ultranationalist, he ordered that bilingual signs be removed from Slovakia's roads in 1993. He was also hypersensitive to criticism from RFE, and tried unsuccessfully to get the U.S. Embassy to intervene to stop it.

Hoffman, Ivan (1952–) Noted singer and journalist. After 1989, was a correspondent for Radio Free Europe, and became the bane of nationalist Slovaks. Editor of *Radio Journal* program on Czech Radio. Has lived in Prague since 1992.

Hoffman, Pavol (1931–2005) Member of VPN, minister for strategic planning in the federal government from June 1990; in 1991 became deputy prime minister for economic issues in the federal government. Earlier active in the Economic Institute of the Slovak Academy of Science (SAV). Family was hidden during the Holocaust and saved by friends and partisans.

Hrušovský, Pavol (1952–) Member of Parliament 1992–present; chairman of the NRSR 2002–6, chairman of the KDH.

Húska, Augustín Marián (1929–) Member of the NRSR for the HZDS 1994–98 and 1998–2002; other positions held in the 1990s included vice chairman of the HZDS and vice speaker of the NRSR.

Klaus, Václav (1941–) Second president of the Czech Republic (2003–). First prime minister of the independent Czech Republic 1993–97; federal minister of finance 1989–92. Klaus is known as a "Euroskeptic" who has significant reservations about the value of European institutions.

Klepáč, Ján (1949–) Elected 1990 as a member of the Slovak National Council for the KDH, he split with Čarnogurský over the issue of Slovak independence and in 1992 became chairman of the Slovak Christian Democratic Movement (SKDH, later Christian Social Movement or KSÚ), which failed to retain any deputies in the parliament elected that June. He became a director in the office of President Rudolf Schuster in 2001, and is presently vice chairman of the Regulatory Office for Network Industries in Bratislava responsible for the gas industry (he started off as an engineer in the Slovnaft company).

Kňažko, Milan (1945–) Slovak foreign minister 1992–93; minister of culture 1998–2002. Educated as an actor, he was one of the "tribunes" of the November 1989 revolution and one of the founders of the HZDS. He left the movement after disagreements with Mečiar.

Korec, Ján Chryzostom (1924–) Named a cardinal by Pope John Paul II in 1991, Korec was imprisoned for underground Church activities from 1960–68. He was a leading member of the underground Church in Slovakia and was ordained a bishop in secret at the age of twenty-seven. He was reimprisoned in 1974, but later released due to poor health. Korec's role became controversial in July 1990 when he dedicated a memorial plaque to Father Jozef Tiso at a school where Tiso had taught in Bánovce. He disagrees with the view that Tiso was justly condemned as a war criminal.

Kováč, Michal (1930–) First president of Slovakia 1993–98. An economist who spent some of his working life in the banking field in London and Havana, Kováč was the speaker of the federal assembly in 1992, during the period when the dissolution of the federation was negotiated. Not known for his charisma, Kováč nonetheless was determined to be an independent president, and his relations with Mečiar gradually deteriorated.

Kováč, Roman (1940–) Chairman of the Slovak Confederation of Trade Unions 1990–92. From 1992 to 1994 was deputy prime minister overseeing the ministry of control. Member of the National Council 1994–98; minister of health 2000–2002. His name was mentioned as a possible candidate for president in 1993, but his namesake Michal Kováč was chosen because of the view that the latter would be more independent of Mečiar. Educated as a physician.

Kozlík, Sergej (1950–) In 1992 named assistant to the chairman of the HZDS for economic affairs; November 1993–March 1994, deputy prime minister in charge of economic affairs; November 1994–January 1998, deputy prime minister and minister of finance. Currently EU Parliament deputy for the ĽS-HZDS.

Kubiš, Ján (1952–) Executive secretary of the UN Economic Commission for Europe (UNECE) since 2009. Slovak minister of foreign affairs 2006–2009. A career diplomat, Kubiš began his service in Ethiopia from 1980 to 1985, and headed the Security and Arms Control Section of the Czechoslovakia Ministry of Foreign Affairs from 1985 to 1988. He was deputy chief of mission in Moscow 1990–91. In the 1990s he held a number of posts first with the federal and later with the Slovak ministry of foreign affairs dealing with European security and economic issues. He was secretary general of the Organization for Security and Cooperation in Europe (OSCE) from 1999–2005.

Lajčák, Miroslav (1963–) A career diplomat, Lajčák was the High Representative for Bosnia and Herzegovina from 2007–2009, at which time he was named to his current position of foreign minister of Slovakia.

Loebl, Evžen (also Eugen) (1907–1987) One of the three survivors of the infamous 1952 Slánský show trial, Loebl was director of the Slovak regional branch of the state bank of Czechoslovakia in 1968 at the time of the Soviet-led invasion. He taught economics and political science after emigrating to the United States, and was a vice president of the Slovak World Congress, specializing in economic issues.

Markuš, Jozef (1944–) Deputy prime minister in the transitional federal governments of 1989–90; head of the Matica Slovenská since 1990. A strong proponent of Slovak nationalist views. In the 1970s and 1980s, he held various positions in the Slovak Academy of Science in the field of economics and prognostics.

Mečiar, Vladimír (1942–) Slovak prime minister 1990–91, 1992–94, 1994–98. Founder and chairman of the Movement for a Democratic Slovakia, HZDS (Hnutie za demokratické Slovensko). The major personality in Slovak politics throughout most of the 1990s. Known for his pugnacious political style and appeals to Slovak populism, as well as acts during his rule that seriously brought into question the rule of law in his country.

Mikloš, Ivan (1960–) Minister for privatization 1991–92; member of Parliament for the SKDÚ; deputy prime minister and minister of finance, 2002–6; deputy prime minister for economic affairs 1998–2002. In the 1980s, he was a professor of economics at the Higher School of Economics in Bratislava.

Mikloško, František (1947–) Chairman of the Slovak National Council (SNR, Parliament) 1990–92; originally a member of the Public Against Violence (VPN), before the 1992 elections he switched to the Christian Democratic Movement (KDH), and represented the KDH in Parliament. He was active in the underground Church before 1989, and was one of the leaders of the "Candlelight Demonstration" of 1988 for religious freedom that was broken up by the police. On February 21, 2008, together with three other parliamentary deputies, he announced he was leaving the KDH because of its "doctrine of opportunism and pragmatism." In July 2008, he and several colleagues established a new party, Conservative Democrats of Slovakia (KDS or Konservatívni Demokrati Slovenska).

Moric, Viťazoslav (1946–) Founding chairman of the SNS in 1990, and later a deputy in the Slovak National Council. He has reflected the ultra-nationalist fringe of his party, with defamatory remarks against the Romanies and attempts to rehabilitate the fascist wartime Slovak state. In 2000, he lost his parliamentary immunity due to incitement against the Romanies. Presently chairman of the Slovak National Coalition, SLNKO.

Nagy, László (1948–) Member of the Slovak National Council for the SMK. He was deputy prime minister 1990–92 for the Independent Hungarian Initiative (MNI) and represents a moderate voice in Hungarian Slovak politics.

Oberhauser, Vilem (1948–) Minister of forestry and water economy 1992–94, he bolted the KDH and aligned with its nationalist wing in the SKDH.

Pittner, Ladislav (1934–2008) Minister of the interior for the KDH 1990–92; appointed after Mečiar demanded the dismissal of the incumbent for incompetence. Returned to this position March–November 1994, again 1998–2001. Director of the Slovak Information Service (SIS) 2003–6.

Rusko, Pavol (1963–) Deputy director of Slovak Television 1989–94; co-founder of Markiza television and first director general 1995–2000; chairman of ANO (Aliancia nového občana) 2001–2007; deputy speaker of National Council 2002–2003; minister of economy 2003–2005. Recalled from that position by then Prime Minister Mikuláš Dzurinda after he was accused of improprieties regarding a loan of 104 million Slovak crowns from a private businessman.

Schuster, Rudolf (1934–) Second president of Slovakia 1999–2004. From 1972 to 1983 he held various functions in the Košice regional government. Was mayor of Košice 1983–86 and 1994–99 and Czechoslovak ambassador to Canada 1990–92. Founder and leader of the Party of Civic Understanding (SOP—Strana občianskeho porozumenia) 1998–99. From 1964 to 1990, he was a member of the KSČ—a political past that negatively affected the trust of the younger generation.

Slobodník, Dušan (1927–2001) Minister of culture and acting minister of education during the 1992–94 Mečiar government. Imprisoned by the Soviets for joining a Nazi SS youth group at the end of World War II, Slobodník did not return to Slovakia until 1953. Was for a time head of the Institute of World Literature. By the early 1990s, he had become a strong advocate of Slovak independence and Slovak nationalism, and was adamantly opposed to the opening of Trnava University in late 1992, because of its "opposition" character. From 1994 to 1998 he was chairman of the committee on foreign affairs of the Slovak National Council.

Slota, Ján (1953–) Head of the Slovak National Party (SNS) since 2003, mayor of Žilina 1990–2006. He has been roundly criticized for his chauvinistic, ultranationalist, anti-Romany, and anti-Hungarian remarks. Elected to the Slovak parliament in 1992, 1994, and 1998. After the ÚPN (Nation's Memory Institute, *see Appendix D*) disclosed information in police files that Slota had in 1971 robbed a shop, the SNS initiated a move in early 2008 to abolish the Institute.

Sokol, Ján (1933–) Appointed bishop of Trnava 1988, archbishop 1989. Sokol in early 2007 stirred controversy when reports mentioned that he had been a collaborator with the Communist secret police (the STB), reports which he denied. Also, in an interview, Sokol described the wartime Slovak regime as a "time of well-being," and was also condemned for whitewashing the wartime Slovak republic. He has previously celebrated masses in memory of Father Jozef Tiso, who was hanged for war crimes in 1947. He retired from that position on reaching seventy-five years of age in 2009.

Stern, Juraj (1940–) Economist, former rector of the Economic University, activist in promoting such areas as European integration. Was one of the few Slovak academicians who accepted the invitation to attend the opening of Trnava University in October 1992. Unsuccessful candidate for mayor of Bratislava 2002. Vice chair of the board of directors of the Slovak Foreign Policy Association.

Tondra, František (1936–) Bishop of Spiš since 1989. While his views in the 1990s were somewhat more flexible than some of his colleagues, in 2006, as chairman of the Slovak Bishops Conference, he warned that Western liberalism was "subverting Christian values."

Traubner, Pavol (1941–) Head of the first neurological clinic in the Faculty of Medicine at Comenius University 1991–present; dean of Faculty of Medicine 2000 and 2003–7; honorary chairman of the Central Union of Jewish Religious Communities of Slovakia.

Tuchyňa, Jozef (1941–) A career military officer during the period of Communist rule, he was commander for the eastern military district in 1992 when tapped to become minister of the interior, a post he held under Mečiar's government until March 1994. He became chief of staff in November 1994. Retired in 1998.

Vášáryová, Magdaléna (1948–) A sociologist by training, an actress in her earlier career, former ambassador of Czechoslovakia to Austria, unsuccessful candidate for president, member of Slovakia's delegation to the European Parliament, state secretary at the ministry of foreign affairs, and currently a member of the National Council for the SDKÚ—DS, Vášáryová is Slovakia's closest approximation to a "renaissance woman."

Weiss, Peter (1952–) A reform-minded Communist before the 1989 revolution, Weiss became the first chairman of the post-Communist SDĽ (1991–96). Chairman of the Foreign Affairs Committee of the National Council 1998–2002. Lecturer at the Faculty of International Relations at the Economic University. Appointed ambassador to Hungary, June 2009.

Zala, Boris (1954–)　From 1990–92 chairman of the Social Democratic Party of Slovakia; moved aside during the 1992 campaign so that Alexander Dubček could take over the position. Member of Parliament for SMER 2002–present. Since 2000, head of the department of political science and European studies at the University of Konštantín Filozof (Constantine the Philosopher) in Nitra. Currently chairman of the Foreign Affairs Committee of the Slovak Parliament.

APPENDIX A: SLOVAK LEADERS, 1993–2008

CURRENT PARTIES

ANO: Alliance of the New Citizen (2001)
HZD: Movement for Democracy (2002)
KDH: Christian Democratic Movement (1990)
KSS: Communist Party of Slovakia (1992)
LS-HZDS: People's Party—Movement for a Democratic Slovakia
(1991/2003)
SDKÚ-DS: Slovak Democratic and Christian Union-Democratic Party (2006)
SMER: "Direction"—Social Democracy (1999/2005)
SMK: Party of the Hungarian Coalition (1998)
SNS: Slovak National Party (1990), ZRS: Slovak Workers' Front (1994)
SZ: Green Party (1990)

FORMER PARTIES AND COALITIONS

DNS: National Democratic Party (1994–95)
DS: Democratic Party (1989–2006)
DÚ: Democratic Union (1994–2000)
HZDS: Movement for a Democratic Slovakia (1991, renamed LS-HZDS
in 2003)
PSNS: Real Slovak National Party (2001–3)
SDA: Social Democratic Alternative (2002–5)
SDK: Slovak Democratic Coalition (1998–2001, comprising DS, SDSS, SZS,
DÚ, and KDH)
SDĽ: Party of Democratic Left (1990–2005)
SDKÚ: Slovak Democratic and Christian Union (2000–2006)
SDSS: Social Democratic Party of Slovakia (1990–2005)
SOP: Party of Civic Understanding (1998–2003)

PRESIDENTS OF THE REPUBLIC

Michal Kováč	March 2, 1993–March 2, 1998	n/p
Vladimír Mečiar	March 2, 1998–August 4, 1998	HZDS (acting)
Ivan Gašparovič	August 4, 1998–October 29, 1998	HZDS (acting)
Jozef Migaš	October 29, 1998–June 15, 1999	SDĽ (acting)

Rudolf Schuster   June 15, 1999–June 15, 2004   SOP, n/p

Ivan Gašparovič   June 15, 2004–   n/p

PRIME MINISTERS

Vladimír Mečiar	January 1, 1993– March 16, 1994	HZDS
Jozef Moravcik	March 16, 1994– 13 December, 1994	DÚ
Vladimír Mečiar	December 13, 1994– October 30, 1998	HZDS
Mikuláš Dzurinda	October 30, 1998– July 4, 2006	KDH/SDK, SDKÚ, SDKÚ-DS(*)
Robert Fico	July 4, 2006–	SMER

(*) Prime Minister Dzurinda was originally a member of KDH and then chairman of the SDK. On February 14, 2000, he registered the SDKÚ as his own party.

DEPUTY PRIME MINISTERS

Milán Kňažko	June 24, 1992– February 25, 1994	HZDS
Sergej Kozlík	June 24, 1992– March 15, 1994	HZDS
Roman Kováč	June 24, 1992– December 13, 1994	HZDS, DÚ
Marián Andel	November 10, 1993– March 15, 1994	SNS
Jozef Prokeš	November 10, 1993– March 15, 1994	SNS
Ivan Šimko	March 15, 1994– December 13, 1994	KDH
Brigita Schmögnerová	March 15, 1994– December 13, 1994	SDĽ
Katarína Tóthová	December 13, 1994– October 30, 1998	HZDS
Sergej Kozlík	December 13, 1994– October 30, 1998	HZDS
Jozef Kalman	December 13, 1994– October 30, 1998	ZRS

Pavol Hamžík	October 30, 1998– May 4, 2001	SOP
Ľubomír Fogaš	October 30, 1998– October 15, 2002	SDĽ
Pál Csáky	October 30, 1998– July 4, 2006	SMK
Ivan Mikloš	October 30, 1998– July 4, 2006	DS/SDK, SDKÚ, SDKÚ-DS
Mária Kadlečíková	May 4, 2001– October 15, 2002	SOP
Robert Nemcsics	October 16, 2002– September 10, 2003	ANO
Daniel Lipšic	October 16, 2002– February 8, 2006	KDH
Pavol Prokopovič	September 10, 2003– September 24, 2003	SDKÚ (acting)
Pavol Rusko	September 24, 2003– August 24, 2005	ANO
Jirko Malchárek	October 4, 2005– July 4, 2006	ANO
Lucia Žitnanská	February 8, 2006– July 4, 2006	n/p
Dušan Čaplovič	July 4, 2006–	SMER
Robert Kaliňák	July 4, 2006–	SMER
Štefan Harabin	July 4, 2006–	LS-HZDS
Ján Mikolaj	July 4, 2006–	SNS

MINISTERS OF FOREIGN AFFAIRS

Milán Kňažko	1993	HZDS
Jozef Moravčik	1993–94	HZDS
Eduard Kukan	1994	DÚ
Juraj Schenk	1994–96	HZDS
Pavol Hamžík	1996–97	HZDS
Zdenka Kramplová	1997–98	HZDS
Jozef Kalman	1998	ZRS (acting)
Eduard Kukan	1998–2006	DÚ/SDK, SDKÚ, SDKÚ-DS
Ján Kubiš	2006–9	n/p
Miroslav Lajčák	2009–	n/p

MINISTERS OF DEFENSE

Imrich Andrejčák	1993–94	HZDS
Pavol Kanis	1994	SDĽ
Ján Sitek	1994–98	SNS
Pavol Kanis	1998–2001	SDĽ
Jozef Stank	2001–2	SDĽ
Ivan Šimko	2002–3	SDKÚ
Eduard Kukan	2003	SDKÚ (acting)
Juraj Liška	2003–6	SDKÚ, SDKÚ-DS
Martin Fedor	2006	SDKÚ-DS
Frantisek Kašický	2006–8	n/p
Jaroslav Baška	2008–	SMER

MINISTERS OF THE INTERIOR

Jozef Tuchyňa	1993–94	
Ladislav Pittner	1994	KDH
Ľudovít Hudek	1994–96	HZDS
Gustáv Krajci	1996–98	HZDS
Ladislav Pittner	1998–2001	KDH/SDK
Ján Čarnogurský	2001	KDH (acting)
Ivan Šimko	2001–2	SDKÚ
Vladimír Palko	2002–6	KDH
Martin Pado	2006	SDKÚ-DS
Robert Kaliňák	2006–	SMER

MINISTERS OF FINANCE

Július Tóth	1993–94	HZDS
Rudolf Filkus	1994	DÚ
Sergej Kozlík	1994–98	HZDS
Miroslav Maxon	1998	HZDS
Brigita Schmögnerová	1998–2002	SDĽ
Frantisek Hajnovič	2002	SDĽ
Ivan Mikloš	2002–6	SDKÚ, SDKÚ-DS
Ján Počiatek	2006–	SMER

MINISTERS OF ECONOMY

Ľudovít Černák	1993	SNS
Jaroslav Kubečka	1993	HZDS
Jozef Ducký	1993–94	HZDS
Peter Magvasi	1994	SDĽ
Ján Ducký	1994–96	HZDS (+1999)a
Karol Česnek	1996–98	n/p
Milan Cagala	1998	HZDS
Ľudovít Černák	1998–99	DÚ/SDK
Lubomír Harach	1999–2	DÚ/SDK, SDKÚ
Robert Nemcsics	2002–3	ANO
Pavol Prokopovič	2003	SDKÚ (acting)
Pavol Rusko	2003–5	ANO
Ivan Mikloš	2005	SDKÚ (acting)
Jirko Malchárek	2005–6	ANO
Ľubomír Jahnátek	2006–	SMER

CHAIRMEN OF THE NATIONAL COUNCIL (PARLIAMENT)

Ivan Gašparovič	1993–98	HZDS
Jozef Migaš	1998–2002	SDĽ
Pavol Hrušovský	2002–6	KDH
Béla Bugár	2006	SMK (acting)
Pavol Paška	2006–	SMER

CHAIRMAN OF SMER

Robert Fico   1999–
SMER was founded by Robert Fico, a former SDĽ member, on October 29, 1999. On January 1, 2005, the party merged with the SDĽ, the SDA, and the SDSS, forming a new party called SMER—Social Democracy.

CHAIRMAN OF HZDS AND LS-HZDS

Vladimír Mečiar   1991–
Vladimír Mečiar left the Public Against Violence (VPN, see Czechoslovakia) on March 6, 1991, and founded the Movement for a Democratic Slovakia (HZDS) on June 22, 1991. The party changed its name by adding the label People's Party (LS-HZDS) on June 14, 2003.

CHAIRMAN OF SDKÚ AND SDKÚ-DS

Mikuláš Dzurinda   2000–
SDKÚ was launched on February 14, 2000, by Prime Minister Dzurinda
with the aim of replacing the SDK in time, although only one of the five
coalition members, DÚ, agreed to merge with SDKÚ. The founding congress
of SDKÚ as a party was held on November 18, 2000. On January 21, 2006,
SDKÚ and DS merged to form SDKÚ-DS.

CHAIRMEN OF SMK

Béla Bugár   1998–2007
Pál Csáky   2007–
SMK was born on June 21, 1998, from the merger of three Magyar parties:
the Hungarian Christian Democratic Movement (MKDM), Coexistence (E),
and the Hungarian Civic Party (MPP).

CHAIRMEN OF KDH

Ján Čarnogurský   1990–2000
Pavol Hrušovský   2000–
KDH was founded in February 1990. In 1998 it was an original partner of
SDK, but in 2000 it refused to join SDKÚ.

CHAIRMEN OF ANO

Pavol Rusko   2001–7
Robert Nemcsics   2007–
ANO was founded by media mogul Pavol Rusko on April 22, 2001.

CHAIRMEN OF KSS

Vladimír Ďaďo   1992–98
Jozef Ševc   1998–2006
Vladimír Ďaďo   2006 (acting)
Jozef Hrdlička   2006–
The current KSS was formed in 1992 from the merger of two Communist,
Marxist-Leninist groups, and adopted the same name as the defunct KSS.

CHAIRMEN OF HZD

Ivan Gašparovič   2002–4
Jozef Grapa   2005–
HZD was registered by splinters of HZDS on July 12, 2002.

CHAIRMEN OF SNS

Víťazoslav Moric   1990
Jozef Prokeš   1990–92
Ľudovít Černák   1992–94
Ján Slota   1994–99
Anna Malíková   1999–2003
Ján Slota   2003–
From October 6, 2001, to May 31, 2003, a splinter faction of the party, the PSNS, existed as independent party. *List courtesy of Michal Kubálek.*

CHAIRMAN OF ZRS

Ján Ľupták   1994–
ZRS was founded in April 1994 by splinters of SDĽ.

CHAIRMEN OF SDĽ (1990–2005)

Peter Weiss   1990–96
Jozef Migaš   1996–2001
Pavel Koncoš   2001–2
Ľubomir Petrák   2002–5
SDĽ was founded in 1990 by members of the defunct KSS. The party ceased to exist on January 1, 2005, as it merged into the SMER party.

CHAIRMEN OF SDSS (1990–2005)

Ivan Paulička   1990
Boris Zala   1990–92
Alexander Dubček   1992
Jaroslav Volf   1992–2001
Ludomir Slahor   2001–2

Peter Baráth   2002–3
Jaroslav Volf   2003–5

SDSS joined other parties to form SDK in 1998. It ceased to exist on January 1, 2005, as it merged into the SMER party. *List courtesy of Michal Kubálek.*

CHAIRMEN OF DS (1989–2006)

Martin Kvetko   1990
Ján Holčik   1990–92
Peter Mattoš   1992–93
Anton Ďuriš   1993–94
Pavel Hagyari   1994
Ivan Mikloš   1994
Peter Osuský   1994–95
Ján Langoš   1995–98
Ivan Brndiar   1998–99 (acting)
Ján Langoš   1999–2001
Ľudovít Kaník   2001–6

DS was first founded in 1944, disbanded in 1948, and refounded on December 10, 1989. In 1994 the party was relaunched as the merger of the Civic Democratic Union (ODÚ), the Civic Democratic Party of Slovakia (ODSS), Democrats 92, the Movement of Czech-Slovak comprehension (HCSP), and the Green League (ZL). In 1998 it joined other parties to form SDK. On December 17, 2005, the party decided to merge with the SDKÚ. The new SDKÚ-DS was launched on January 21, 2006. *List courtesy of Ondrej Dostal.*

CHAIRMAN OF SDA (2002–5)

Milán Ftáčnik   2002–5

SDA was founded on February 21, 2002, by splinters of SDĽ. It ceased to exist on January 1, 2005, as it merged into the SMER party.

CHAIRMEN OF SOP (1998–2003)

Rudolf Schuster   1998–99
Pavol Hamžík   1999–2003

SOP was founded on April 5, 1998, and ceased to exist on March 1, 2003, as it merged into the SMER party.

CHAIRMAN OF SDK (1998–2001)

Mikuláš Dzurinda   1998–2001
SDK was born on July 4, 1998, as a federation of five parties: DS, SDSS, SZS, DÚ, and KDH. On February 14, 2000, Dzurinda introduced his own party, SDKÚ, as a new and temporary member of SDK, which was intended to be disbanded and replaced by SDKÚ before the 2002 general elections. Throughout 2001 the old SDK suffered a process of disintegration, so DS, SDSS, SZS, and KDH continued separately, while DÚ joined SDKÚ.

CHAIRMEN OF DÚ (1994–2000)

Jozef Moravčík   1994–99
Ľubomír Harach   1999–2000
DÚ was born on April 23, 1994, as the merger of the Alliance of Democrats (chairman, Milán Knažko) and the Democratic Union of Slovakia (chairman, Jozef Moravčík), both of them splinter factions of HZDS, and these were then allied in the so-called Center Bloc. DÚ joined other parties to form SDK in 1998 and in July 2000 decided to merge into Prime Minister Dzurinda's new SDKÚ, ceasing to exist.

CHAIRMAN OF DNS (1994–95)

Ľudovít Černák   1994–95
DNS was founded in February 1994 by splinters of SNS. On March 25, 1995, it merged with DÚ and ceased to exist.

CHAIRMAN OF PSNS (2001–3)

Ján Slota   2001–3
PSNS was founded on October 6, 2001, by former SNS chairman J. Slota. PSNS and SNS reunited again on May 31, 2003, under the name SNS.

List of Slovak leaders © Copyright ZPC, Roberto Ortiz de Zárate, 1996–2008. http://www.terra.es/personal2/monolith/slovakia.htm. *Used by permission of author.*

Party	1990 %	1990 seats	1992 %	1992 seats	1994 %	1994 seats	1998 %	1998 seats	2002 %	2002 seats	2006 %	2006 seats
HZDS			37.3	74	35.0	61	27.0	43	19.5	36	8.8	15
SDKÚ									15.1	28	18.4	31
SDK							26.3	42				
SMER									13.5	25	29.1	50
MK	8.6	14	7.4	14	10.1	17	9.1	14	11.2	20	11.7	20
KDH	19.2	31	8.9	18	10.1	17	26.3	16	8.3	15	8.3	14
DÚ					8.6	15						
DS	4.4	7	3.3		3.4							
SDSS			4.0									
SP. VOLBA					10.4	18						
SZS												
SDĽ	13.3	22	14.7	29			14.7	24	1.4			
KSS			0.8		2.7		2.8		6.3	11	3.9	
SNS	13.9	22	7.9	15	5.4	9	9.1	14	3.3		11.7	20
ZRS					7.3	13	1.4		0.6			
SOP									8.0	13		
VPN	29.3	48	4.0									

HZDS: Movement for a Democratic Slovakia; SDKÚ: Slovak Democratic and Christian Union; SDK: Slovak Democratic Coalition; SMER: Direction; MK: Hungarian Coalition; KDH: Christian Democratic Movement; DÚ: Democratic Union; DS: Democratic Party; SDSS: Social Democratic Party of Slovakia; SP. VOLBA: Common Choice (SDSS, SDĽ, three other Left parties, 1994 only); SZS: Green Party of Slovakia; SDĽ: Democratic Left Party; KSS: Communist Party of Slovakia; SNS: Slovak National Party; ZRS: Slovak Workers' Union; SOP: Party of Civic Understanding; VPN: Public Against Violence (1992: Democratic Civic Union). Sources: Ministerstvo Vnútra Slovenskej Republiky; Studies on Parties and Elections.

A detailed official tabulation of all Slovak election and referendum results 1990–2006 is available on the site of the Slovak Statistical Office at http://www.statistics.sk/struk/volby.htm.

APPENDIX C:
CHRONOLOGY OF DEVELOPMENTS ON
THE SLOVAK LANGUAGE ISSUE

January 1, 1996	Law on the State Language passed by the Mečiar government. Strict use of Slovak; no right to use minority languages; Slovak is the exclusive official language of the Slovak Republic. Previous law that had guaranteed ethnic minorities the use of their language in official and unofficial contacts was canceled.
1996–97	European Union demands restoration of ethnic minority language rights as a prerequisite for entry into EU. In part because of this, Slovakia is excluded from first phase of EU expansion.
Fall 1997	Slovak Constitutional Court rules 1996 law unconstitutional. Slovak Constitution: Article 6: "The use of other languages than the state language in official contacts is guaranteed by law"; Article 34: "Members of national minorities have the right to use their languages in official state contacts."
1997–98	Mečiar makes no movement on his unconstitutional law.
June 17, 1999	Mečiar's HZDS Party threatens to call a referendum on language laws and privatization.
First week of July 1999	Slovak Parliament debates two versions of new law
July 6, 1999	Hungarian Coalition Party (SMK) version defeated
July 11, 1999	Law on the Use of Minority Languages passes 70 to 18

Source: U.S. English Foundation, online at http://www.us-english.org/foundation/research/olp/viewLegislation.asp?CID=34&LID=100. Used by permission.

APPENDIX D: INSTITUTIONAL LINKS

CEP: Centrum pre európsku politiku (Center for European Policy). Web site: http://www.cpep.sk

EAC: Euroatlantické centrum (Euroatlantic Center). Web site: http://www.eac.sk

EU: Ekonomická univerzita v Bratislave (Economic University in Bratislava). English Web site: http://193.87.16.10/english Slovak Web site: http://193.87.16.10

F. A. Hayek Foundation: Nadácia F. A. Hayeka. Web site: http://www.hayek.sk

FFUK: Filozofická fakulta university komenského katedra politólogie (Department of Political Science, Philosophical Faculty Comenius University [Bratislava]). Web site: http://www.fphil.uniba.sk/index.php?id=kpol

Friends of Slovakia (U.S.-based organization). Web site: http://www.friendsofslovakia.org

INEKO: Inštitut pre ekonomické a sociálné reformy (Institute for Economic and Social Reforms). Web site: http://www.ineko.sk

IVO: Inštitút pre verejné otázky (Institute for Public Affairs). Web site: http://www.ivo.sk

KI: Konzervatívny inštitút Milana Rastislava Štefánika (The Milan Rastislav Štefánik Conservative Institute). Web site: www.institute.sk

M.E.S.A. 10 Centrum pre ekonomické a sociálne analýzy (Center for Social and Economic Analyses). Web site: http://www.mesa10.sk

OSF: Nadácia otvorenej spoločnosti (Open Society Foundation). Web site: http://www.osf.sk

SAIA: Slovenská akademická informačná agentúra (Slovak Academic Information Agency). Web site: http://www.saia.sk

SFPA: Slovenská spoločnosť pre zahraničnú politiku (Slovak Foreign Policy Association). Web site: http://www.sfpa.sk

SGI: Inštitút pre dobre spravovanú spoločnost (Slovak Governance Institute). Web site: http://www.governance.sk

SHU MS: Slovenský Historický Ústav Matice Slovenskej (Slovak Historical Institute of the Slovak Heritage Society). Web site: http://www.matica.sk/index.php?M=67&lang=sk

Slovak Media Links: http://www.abyznewslinks.com/slova.htm

Slovak Youth Research: http://www.vyskummladeze.sk

SSA: Slovak Studies Association (U.S.). Web site: http://web.as.uky.edu/ssa

ÚEŠMV: Ústav európskych štúdií a medzinárodných vzťahov (Institute of European Studies and International Relations, Comenius University, Bratislava). Web site: http://www.fses.uniba.sk/index.php?id=2046

ÚPN: Ústav pamäti národa (Nation's Memory Institute; documentation of oppression from 1939–89). Web site: http://www.upn.gov.sk

TRANSCRIPT OF DECEMBER 3, 1992, PRESS CONFERENCE OF DEPARTMENT OF STATE SPOKESMAN RICHARD BOUCHER ON THE MICROPHONE AFFAIR

Note: *This contains the text of the briefing by the spokesman dealing with the Microphone Affair. The author was never informed that he was mentioned in this briefing (the only such mention in his career), and learned about it years later when doing research for this book.*

US Department of State Daily Briefing #176: Thursday, 12/3/1992
[Slovakia: US Discovers Listening Devices in Bratislava Consulate]

Q: New subject: Richard, on the U.S. Consulate in Slovakia, does the United States accept today's explanation by the Slovak Prime Minister that this happened five or six years ago and had nothing to do with the new government there?

MR. BOUCHER: I haven't seen today's explanation, so I can't give you a judgment on it at this point.

For those who don't know what we're talking about, however, the U.S. Government was dismayed to find listening devices in the Consulate General in Bratislava. This kind of activity we think cannot be helpful to the bilateral relationship.

We have asked senior officials of both the Federal and the Slovak Governments to investigate this incident, to urgently provide us with full details, and for their assurances that this kind of activity will not continue. We hope the incident can be put behind us.

Q: Have you been able to determine how long those devices might have been in there?

MR. BOUCHER: I don't have that information. I don't know.

Q: The building was standing empty until about a year ago, and then there were extensive renovations, and it was opened as a consulate in the fall of 1991. Who carried out the renovations? Was any local labor used?

MR. BOUCHER: I don't know. I'd have to check on that. I understand that these devices were found during the process of reconstruction and repair.

Q:	Are you confident that you found all the bugs?
MR. BOUCHER:	I don't know, Sid. That's for experts to decide and not usually for us to talk about.
Q:	Is there any thought to abandoning the mission?
MR. BOUCHER:	Not that I've heard of.
Q:	Richard—
MR. BOUCHER:	I guess that would depend on further investigation, though.
Q:	Could you tell me, please, Ralph Johnson met on a Friday the Czech Ambassador here in Washington. Was delivered some diplomatic note or verbal protest? What was the subject of discussion?
MR. BOUCHER:	I don't know. I'll have to check on that meeting.
Q:	Could you confirm, please, or deny today's report in Slovak press, leading Slovak daily which is called *Narodna Obroda,* which quotes that Larry Eagleburger, realizing that this happened, was so angered that plaster from the walls in his cabinet was falling apart? (Laughter)
MR. BOUCHER:	I haven't seen any plaster falling up in his office, but I also haven't seen the Slovak press. I'm afraid that's not the kind of thing I can talk about.
Q:	Another follow-up: Today's Slovak press is—I am quoting today's Slovak press that there was certain—that it will be provocation against Slovakia which is going to establish diplomatic relationship in a few weeks with United States. In connection with the leakage, quoting Czech television from Friday night, that whole affair was leaked by the American Embassy in Prague. Could you comment on that?
MR. BOUCHER:	No, I can't comment on that. I haven't been reading the Slovak press. I don't ever try to explain leaks. I think that's for people—our friends in the press corps to explain rather than us.
Q:	Richard, is the U.S. Consul, Paul Hacker, is he still in the United States? Or has he gone back?
MR. BOUCHER:	I don't know where he is.
Q:	Can you check into that?
MR. BOUCHER:	I'll check if it's relevant. I don't know that it is.
Q:	Well, he came here presumably to inform the State Department about what was going on there.
MR. BOUCHER:	You're making assumptions. I'll try to check on where he is.
Q:	Richard, when were the bugs first discovered, and why has it not come out until this weekend?

MR. BOUCHER: My understanding is they were discovered during reconstruction work that's fairly recent, but I'm not sure exactly when it was.

Q: And why did it not come out until so recently?

MR. BOUCHER: We don't usually advertise these things.

Q: Well, actually in the case of the former Soviet Union, you advertised them quite extensively—

MR. BOUCHER: I guess it depends.

Q: —to the tune of several hundred million dollars worth of reconstruction plans.

MR. BOUCHER: It depends. I said "usually," Ralph.

Q: How many more of these do you have that haven't been announced?

MR. BOUCHER: I don't know, Norm.

Source: http://dosfan.lib.uic.edu/ERC/briefing/daily_briefings/1992/9212/176.html.

APPENDIX F:
FIRST TWO CABLES SENT AFTER
SLOVAK INDEPENDENCE

```
PAGE 01        VIENNA  00031  01 OF 03  041640Z
ACTION EUR-01

INFO  LOG-00   AID-01   CIAE-00  C-01      OASY-00  DODE-00  HA-09
      H-01     INRE-00  INR-01   L-03      ADS-00   NSAE-00  NSCE-00
      OMB-01   PA-01    PM-02    PRS-01    P-01     SCT-03   SNP-00
      SP-00    SS-00    TRSE-00  T-01      USIE-00  /027W
                ------------------8C9A2C  041641Z /38

O 041640Z JAN 93
FM AMEMBASSY VIENNA
TO SECSTATE WASHDC IMMEDIATE 3308
INFO EASTERN EUROPEAN POSTS COLLECTIVE


LIMITED OFFICIAL USE SECTION 01 OF 03 VIENNA 00031


THIS IS BRATISLAVA 002

DEPARTMENT PLEASE PASS AID

E.O. 12356:N/A
TAGS:  PGOV, LO
SUBJECT:  INDEPENDENT SLOVAKIA ENTERS THE WORLD STAGE

1.  LIMITED OFFICIAL USE -- ENTIRE TEXT

2.  SUMMARY:  WITH THE FANFARE OF FIREWORKS, THE ROAR OF
THOUSANDS OF ROCKETS, THE UNCORKING OF HUNDREDS OF
THOUSANDS OF BOTTLES OF CHAMPAGNE, SLOVAKS CELEBRATED
NOT ONLY THE COMING OF THE NEW YEAR JANUARY 1 BUT ALSO
                LIMITED OFFICIAL USE


                LIMITED OFFICIAL USE

PAGE 02        VIENNA  00031  01 OF 03  041640Z
THE MILENNIAL ACHIEVEMENT OF AN INDEPENDENT STATE.  THE
SLOVAK PARLIAMENT, MEETING ON THAT DAY, FORMALLY ISSUED
A DECLARATION OF INDEPENDENCE.  OFFICIALS ATTENDED A
HIGH MASS THAT DAY, AND HELD A RECEPTION FOR AMBASSADORS
OR CHARGES FROM THE SEVENTYODD COUNTRIES THAT HAVE
ALREADY RECOGNIZED SLOVAKIA.  THE SPIRIT OF THE DAY
SEEMED TO BE "WE CAN DO IT;" A SUBTLE PSYCHOLOGICAL TURN
SEEMS TO HAVE OCCURRED TO THE REALIZATION THAT SLOVAKS
NOW ARE TRULY ON THEIR OWN.  THE MAKINGS OF A NEW STATE
ARE STILL INCOMPLETE, AND THE UNCERTAINTIES OF OUTSIDERS
WILL TAKE SOME TIME TO BE RELIEVED.  AS SLOVAKS RETURN
```

TO THEIR EVERYDAY CARES, THEY WILL SOON FIND OUT WHAT IS
IN STORE ON THE OTHER SIDE OF THE COIN OF INDEPENDENCE.
END SUMMARY

3. THE SQUARE OF THE SLOVAK NATIONAL UPRISING,
BRATISLAVA'S MAIN SQUARE, WHICH HAS WITNESSED MANY
DRAMAS OF SLOVAK HISTORY SINCE IT WAS FILLED TO
OVERFLOWING IN THE HEADY DAYS OF THE NOVEMBER 1989
REVOLUTION WAS THE SCENE OF ONE MORE EPOCHAL EVENT AS
CHURCH BELLS RANG IN THE NEW YEAR OVER THE SLOVAK
CAPITAL. DESPITE THE COLD, THOUSANDS OF MERRY-MAKERS
FILLED THE SQUARE'S LOWER PORTION, TO HEAR PRIME
MINISTER VLADIMIR MECIAR ANNOUNCE
THAT SLOVAKIA WAS NOW INDEPENDENT. MANY, HOWEVER, WERE
TOO INVOLVED IN THE MERRIMENT OF THE MOMENT TO HEAR HIS
WORDS. THE NEXT MORNING, HUNDREDS OF SLOVAKS LINED THE
STREETS WAITING TO BUY THE FIRST POSTAGE STAMPS OF THE NEW
REPUBLIC.

4. IN A NEW YEAR'S SPEECH TO THE NATION, MECIAR CALLED
LIMITED OFFICIAL USE

LIMITED OFFICIAL USE

PAGE 03   VIENNA 00031 01 OF 03 041640Z
THE DEMISE OF THE CSFR PART OF THE GEOPOLITICAL CHANGES
OCCURRING IN THE WORLD, AND ALSO OF THE DIFFERENT
POLITICAL AND ECONOMIC DEVELOPMENT IN THE CZECH AND SLOVAK
REPUBLICS AFTER 1989, AND OF THE "MISTAKES" MADE DURING
THAT TIME. HE SAID THERE IS INDEED SOMETHING TO
CELEBRATE: NOT ONLY THE CULMINATION OF A MILLENIAL LONGING
FOR ONE'S OWN STATE, BUT ALSO THE POSSIBILITY OF DIRECTLY
PARTICIPATING IN EUROPEAN AND WORLD-WIDE INTEGRATION.
SLOVAK SECURITY WOULD BE GUARANTEED IN AN "ALL EUROPEAN
SECURITY SYSTEM." (NOTE: ON JANUARY 4, IN A SPEECH TO THE
BUDDING SLOVAK MILITARY, MECIAR SAID THAT AN ARMY IS NEED
BECAUSE, "WHILE WE HAVE NO ENEMIES, WE HAVE NO ALLIES
EITHER"). MECIAR DENIED THAT SLOVAKIA WOULD BE ISOLATED
INTERNATIONALLY, AND POINTED TO RAPID RECOGNITION BY OTHER
STATES.

5. IN DESCRIBING RELATIONS WITH THE U.S., MECIAR CALLED
THEM "IMPORTANT." HE SAID THAT, WHILE SOMEONE TRIED TO
"EMBITTER" THOSE RELATIONS TOWARD THE END OF LAST YEAR, HE
BELIEVED THAT THEY WOULD NOT BE AFFECTED (MECIAR REFERRED
TO THE EAVESDROPPING INCIDENT IMPLICITLY ONLY). WHILE NOT
EXPLICITLY VOWING TO INSURE THAT SUCH INCIDENTS NOT REPEAT
THEMSELVES, MECIAR DID STATE THAT SLOVAKIA WILL RESPECT
THE INVIOLABILITY OF THE DIPLOMATIC OFFICES OF ALL STATES

UNCLASSIFIED
AND ALL OBLIGATIONS ARISING FROM INTERNATIONAL
CONVENTIONS. AFTER MENTIONING THE U.S., MECIAR PLACED
RELATIONS WITH RUSSIA AND THE UKRAINE AND THEN WITH THE
CZECH REPUBLIC, RELATIONS WHICH HE SAID WOULD BE THE "MOST
NUMEROUS." RELATIONS WITH AUSTRIA ARE IMPORTANT BECAUSE
OF THE COUNTRY'S CHARACTER AS A MARKET ECONOMY AND
ADVANCED DEMOCRACY, AND WITH HUNGARY ON THE BASIS OF
                    LIMITED OFFICIAL USE

                    LIMITED OFFICIAL USE

PAGE 04   VIENNA 00031 01 OF 03 041640Z
"NON-INTERFERENCE IN INTERNAL AFFAIRS" AND "INVOLABILITY
OF BORDERS." THE GABCIKOVO PROBLEM, MECIAR SAID, SHOULD
BE SOLVED BY MUTUAL AGREEMENT.

6. MECIAR SAID THAT THE STRUCTURE OF SLOVAK
ADMINISTRATION WOULD BE COMPLETED IN THE NEXT FEW MONTHS,
STARTING WITH CENTRAL STATE ORGANS AND CONTINUING WITH
LOCAL GOVERNMENT AND ADMINISTRATION; HE ASSURED THERE
WOULD BE NO "BLAVO(BRATISLAVA)CENTRALISM" TO MAKE UP FOR
THE DETESTED "PRAGOCENTRALISM." THE COUNTRY WOULD BE
BUILT UP ACCORDING TO LEGAL NORMS PREVALENT IN THE EC.
PRIVATIZATION WOULD CONTINUE WITH THE AIM OF ESTABLISHING
AN ENTREPRENEURIAL CLASS. MECIAR CLOSED BY NOTING THAT

                    LIMITED OFFICIAL USE

NNNN

                    LIMITED OFFICIAL USE

PAGE 01   VIENNA 00031 02 OF 03 041641Z
ACTION EUR-01

INFO LOG-00   AID-01   CIAE-00 C-01   OASY-00 DODE-00 HA-09
      H-01   INRE-00 INR-01   L-03   ADS-00   NSAE-00 NSCE-00
      OMB-01   PA-01   PM-02   PRS-01 P-01   SCT-03   SNP-00
      SP-00   SS-00   TRSE-00 T-01   USIE-00 /027W
               -----------------8C9A3C 041642Z /38

                    UNCLASSIFIED

O 041640Z JAN 93
FM AMEMBASSY VIENNA
TO SECSTATE WASHDC IMMEDIATE 3309
INFO EASTERN EUROPEAN POSTS COLLECTIVE

UNCLASSIFIED

LIMITED OFFICIAL USE SECTION 02 OF 03 VIENNA 00031

THIS IS BRATISLAVA 002

DEPARTMENT PLEASE PASS AID

E.O. 12356:N/A
TAGS: PGOV, LO
SUBJECT: INDEPENDENT SLOVAKIA ENTERS THE WORLD STAGE

"IF WE BELIEVE OURSELVES, THE WORLD WILL BELIEVE US AS
WELL."

7. AT A SESSION HELD ON THE MORNING OF JANUARY 1, THE
SLOVAK PARLIAMENT APPROVED A DECLARATION ANNOUNCING
SLOVAKIA AS ONE OF THE TWO SUCCESSOR STATES TO THE CSFR.
                    LIMITED OFFICIAL USE

                LIMITED OFFICIAL USE

PAGE 02   VIENNA 00031 02 OF 03 041641Z
THE DECLARATION ASSURED THAT SLOVAKIA WOULD ASSUME ITS
INTERNATIONAL LEGAL COMMITMENTS AND BE GOVERNED ACCORDING
TO THE RULES OF A PLURALISTIC DEMOCRACY. THE PARLIAMENT
DECLARED SLOVAKIA'S INTENTION OF JOINING THE UN AND
COUNCIL OF EUROPE AND ITS READINESS TO EXCHANGE DIPLOMATIC
RELATIONS WITH ALL STATES BASED ON "FRIENDSHIP AND
PEACEFUL COEXISTENCE (NA MIEROVOM SPOLUNAZIVANI), ON THE
BASIS OF EQUALITY, NON-INTERFERENCE IN INTERNAL AFFAIRS,
AND INVOLABILITY OF BORDERS. IN REMARKS BEFORE PARLIAMENT
THAT MORNING, MECIAR WARNED THAT THE COMING YEAR WOULD BE
"DIFFICULT," BUT NOT NECESSARILY MORE SO THAN PAST ONES."
PARLIAMENT SPEAKER IVAN GASPAROVIC, FOR HIS PART, ASKED
HIS COLLEAGUES FOR "UNITY," NOT IN THE FORMAL SENSE THAT
DISREGARDS THE NATURAL DIFFERENTIATION OF INTERESTS, BUT
ONE THAT PLACES POLITICAL STABILITY, SPIRITUAL RENEWAL,
AND ECONOMIC PROSPERITY AS AIMS FOR EVERYONE REGARDLESS OF
PARTY. IN THE JANUARY 4 "PRACA," GASPAROVIC URGED HIS
FELLOW-COUNTRYMEN TO BE REALISTIC -- NOT TO UNDERESTIMATE
THEIR OWN POTENTIAL, BUT TO REALISTICALLY JUDGE THE
ECONOMIC, MORAL, AND PHYSICAL RESERVES OF THE COUNTRY AND
ITS POPULATION.

                UNCLASSIFIED

UNCLASSIFIED

8. FOREIGN MINISTER MILAN KNAZKO, IN A JANUARY 1 PRESS
CONFERENCE, SOUGHT TO PLACE SLOVAK FOREIGN POLICY IN THE
CONTOURS OF EUROPEAN INTEGRATION AND SECURITY. HE SAID
SLOVAKIA WANTS TO BE INVOLVED WITH THE VISEGRAD FOUR, AND
THAT AS FAR AS ARMS SALES ARE CONCERNED, SLOVAKIA WOULD
NOT EXPORT TO RISK AREAS AND WOULD SEEK TO COORDINATE ITS
APPROACH WITH SUCH STATES AS THE U.S. AND FRANCE. HE
REJECTED THE NOTION OF A RENEWED "LITTLE ENTENTE" AGAINST
POSSIBLE FUTURE HUNGARIAN EXPANSIONISM. FINALLY, HE
LIMITED OFFICIAL USE

LIMITED OFFICIAL USE

PAGE 03   VIENNA 00031 02 OF 03 041641Z
CAREFULLY FIELDED A JOURNALIST'S QUESTION WHICH SOUGHT TO
FORCE HIM TO DIFFERENTIATE HIS CONCEPTION OF FOREIGN
POLICY FROM MECIAR'S (MECIAR HAD PLACED THE U.S. FIRST IN
DISCUSSING FOREIGN RELATIONS, WHEREAS KNAZKO HAD SAID THAT
RELATIONS WITH SLOVAKIA'S NEIGHBORS, ESPECIALLY THE CZECH
REPUBLIC, WOULD BE ITS PRIORITIES).
9. MARIAN TKAC, WHO IS ORGANIZING THE SLOVAK NATIONAL
BANK, PREDICTED IN A JANUARY 4 INTERVIEW IN "NARODNA
OBRODA" THAT ONCE FLOATED, SLOVAKIA'S CURRENCY SHOULD NOT
LOSE MORE THAN 10 PCT OF ITS VALUE, WHICH HE CONSIDERS A
"FANTASTIC SUCCESS" GIVEN THE MUCH LARGER FALL IN THE
CZECHOSLOVAK KORUNA'S VALUE SINCE 1990. TKAC ALSO SAW ONE
OF THE MAIN ADVANTAGES OF INDEPENDENCE BEING THAT IT
ALLOWS SLOVAKIA TO EXECUTE ITS OWN ECONOMIC AND FINANCIAL
STRATEGY.

10. COMMENT: WHILE TEARS SHED LAST WEEKEND WERE MOSTLY
TEARS OF JOY, A FEW DIE-HARDS GATHERED NEW YEAR'S EVE TO
GRIEVE THE LOSS OF THEIR CZECH CONNECTION AT THE CZECH
LION -- THE TRADITIONAL MONUMENT TO CZECH-SLOVAK
STATEHOOD. IN THE RECENT PAST, MANY SLOVAKS HAVE BEEN
GLOOMY ABOUT THE EFFECT OF INDEPENDENCE ON THEIR ECONOMIC
FUTURE. THOSE THAT CELEBRATED, HOWEVER, SEEMED TO BE
GENUINELY ELATED AT THE NOVELTY OF LIVING IN THEIR OWN
STATE AND RESPONSIBLE FOR THEIR OWN FUTURE. ONE CAN
EXPECT THAT QUESTIONS ABOUT POLITICAL PLURALITY WILL
CONTINUE TO PLAGUE THE RULING HZDS AS SLOVAKIA LOOKS AWAY
FROM THE CONSTITUTIONAL ISSUE AND MORE TOWARD DEVELOPING
BOTH POLITICALLY AND ECONOMICALLY AS A STATE.
INTERESTINGLY ENOUGH, KNAZKO AGAIN TOOK THE ROLE OF
DISSIDENT WITHIN HIS OWN MOVEMENT; IN REPLY TO A POLL
LIMITED OFFICIAL USE

UNCLASSIFIED

UNCLASSIFIED   E1

RELEASED IN FULL

PAGE 01   VIENNA 00018 041409Z
ACTION EUR-01

INFO LOG-00   AID-01   AMAD-01 A-01   CIAE-00 C-01   OASY-00
      DODE-00 FOE-00   HA-09   H-01   INRE-00 INR-01 L-03
      ADS-00   NSAE-00 NSCE-00 OMB-01   PA-02   PER-01 PM-02
      PRS-01   P-01   SNP-00   SP-00   SSC-01   TRSE-00 T-01
      USIE-00 /029W
                       ------------------8C8BDF 041410Z /38
O 041411Z JAN 93
FM AMEMBASSY VIENNA
TO SECSTATE WASHDC IMMEDIATE 3294
INFO EASTERN EUROPEAN POSTS COLLECTIVE
USOFFICE RAMC TEXT PARIS

UNCLAS VIENNA 00018

THIS IS BRATISLAVA 001

DEPARTMENT PLEASE PASS AID

E.O. 12356:N/A
TAGS: AMGT, PREL, LO, US
SUBJECT: ESTABLISHMENT OF US EMBASSY BRATISLAVA

REF: 92 STATE 417667

1. IN ACCORDANCE WITH INSTRUCTIONS REFTEL, CONSUL
GENERAL DELIVERED TO SLOVAK FOREIGN MINISTER MILAN
KNAZKO COPY OF PRESIDENT'S LETTER TO SLOVAK PRIME
                      UNCLASSIFIED

                      UNCLASSIFIED

PAGE 02   VIENNA 00018 041409Z
MINISTER VLADIMIR MECIAR AND RECEIVED ORIGINAL OF
MECIAR'S REPLY AT 3:23 PM JANUARY 1. CEREMONY TOOK
PLACE IN THE APPROPRIATELY NAMED CONSUL ROOM AT THE
BRATISLAVA FORUM HOTEL. COPY HAS BEEN FAXED TO
OPERATIONS CENTER AND ORIGINAL WILL BE POUCHED TO
EUR/EE. ACCORDINGLY, DIPLOMATIC RELATIONS HAVE BEEN
ESTABLISHED BETWEEN THE UNITED STATES AND THE SLOVAK
REPUBLIC AND CONSUL GENERAL PAUL HACKER HAS ASSUMED
CHARGE OF THE U.S. EMBASSY IN BRATISLAVA AS OF JANUARY 1
UNTIL THE ARRIVAL OF A PERMANENT AMBASSADOR. PENDING
INSTALLATION OF COMMUNICATIONS IN BRATISLAVA,

UNCLASSIFIED

UNCLASSIFIED

TELEGRAPHIC COMMUNICATIONS WILL CONTINUE TO BE CONDUCTED THROUGH VIENNA.

2. WITH THIS ACT, THE U.S. CONSULATE GENERAL IN BRATISLAVA, ALONG WITH THE CZECH AND SLOVAK FEDERAL REPUBLIC, HAS NOW PASSED INTO HISTORY. THE CONSULATE GENERAL WAS OPENED BY VICE CONSUL (ACTING CONSUL GENERAL) CLAIBORNE PELL ON MARCH 1, 1948, AND CLOSED DURING THE HEIGHT OF STALINIST REPRESSION ON MAY 27, 1950. CONSUL HACKER ARRIVED IN BRATISLAVA OCTOBER 3, 1990 TO REOPEN THE CONSULATE, AND THE BUILDING WAS FORMALLY REDEDICATED MAY 27, 1991, 41 YEARS TO THE DAY AFTER IT WAS CLOSED, WITH THE PARTICIPATION OF NOW SENATE FOREIGN RELATIONS COMMITTEE CHAIRMAN PELL. THE CONSULATE WAS UPGRADED TO CONSULATE GENERAL STATUS BY THE DEPARTMENT OF STATE ON OCTOBER 21, 1991. IT CEASED OPERATIONS AND THE U.S. FLAG WAS LOWERED FOR THE LAST TIME AT COB DECEMBER 31, 1992.

3. THE U.S. EMBASSY WAS FORMALLY OPENED BY CHARGE
                    UNCLASSIFIED

                    UNCLASSIFIED

PAGE 03   VIENNA 00018 041409Z
HACKER ON JANUARY 4, IN A SHORT CEREMONY THAT INCLUDED RAISING A NEW U.S. FLAG, ISSUING THE FIRST DIPLOMATIC VISA TO THE GUEST OF HONOR, FOREIGN MINISTER KNAZKO (WHO WILL BE ARRIVING IN NEW YORK JANUARY 15 TO BEGIN SLOVAKIA'S MEMBERSHIP IN THE U.N.), AND CHANGING THE SHIELDS IN FRONT OF THE BUILDING. IN HIS REMARKS, CHARGE STRESSED THE CLOSE TIES AND COOPERATION THAT HAVE BOUND THE PEOPLE OF THE U.S. AND SLOVAKIA AND OUR EXPECTATION THAT THESE RELATIONS WILL CONTINUE AND EXPAND IN THE FUTURE.

4. ON THIS HISTORIC OPENING DAY OF THE U.S. EMBASSY IN BRATISLAVA, WE EXPRESS THE HOPE THAT OUR RELATIONS WITH THE SLOVAK REPUBLIC WILL ALWAYS BE TRUE TO OUR TRADITIONS AS A NATION, AND THAT THE PEOPLE OF SLOVAKIA, NOW JOINED TO THE REST OF THE WORLD AS AN INDEPENDENT SUBJECT, WILL ENJOY THE BLESSINGS OF PEACE, FREEDOM, AND PROSPERITY. HACKER UNQUOTE SWIHART

                    UNCLASSIFIED

                    UNCLASSIFIED

JIMMY CARTER

July 16, 1993

To Chargé Paul Hacker

    Thank you for the many courtesies that were
extended to Rosalynn and me during our visit to
Slovakia. We had a wonderful visit and appreciate all
the Embassy did to make it possible.

    With thanks and warm best wishes to you and Eeva,

        Sincerely,

Jimmy Carter

Chargé d'Affaires
Paul Hacker
United States Embassy
Bratislava, Slovakia

NOTES

INTRODUCTION

1. Our car was once stopped by the police for speeding just outside of Vienna, and the officer involved threatened to confiscate our consulate car radio when our driver told him he had no money to pay the fine he demanded. When I objected that the car and its radio were property of the U.S. government, he finally relented. The hapless Austrian consul in Bratislava was constantly bombarded by complaints from his consular colleagues about rough treatment at the hands of the Austrian police, who usually did nothing to facilitate the passage of diplomatic vehicles through their border with Slovakia, and who even tried to fine one of my colleagues when she tried to jump the two-mile-long waiting line of cars when returning one evening to Bratislava. However, since it was the Austrian Ministry of the Interior and not the Ministry of Foreign Affairs that controlled the police, there was little he could do. Our lack of communications meant that Vienna, for us, was an extension of our workplace more than a convenient R&R point, but our diplomatic status ended at the Austrian border. Our first unclassified telegraphic communications were not installed until shortly before my departure in July 1993. What is described here is now a part of history as, since Slovakia and the Czech Republic both entered the Schengen zone allowing travel between member states without border formalities on December 21, 2007, travel across what was once the Iron Curtain takes place without border controls or delays, and the Czech-Slovak border is again freely open as was the case before January 1, 1993.

2. On March 25, 1988, police broke up a demonstration with more than two thousand participants demanding religious and civic freedoms in the "Candlelight Demonstration" that took place almost outside the front door of our then-closed consulate. For a full account, please see "Sviečková manifestácia—25. marec 1988," at http://www.sviockovamanifestacia.sk.

3. The one clear exception to this policy was the USSR—the United States had never recognized the forceful incorporation of the Baltic states into its territory in 1940.

4. Pell and Hvasta maintained close ties after Hvasta's return to the United States. Typically, on February 7, 1990, Pell inserted into the *Congressional Record* a *Washington Post* article on Hvasta's exploits that had been published four days earlier. This account is available at http://fas.org/irp/congress/1990_cr/s900702-tribute.htm.

5. Slovak Americans who favored the continuation of a joint Czech-Slovak state were grouped with Czechs in the Czechoslovak National Council of the United States, which dated back to the foundation of the Czechoslovak Republic in 1918. They were referred to derisively as "Czechoslovakists" by other Slovaks who wanted to separate from the Czechs.

6. Perhaps his best-known work is *Slovakia: Nation at the Crossroads of Central Europe*.

CHAPTER 1

1. In 1988, while serving as political counselor in our embassy in Helsinki, I put this principle to use by inserting a few choice words of greeting in Finnish into an address President Ronald Reagan made to a Finnish audience while on the way to Moscow. When Reagan died, the one passage that made it to Finnish television was a shot of the president trying his best to say the words I had drafted.

2. For an excellent overview of the practice of library censorship during and prior to the period of "normalization," see Skaláková, "'Libri prohibiti.'" According to the author, more than nine hundred thousand items had been removed from general library collections as of August 15, 1973.

CHAPTER 4

1. Svěchota, as deputy chief of the Slovak Information (Security) Service, was implicated in a number of crimes involving misuse of power. Please see chapter 22 for further details.

CHAPTER 5

1. In a 1999 interview, Gál was asked why he never assumed any function in the state administration. He explained that there were too many things to do in his VPN role and not enough time to devote to the legislature or service in a ministry. He also said, "I never strived to be a professional politician," but thought he would go back to his career as a social scientist. He concluded that "today, I know I made a mistake." See Gál, "Naša misia bola provizórna."

CHAPTER 6

1. When President George W. Bush addressed a Slovak audience on Hviezdoslav Square close to the U.S. Embassy building in Bratislava during his February 23–25, 2005, visit to the capital for a summit meeting with Russian president Vladimir Putin, the president's handlers allowed him two words in Slovak to open his speech: *Dobrý den* (Good day!).

2. The U.S. Embassy in Bratislava recently translated into Slovak a work by an American author on the Green Mission, and it actively promotes commemorations of our participation in the Slovak National Uprising. Please see Downs, *World War II*.

3. Curiously, I was informed by one of my Washington-based colleagues that Ambassador Black had given an interview to a journalist that went beyond our current line of trying to hold Czechoslovakia together—she predicted that the country would split. My colleague pleaded with the journalist to hold the story to avoid embarrassing the ambassador, and it never saw the light of day.

CHAPTER 7

1. For an online bibliography of sources on this issue, please see http://www.international waterlaw.org/bibliography/danube.html.

CHAPTER 8

1. An agreement reached by the two national councils in February 1992 for a continuation of the common state quickly broke down. For a comprehensive account of that period, see Innes, *Czechoslovakia*.

CHAPTER 11

1. A comprehensive compendium of Slovak sources on the sovereignty issue is available: Štátna vedecká knižnica v Prešove, "*Deklarácia o zvrchovanosti Slovenskej Republiky*" (Declaration of Sovereignty of the Slovak Republic) Prešov, 2007, http://www.svkpo.sk/uplsub/resers_julo7.pdf.

CHAPTER 12

1. Zelenay died tragically when a car in which he was riding crashed into a truck at the Slovak-Czech border on November 1, 1993. At the time, he was state secretary in the Ministry of Culture and deputy chairman of the HZDS.

2. Johnson served as U.S. ambassador to Slovakia from 1996 to 1999.

3. Actually, RFE broadcasts to Slovakia, as well as to Bulgaria, Croatia, and the Baltic states, ended on January 31, 2004, due to the decision of the Bush administration to concentrate broadcasting efforts in other regions of the world deemed more critical to U.S. concerns in the early twenty-first century. See "RFE/RL to End Broadcasts in Seven European Languages," http://www.america.gov/st/washfile-english/2003/November/20031128153405osnhojaco.5005152.html.

But Hofbauer continued his crusade during the tenure of Ambassador Theodore Russell, sending a note protesting "non-objective" reporting on Slovakia in the U.S. media. According to a July 26, 1995, report of the TASR press agency, the U.S. Embassy responded by issuing a statement saying that Hofbauer "demonstrated regrettable ignorance about how the independent press functions in a democratic society." See "Signs of the Times," *Post-Soviet Media Law and Policy Newsletter*, no. 21, September 27, 1995, Benjamin N. Cardozo School of Law, http://www.vii.org/monroe/issue21/signs.html.

CHAPTER 13

1. For a summary of events connected with the fate of Slovak Jewry during World War II, see "This Month in Holocaust History July," Yad Vashem Documentation Center, Jerusalem, http://www1.yadvashem.org/about_HOLocaust/month_in_HOLocaust/july/july_lexicon/SLOVAKIA.html.

2. In 1997, however, on the fiftieth anniversary of Tiso's execution for war crimes, Korec officiated at a mass held in Nitra in commemoration of Slovakia's wartime leader. Korec regards Tiso's execution as a "profound injustice" and views the wartime period through the prism of someone who was persecuted for his religious activities and who, in that context, considers the Communist era to have been much more destructive for Slovakia than the fascist period. For a detailed analysis of Korec's views, see Luxor, "Cardinal's Life."

3. In early 2007, Sokol caused an uproar in an interview with Slovak television station TA3, in which he said he "highly esteemed" wartime President Jozef Tiso (later hanged as a war criminal). See discussion in Cameron, "Slovak Bishop."

4. The text of the ruling and background in the case may be found in *Case of Feldek vs. Slovakia*, European Court of Human Rights, July 12, 2001, http://www.iidh.ed.cr/comunidades/libertadexpresion/docs/le_europeo/feldek%20vs%20slovakia%202001.htm.

CHAPTER 14

1. He served as Slovakia's ambassador to Croatia later on in the decade. When the Dzurinda government took over power, he was one of many former HZDS officials who were removed from their positions.

CHAPTER 15

1. I even became, for the only time in my career, the subject of a question at the Department of State's Noon Press Briefing. Richard Boucher, the Department spokesman, was asked

whether I was still in the United States and whether my trip to Washington was connected with the discovery of the microphones (it wasn't). I was never told of this at the time, and only found out years later by accident. See "US Department of State Daily Briefing" #176:Thursday, 12/3/1992, http://dosfan.lib.uic.edu/ERC/briefing/daily_briefings/1992/9212/176.html. A copy of the transcript is available in appendix E below.

CHAPTER 17

1. One should take his statements figuratively rather than literally; in any case, the EU flag retains twelve stars despite the expansion of membership to twenty-seven states in recent years.

CHAPTER 18

1. See U.S. Department of State, *SEED Act Implementation Report*.

2. But once out of power, Mečiar returned to the populist game vis-à-vis the West. In April 1999, during the air war against Yugoslavia, he pointedly invited Yugoslav President Slobodan Milosević to Slovakia for "hunting" and likened NATO air strikes to the 1968 Warsaw Pact invasion of Czechoslovakia. See "Election Could Affect Slovakia's Emergence from Isolation," *New York Times*, May 13, 1999, http://www.nytimes.com/1999/05/13/world/election-could-affect-slovakia-s-emergence-from-isolation.html.

CHAPTER 19

1. We always thought that Černák was out of his element in the SNS. In February 1994, he was expelled from the Party and later that year was elected to Parliament on the ticket of the Democratic Union (DÚ), whose vice chairman he was until 1997. He became a member of the SDK in 1998.

POSTSCRIPT

1. At the same time, public opinion polls carried out in Slovakia show that Mečiar had fallen to sixth place by late 2008. "Ficovi, Gašparovičovi a Slotovi rastie dôvera" [Trust of Citizens in Fico, Gašparovič, and Slota Is Growing], SME.sk, December 18, 2008, http://www.sme.sk/c/4230555/ficovi-gasparovicovi-a-slotovi-rastie-dovera.html. As late as February 2003, Mečiar was still in second place among all politicians in the popularity contest, coming out only behind Robert Fico of ANO, who was elected prime minister in 2006. See "Dôvera občanov k politikom," October 7, 2003, http://www.ivo.sk/buxus/docs/vyskum/subor/produkt_4132.pdf, and Štatistický úrad Slovenskej Republiky, "Dôvera občanov k politikom v roku 2008," http://portal.statistics.sk/showdoc.do?docid=10814. Gašparovič was reelected in April 2009 with 55.5 percent of the votes, opposed by the sociologist and former minister of labor, Iveta Radičová, who received 45.5 percent.

2. For an excellent overview of the relationship between the HZDS and its two coalition partners in the 1994–98 period, see Haughton, "Vladimír Mečiar and His Role." Haughton argues that Mečiar was the dominant figure in the government (as might be expected), but that others were not without influence on his policies.

3. For a comprehensive account of the kidnapping (in Slovak), see "Zločiny Ivana Lexu" [The Crimes of Ivan Lexa], http://www.geocities.com/ivanlexa2002/index.html.

4. The Lexa case was finally decided by the European Court of Human Rights (Strasbourg), which ruled that Lexa's detention by Slovak police in 1999 on suspicion of involvement in the 1995 kidnapping of the son of President Kováč violated Lexa's rights because Lexa was covered by

an amnesty issued by Mečiar in 1998 when he was acting president. The Court's judgment, which the Slovak government decided not to appeal, did not address the issue of whether Lexa was actually involved in that crime, but only the narrower issue of whether the amnesty allowed him to escape prosecution. For the text of the ruling, see *Case of Lexa v. Slovakia*, http://www.ius-software.si/EUII/EUCHR/dokumenti/2008/09/CASE_OF_LEXA_v._SLOVAKIA_23_09_2008 .html. For a collection of documents and views on the subject of the misuse of the SIS see *SIS-Meciarova MAFIA alebo SIS ako politicky nastroj* [SIS = Mečiar's Mafia or SIS as a Political Tool (in Slovak)], http://www.geocities.com/Area51/6199/RR3.html, or in English, Williams, "Slovakia Since 1993."

5. See Márius Kopcsay, "Svěchota odsúdený, potrestaný" [Svěchota Condemned and Punished], *Národná Obroda*, June 16, 2004, http://www.obroda.sk/clanok/9666/Svechota-odsudeny,-potrestany---%28Marius-Kopcsay%29. Svěchota's full interview is available (in Slovak) in *Plus 7 dní*, nos. 30 and 31, 1999; see Ľuba Lesná, "Svěchota Prehovoril" [Svěchota Spoke Up], http://www.geocities.com/Area51/6199/OKNO-HOTNEWS.html. See the bibliography for reference to Lesná's book on the subject. Svěchota died on November 8, 2004.

6. Siegfried Mortkowitz gives an account of the episode in "Slovak Spy Unit Broke the Law," *Prague Post*, February 24, 1999, http://www.praguepost.cz/news022499b.html .

7. The original question only concerned NATO membership, but the HZDS leadership added two more questions—one on the stationing of foreign troops in Slovakia and the other on the stationing of nuclear weapons. The purpose of the two additional questions was to associate two notions strongly opposed by public opinion—stationing of foreign troops and placement of nuclear weapons—as a counterpoint to the NATO accession issue. For a comprehensive summary of the events surrounding the referendum, see "Constitution Watch," *East European Constitutional Review* 6, nos. 2–3 (Spring–Summer 1997), http://www.law.nyu.edu/eecr/vol6num2/constitutionwatch/slovakia.html.

8. The State Department spokesman, for example, issued a strong statement on March 5, 1998, denouncing the government's issuance of amnesties for those accused of breaking the law both in the kidnapping episode and in the thwarting of the referendum on direct election of the president. The statement stated, "These actions are not consistent with the behavior of a government that respects the rule of law. They invite further abuses of the law and the constitution by those who claim to be serving the national interest." See U.S. Department of State Daily Press Briefing #29, March 5, 1998, http://www.hri.org/news/usa/std/1998/98-03-05.std.html. Earlier, Ambassador Ralph Johnson, in a widely noted speech, spoke of intolerance for those with differing views and a concentration of power as reasons for strong U.S. concern. For this, he was denounced by Mečiar, who likened his stance to that of Soviet Ambassador Chervonenko just before the 1968 Warsaw Pact invasion of Czechoslovakia. While Gašparovič, as speaker of Parliament, echoed these views, President Kováč pointedly disassociated himself from the criticism of Johnson. See "Ralph Johnson About Slovakia and NATO," http://www.geocities.com/CapitolHill/7502/1ralph.html, as well as "Slovak President Criticizes Attacks on U.S. Ambassador," *RFE/RL Newsline* 1, no. 78, pt. II, July 22, 1997, http://www.friends-partners.org/friends/news/omri/1997/07/970722II.html.

9. "Constitution Watch."

10. See International Helsinki Federation for Human Rights, "Slovakia."

11. Bútora and Bútorová, "Slovakia's Democratic Awakening," 81.

12. See U.S. Department of State, *Slovak Country Report on Human Rights Practices for 1998*.

13. Bútora and Bútorová, "Slovakia's Democratic Awakening," 86.

14. Javurek, "Slovak Opposition Deputy."

15. See, for example, U.S. Department of State, *Slovak Country Report on Human Rights Practices for 2006*, especially sections 1 c. and f.; also section 5, National/Racial/Ethnic Minorities. An excellent summary of the current situation surrounding the Roma is contained in British Helsinki Human Rights Group, *Slovakia's Roma Shame*.

16. Gyárfašová, "Slovakia from Black Hole to Leading Light."

17. Quoted in BBC monitoring, http://news.bbc.co.uk/1/hi/world/monitoring/media_reports/2072385.stm.

18. See "Slovakia: EU Hails Referendum Results," RFE/RL news, http://www.globalsecurity
.org/military/library/news/2003/05/mil-030517-rfel-000752.htm.

19. Details of the summit may be found in "President George W. Bush's Visit to Bratislava,
Slovakia (February 24, 2005)," on the Web site of the U.S. Embassy in Moscow, http://moscow
.usembassy.gov/bilateral/bilateral.php?record_id=visit_bratislava.

20. For a detailed description of the 1995 law, please see Balla, "New Language Law in
Slovakia."

21. See, for example, "Human Rights Watch World Report 1998—Slovakia."

22. A detailed analysis of the 1999 law is found in Kopanic, "New Minority Language Law in
Slovakia."

23. See Deegan-Krause, "Slovakia's Second Transition." Deegan-Krause provides one of the
best analyses of recent Slovak political trends.

24. See Fürst, "Hungarian-Slovakian Conflict."

25. For an excellent overview of the changing realities of public opinion in the former Communist countries, see Druker, "Gauging the Extent of the Transatlantic Rift."

26. See, for example, Warhola, "2004 Slovak Presidential Election."

27. See https://esta.cbp.dhs.gov/esta/esta.html?_flowExecutionKey=_c4A7ED5F7-1DDA-CDE8-
E50F-BF5866831766_k980800EA-434F-FD28-41AD-854215290433 for more detailed information.

28. For more information, see Sharon Fisher, "Slovak Presidential Elections."

29. For a recent analysis of Slota's statements, see "Beata Balogová, The journalist's dilemma:
how to report Ján Slota," *Slovak Spectator*, October 13, 2008.

30. "Slovakia Pulls Troops From Iraq," *Herald Sun,* February 3, 2007, http://www.globalpolicy
.org/security/issues/iraq/withdraw/2007/0203slovakiawithdraw.htm. See also "Slovak PM criticizes U.S. over Iraq war," CBS News (via AP) http://www.cbsnews.com/stories/2009/10/22/ap/
world/main5408781.shtml.

31. Martina Jurinová, "Fico Snubs US Missile Plan for Czechs, Poles," *Slovak Spectator,* January 29–February 4, 2007, http://www.slovakspectator.sk/clanok.asp?cl=26422.

32. Mikulova, "Concern over New Slovak Government."

33. For a review of the activities of NGOs in the 1998 elections, see Potocki, "Slovakia's Elections," and Institute of Development Studies, "Case Study: Civil Campaign 'OK 98.'" For a general
overview, see Svitkova, "Evolution of the Third Sector in Slovakia."

34. For a comprehensive overview of U.S. assistance, see U.S. Department of State, *U.S. Government Assistance to Eastern Europe.* An overview of the PHARE aid program of the European
Commission in Slovakia is available at http://www.europa.sk/test/funds/phare_en.htm.

35. One result of the political transformation in the last few years is that the KDH has
turned more to the Right and has fashioned itself into a defender of "traditional values." Vladimír Palko, the KDH's minister of the interior, recently attacked liberals as "Lenin's cousins" and
strongly denounced a one-month sentence given in Sweden to a priest who referred to homo-
sexuals as "the cancer of humanity." As the need to unite against Mečiar as the "common enemy"
recedes, the liberal-conservative cleavage will come more to the forefront in Slovakia. For an
excellent analysis of this trend, see Mesežnikov, "Na Slovensku probíhá spor o character země."
The debates on "moral issues," as well as conservativism versus liberalism, will be strikingly
familiar to anyone who followed the 2004 U.S. presidential campaign.

36. For a comprehensive survey of the current status of the abortion controversy, as well
as other issues related to women's rights, please see ProChoice (online database), http://
moznostvolby.host.sk. Also see Martina Pisárová, "Ruling Coalition Settles Abortion Dispute,"
Slovak Spectator, September 15, 2003, http://www.slovakspectator.sk/clanok-13835.html.

37. See his interview in the Czech daily *Lidové Noviny,* November 16, 2004: Luboš Palata,
"Čarnogurský: Čalfu jsem chtěl, ale Dubčeka ne" [Čarnogurský: I Wanted Čalfa but not Dubček],"
http://lidovky.centrum.cz/clanek.phtml?id=307895.

38. For a recent summary of Slovakia's economic situation, please see Fisher, "Slovak
Economy."

39. Márius Kopcsay and Daniel Forgács, "Prečo novembrová revolúcia nežne zožrala vlastné
deti" [Why The November Revolution Softly Devoured Its Own Children], *Národná Obroda,*

November 17, 2004, http://www.narodnaobroda.sk/clanok/18701/Preco-novembrova-revolucia-nezne-zozrala-vlastne-deti.

40. A critical analysis of the new law by the Hungarian SMK is available from the party's Web site MK, Zákon o štátnom jazyku—Analýza SMK, which criticizes the "negation of the civic principle at the expense of the national principle": http://www.smk.sk/index.php?option=com_content&task=view&id=734&Itemid=35.

41. "Hovorte po slovensky" [Speak Slovak], July 30, 2009, http://www.economist.com/world/europe/displayStory.cfm?story_id=14140437.

42. "German MEP Slams Slovak language law," *Euroaktiv.com*, July 10, 2009, http://www.euractiv.com/en/culture/german-mep-slams-slovak-language-law/article-183982?.

43. See, for example, "Novela o štátnom jazyku," in the blog Cogito, ergo sum, http://janhruby.blog.sme.sk/c/200155/Novela-o-statnom-jazyku.html

44. Institute for Public Affairs, "PM Fico: IVO Survey Aimed to Help Opposition Parties," http://www.ivo.sk/5795/en/news/pm-fico-ivo-survey-aimed-to-help-opposition-parties, and "IVO Barometer: Quality of Democracy in the 2nd Quarter-Year of 2009: Decline to 3,3," http://www.ivo.sk/5779/en/news/ivo-barometer-quality-of-democracy-in-the-2nd-quarter-year-of-2009-decline-to-3-3. The issues raised in this report are explored in more detail in Mesežnikov, Kollár, and Vašečka, "Slovakia." The authors are all associated with the IVO.

45. For an overview of press freedom issues in Slovakia, see David Smith, "Pricing Out the Free Press," Guardian.co.uk October 31, 2009, http://www.guardian.co.uk/commentisfree/libertycentral/2009/oct/31/slovakia-free-press-libel and "Eastern Europe's Media Woes: Shut Up or be Sued," *The Economist,* October 22, 2009, http://www.economist.com/world/europe/displaystory.cfm?story_id=14710816.

46. "Something Is Rotten," *Slovak Spectator,* July 20, 2009, http://www.spectator.sk/articles/view/35992/11/something_is_rotten.html.

BIBLIOGRAPHY

Armitage, Richard M. "Media Roundtable in Slovakia." http://www.state.gov/s/d/rm/36189.htm.

Baer, J. "Boxing and Politics in Slovakia: Mečiarism's Roots, Theory, Practice." *Democratization* 8, no. 2 (Summer 2001): 97–116.

Balla, Kálmán. "New Language Law in Slovakia." http://www.hhrf.org/minoritiesresearch/mr11.htm.

Bekker, Peter. "Gabčikovo-Nagymaros [Hungary/Slovakia], Judgment." *American Journal of International Law* 92, no. 2 (April 1998): 273–78.

British Helsinki Human Rights Group. *Slovakia's Roma Shame: Welcome to the New Europe.* http://www.bhhrg.org/CountryReport.asp?ChapterID=672&CountryID=21&ReportID=212&keyword=.

Bútora, Martin, et al. *Slovenské voľby '06: Výsledky, príčiny súvislosti* [Slovak Elections '06: Results, Causes, Consequences]. Bratislava, Slovakia: Institute for Public Affairs (IVO), 2006.

Bútora, Martin, and Zora Bútorova. "Slovakia's Democratic Awakening." *Journal of Democracy* 10, no. 1 (1999): 80–95.

Cameron, Rob. "Slovak Bishop Praises Nazi Regime." BBC News, http://news.bbc.co.uk/2/hi/europe/6231163.stm.

Čarnogurský, Jan. "The Fall of Communism in Czechoslovakia," 2006: 43–49. http://www.clovekvtisni.cz/download/pdf/static/chapter4.pdf .

Cohen, Shari J. *Politics Without a Past: The Absence of History in Post-Communist Nationalism.* Durham: Duke University Press, 1999.

"Constitution Watch." *East European Constitutional Review* 6, nos. 2–3 (Spring–Summer 1997). http://www.law.nyu.edu/eecr/vol6num2/constitutionwatch/slovakia.html.

Deegan-Krause, Kevin. "Slovakia." In *Handbook of Political Change in Eastern Europe,* edited by Sten Berglund, Joakim Ekman, and Frank Aarebrot, 255–88. London: Edward Elgar, 2004.

———. "Slovakia's Second Transition." *Journal of Democracy* 14, no. 2 (April 2003): 65–79.

Demeš, Pavol, and Joerg Forbrig, eds. *Reclaiming Democracy: Civil Society and Electoral Change in Central and Eastern Europe.* New York: German Marshall Fund, 2007.

DeHoog, Ruth Hoogland, and Luba Racanska. "The Role of the Nonprofit Sector amid Political Change: Contrasting Approaches to Slovakian Civil Society." *Voluntas* 14, no. 2 (September 2003): 263–82.

Diko, Lukas. "Slovakia: A Lexa-con of Slovak Justice." *Transitions Online* (January 31, 2005). Available from Columbia International Affairs Online at http://www.ciaonet.org/pbei-2/tol/tol_2005/jan25-jan31/jan25-jan31d.html.old.

Downs, Jim. *World War II: OSS Tragedy in Slovakia.* Oceanside, Calif.: Liefrinck, 2002. Excerpt at http://www.sffworld.com/authors/d/downs_jim/excerpts/wwiioss1.html.

Druker, Jeremy. "Gauging the Extent of the Transatlantic Rift." Center for Defense Information, September 21, 2004. http://www.cdi.org/program/document.cfm?DocumentID=2481&from_page=../index.cfm.

Fisher, Sharon. *Political Change in Post-Communist Slovakia and Croatia: From Nationalist to Europeanist.* New York: Palgrave Macmillan, 2006.

———. "The Slovak Economy: Surging Forward." Global Insight Inc. CSIS Slovak Roundtable, May 4, 2004. http://csis.org/ee/events/040504fisher.pdf.

———. "The Slovak Presidential Elections: The Final Defeat of Mečiarism?" http://www.wilsoncenter.org/topics/pubs/MR300Fisher.doc.

Fisher, Sharon, John Gould, and Tim Haughton. "Slovakia's Neoliberal Turn." *Europe-Asia Studies* 59, no. 6 (September 2007): 977–98.

Fitzmaurice, John. *Damming the Danube: Gabčikovo and Post-Communist Politics in Europe*. Boulder, Colo.: Westview Press, 1996.

Fürst, Heiko. "The Hungarian-Slovakian Conflict over the Gabcikovo-Nagymaros Dams: An Analysis." *Intermarium* 6, no. 3 (2003). http://www.sipa.columbia.edu/ece/research/intermarium/vol6no2/furst3.pdf.

Gál, Fedor. "Naša misia bola provizórna" [Our Mission Was Provisional]. *Nové Slovo*, October 20–26, 1999. http://www.noveslovo.sk/archiv/1999-35/shostom.html.

Glenn, John K. "International Actors and Democratization: U.S. Assistance to New Political Parties in the Czech Republic and Slovakia." EUI Working Paper SPS No. 99/7. Florence, Italy: European University Institute, 1999. http://cadmus.iue.it/dspace/bitstream/1814/307/1/sps99_7.pdf.

Goldman, Minton F. *Slovakia Since Independence: A Struggle for Democracy*. Westport, Conn.: Greenwood, 1999.

Gould, John, and Soňa Szomolanyi. "Elite Fragmentation, Industry and the Prospects for Democracy in Slovakia: Insights from New Elite Theory." *Intermarium* 1, no. 2 (March 2002). Available from Columbia International Affairs Online at http://www.ciaonet.org/olj/int/int_0102c.html.

Grzymała-Busse, Anna. "Political Competition and the Politicization of the State in East Central Europe." *Comparative Political Studies* 36, no. 10 (December 2003): 1123–47.

Gyárfašová, Oľga. "Slovakia from Black Hole to Leading Light." *Transitions Online* (October 6, 2004). Available from Institute for Public Affairs (IVO), Bratislava, at http://www.ivo.sk/buxus/docs/publicistika/subor/produkt_2264.pdf.

Gyárfašová, Oľga, and Sharon Fisher. "On the Threshold of Change." *Annual Survey 2003, CIAO Atlas*. Available from Columbia International Affairs Online at http://www.ciaonet.org/atlas/countries/sk_data_tol.html.

Harris, E. "Europeanization of Slovakia." *Comparative European Politics* 2, no. 2 (2004): 185–211.

Haughton, Tim. *Constraints and Opportunities of Leadership in Post-Communist Europe*. London: Ashgate, 2005.

———. "Explaining the Limited Success of the Communist-Successor Left in Slovakia: The Case of the Party of the Democratic Left (SDĽ)." *Party Politics* 10, no. 2 (2004): 177–91.

———. "Facilitator and Impeder: The Institutional Framework of Slovak Politics During the Premiership of Vladimír Mečiar." *Slavonic and East European Review* 81, no. 2 (April 2003): 267–90.

———. "HZDS: The Ideology, Organisation, and Support Base of Slovakia's Most Successful Party." *Europe-Asia Studies* 53, no. 5 (July 2001): 745–69.

———. "Vladimír Mečiar and His Role in the 1994–1998 Slovak Coalition Government." *Europe-Asia Studies* 54, no. 8 (December 2002): 1319–38.

———. "'We'll finish what we've started': The 2002 Slovak Parliamentary Elections." *Journal of Communist Studies and Transition Politics* 19, no. 4 (December 2003): 65–90.

Haughton, Tim, and Darina Malová. "Emerging Patterns of EU Membership: Drawing Lessons from Slovakia's First Two Years as a Member State." *Politics* 27, no. 2 (June 2007): 69–75.

Haughton, Tim, and Marek Rybář. "All Right Now: Explaining the Successes and Failures of the Slovak Centre-Right." *Journal of Communist Studies and Transition Politics* 20, no. 3 (September 2004): 115–32.

———. "The Communist Party of Slovakia (KSS): A Threat to Slovak Democracy?" Paper prepared for the Second ECPR Conference, Marburg, September 18–21, 2003. http://www.essex.ac.uk/ecpr/events/generalconference/marburg/ papers/10/2/ Haughton.pdf.

Henderson, Karen. "The EU Parliament Elections in Slovakia, 2004 European Parliament Election." Briefing No. 10. Brighton, U.K.: Sussex European Institute, 2004. http://www.sussex.ac.uk/sei/documents/epernep2004slovakia.pdf, 1–14.

———. Election Briefing No. 26 Europe and the Slovak Parliamentary Election of June 2006. EPERN http://www.sussex.ac.uk/sei/documents/epern.pdf.

———. "Europe and the Slovak Parliamentary Election of September 2002." *RIIA/ OERN Election Briefing No. 7.* London: Royal Institute of International Affairs, 2002, http://www.sussex.ac.uk/sei/documents/paper7slovak.pdf, 1–8.

———. "Euroscepticism or Europhobia: Opposition attitudes to the EU in the Slovak Republic." *SEI Working Paper No. 50/OERN Paper No. 5.* Brighton, U.K.: Sussex European Institute, 2001. http://www.sussex.ac.uk/sei/documents/wp50.pdf, 3–24.

———. "The Slovak EU Accession Referendum 16–17 May 2003, Referendum Briefing No. 7." Brighton, U.K.: Sussex European Institute, 2003. http://www.sussex.ac .uk/sei/documents/epernbrefslovak.pdf, 1–8.

———. *Slovakia: The Escape from Invisibility.* New York: Routledge, 2002.

———. "The Slovak Presidential Elections 3/17 April 2004." Brighton, U.K.: Sussex European Institute, 2004. http://www.sussex.ac.uk/sei/documents/slovak_pres_ election_briefing3.pdf, 1–12.

———. "The Slovak Republic: Eurosceptics and Phoney Europhiles." In *The Party Politics of Euroscepticism,* edited by A. Szczerbiak and P. Taggart, 277–94. Oxford: Oxford University Press, 2007.

———. "The Slovak Republic: Explaining Defects in Democracy." *Democratization* 11, no. 5 (2004), 133–55.

Hilde, Paal Sigurd. "Slovak Nationalism and the Break-up of Czechoslovakia." *Europe-Asia Studies* 51, no. 4 (June 1999): 647–65.

Horná, Dagmar. "The Political Science Department at Comenius University, Bratislava: The Vanguard of Political Science in Slovakia." http://www.epsnet.org/publications/ KioskPlus1/Horna.htm.

Human Rights Watch. "Human Rights Watch World Report 1998—Slovakia." http:// www.hrw.org/worldreport/Helsinki-21.htm.

"Hungary/Slovakia: Judgment on Gabčikovo." *Environmental Policy and Law* 27, no. 6 (December 1997): 459.

Innes, Abby. *Czechoslovakia: The Short Goodbye.* New Haven: Yale University Press, 2001.

Institute of Development Studies. "Case Study: Civil Campaign 'OK 98.'" http://www .ids.ac.uk/ids/civsoc/final/slovakia/slo2.doc.

International Helsinki Federation for Human Rights. "Slovakia." In *Annual Report 1997.* http://www.ihf-hr.org/viewbinary/viewhtml.php?doc_id=4934.

Javurek, Peter. "Slovak Opposition Deputy to Face Kidnapping Probe." http://www .slovakia.org/fa-lexa.htm.

Kirschbaum, Joseph M. *Slovakia: Nation at the Crossroads of Central Europe*. New York: Robert Speller and Sons, 1960.

Kirschbaum, Stanislav J. *A History of Slovakia: The Struggle for Survival*. New York: St. Martin's Press, 1995.

Konečný, Miroslav, and Karel Zetocha. "Slovenská národní strana: Druhá šance" [Slovak National Party: Second Chance] (in Czech with English summary). *Středoevropské politické studie—Central European Political Studies Review* 7, nos. 2, 3 (Spring–Summer 2005), http://www.cepsr.com/clanek.php?ID=235.

Kopanic, Michael J. "The New Minority Language Law in Slovakia." *Central Europe Review* 1, no. 2 (July 5, 1999). http://www.ce-review.org/99/2/kopanic2.html.

Kopeček, Lubomír. "The Ambivalent Influence of the European Union on Democratization in Slovakia." In *The European Union and Reluctant Democratizers*, edited by Paul Kubicek, 58–86. London: Routledge, 2003.

———. *Demokracie, diktatury a politické stranictví na Slovensku* [Democracy, Dictatorships and Political Parties in Slovakia] (in Czech). Brno: Centrum pro studium demokracie a kultury, 2006.

———. "Institutionalization of Slovak Political Parties and Charismatic Leaders." *Středoevropské Politické Studie—Central European Political Studies Review* 6, no. 1 (Winter 2004). http://www.cepsr.com/clanek.php?ID=188.

———. "Křesťanská demokracie na Slovensku po roce 1989" [Christian Democracy in Slovakia After 1989] (in Czech). *Obzory* (3), 1:41–51. http://www.ead.cz/obzory/1_2006.pdf.

Korec, Ján Chryzostom. *Night of the Barbarians*. Wauconda, Ill.: Bolchazy-Carducci, 2002.

"Law on the Use of Minority Languages Passed into Law by the 17th Session of the Slovak Parliament on July 11, 1999." http://www.legacyrus.com/library/LawonMinorityLanguagesSlovakia071799.html.

Leff, Carol Skalnik. *The Czech and Slovak Republics: Nation Versus State*. Boulder, Colo.: Westview Press, 1996.

Lesná, Ľuba. *Únos demokracie: Zo zákulisia slovenskej tajnej služby* [The Kidnapping of Democracy: Behind the Scenes of the Slovak Secret Service]. Bratislava, Slovakia: Institute for Public Affairs (IVO) and G plus G, 2001.

Luxor, Jonathan. "Cardinal's Life Shaped by Slovakia's Troubles." *National Catholic Reporter* (December 17, 1999). http://www.natcath.com/NCR_Online/archives/121799/121799h.htm.

Malová, Darina, and Silvia Miháliková. "Political Science Slovakia." Knowledge Base Social Sciences in Eastern Europe (2002). http://www.cee-socialscience.net/archive/politicalscience/slovakia/report1.html.

Marušiak, Juraj. "Fenomén strany Smer: Medzi 'pragmatizmom' a sociálnou demokraciou" [Political Party "Smer": Between "Pragmatism" and Social Democracy] (in Slovak). *Středoevropské Politické Studie—Central European Political Studies Review* 8, no. 1 (Winter 2006). http://www.cepsr.com/clanek.php?ID=258.

Matejčíková, Daša, and Roman Krpelan. "Mikloško: S nádejou čakám rok 2008" [Mikloško: I Look Forward with Hope to the Year 2008]. *Sme*, December 29, 2002. http://zaujimavosti.sme.sk/clanok.asp?cl=770775.

Mathernova, Katarina, and Juraj Renčko. *Antisemitizmus v politickom vývoji slovenska 2003–2005* [Anti-Semitism in the Political Development of Slovakia]. Bratislava, Slovakia: Múzeum židovskej kultúry, SNM (Slovak National Museum), 2006.

———. "'Reformology': The Case of Slovakia." *Orbis* 50, no. 4 (Fall 2006): 629–40.

Mesežnikov, Grigorij. "Na Slovensku probíhá spor o charakter země" [In Slovakia a Dispute is Taking Place over the Character of the Country]. *Rešpekt*, no. 36 (September 2004). Available from Institute for Public Affairs (IVO), Bratislava, at http://www.ivo.sk/ftp_folder/produkt_2260.pdf.

Mesežnikov, Grigorij, Miroslav Kollár, and Michal Vašečka. "Slovakia." In *Nations in Transit*. New York: Freedom House, 2009. http://www.freedomhouse.hu/images/nit2009/slovakia.pdf.

Mešťan, Pavol. *Antisemitizmus v politickom vývoji slovenska 1989–99* [Anti-Semitism in the Political Development of Slovakia]. Bratislava, Slovakia: Múzeum židovskej kultúry, SNM (Slovak National Museum), 2000.

Miháliková, Silvia. *Political Culture and Civil-Military Relations in Slovakia*. Groningen: Centre for European Security Studies, 2000.

———. "Understanding Slovak Political Culture." In *Political Culture in East Central Europe*, edited by Fritz Plasser and Andreas Pribersky, 167–79. Brookfield, Vt.: Avebury, 1996.

———. "Slovakia: Pathways to a Democratic Community." In *Democracy and Political Culture in Eastern Europe*, edited by Hans-Dieter Klingemann, Dieter Fuchs, and Jan Zielonka, 172–202. New York: Routledge, 2006.

Mikulova, Kristina. "Concern over New Slovak Government." Center for European Policy Analysis, July 12, 2006. http://cepa.ncpa.org/digest/concern-over-new-slovak-government.

Musil, Jiři. *The End of Czechoslovakia*. Budapest: Central European University Press, 1995.

Nedelsky, Nadia. "Constitutional Nationalism's Implications for Minority Rights and Democratization: The Case of Slovakia." *Ethnic and Racial Studies* 26, no. 1 (January 2003): 102–28.

Paul, Ellen L. "Perception vs. Reality: Slovak Views of the Hungarian Minority in Slovakia." *Nationalities Papers* 31, no. 4 (December 2003): 485–93.

Potocki, Roger. "Slovakia's Elections: Outcomes and Consequences." Lecture at Woodrow Wilson Center, Washington, D.C. http://www.wilsoncenter.org/index.cfm?topic_id=1422&fuseaction=topics.publications&doc_id=18876&group_id=7427.

Pridham, Geoffrey. "Coalition Behaviour in New Democracies of Central and Eastern Europe: The Case of Slovakia." *Journal of Communist Studies and Transition Politics* 18, no. 2 (2002): 75–102.

———. "The European Union's Democratic Conditionality and Domestic Politics in Slovakia: The Mečiar and Dzurinda Governments Compared." *Europe-Asia Studies* 54, no. 2 (2002): 203–27.

———. "The EU's Political Conditionality and Post-Accession Tendencies: Comparisons from Slovakia and Latvia." *JCMS* 46, no. 2 (2008): 365–87.

———. "Status Quo Bias or Institutionalisation for Reversibility? The EU's Political Conditionality, Post-Accession Tendencies, and Democratic Consolidation in Slovakia." *Europe-Asia Studies* 60 (2008): 423–54.

———. "Uneasy Democratizations—Pariah Regimes, Political Conditionality, and Reborn Transitions in Central and Eastern Europe." *Democratization* 8, no. 4 (Winter 2001): 65–94.

Riishøj, Søren. *Development of Parties and Party Systems in Central Europe, 1989–2003, Part IV*. Esbjerg, Denmark: Syddansk Universitet, 2006. http://www.sam.sdu.dk/~sr/partIV.pdf, 16–38.

Ronen, Dov. "Managing Cultural, Ethnic, and Religious Diversities on Local, State, and International Levels in Central Europe: The Case of Slovakia." Vienna: Institut für Konfliktforschung, 1999. http://www.unesco.org/most/ronen.htm.

Rybář, Marek. "Powered by the State: The Role of Public Resources in Party-Building in Slovakia." *Journal of Communist Studies and Transition Politics* 22, no. 3 (September 2006): 320–40.

Rybář, Marek, and Kevin Deegan-Krause. "Slovakia's Communist Successor Parties in Comparative Perspective." *Communist and Post-Communist Studies* 41, no. 4 (December 2008): 497–519.

Salner, Peter, and Eva Salnerova. "Treatment of Jewish Themes in Slovak Schools." New York: American Jewish Committee, 1999. http://www.ajc.org/InTheMedia/PublicationsPrint.asp?did=154.

Shepherd, Robin H. E. *Czechoslovakia: The Velvet Revolution and Beyond.* New York: Macmillan, 2000.

Simon, Jeffrey. *NATO and the Czech and Slovak Republics: A Comparative Study in Civil Military Relations.* Lanham, Md.: Rowman and Littlefield, 2004.

Skaláková, Eva. "'Libri prohibiti': 70. let ve fondu Knihovny Akademie věd České Republiky" [Libri Prohibiti: The 1970s in the Collections of the Library of the Academy of Science of the Czech Republic]. In *Zpráva o činnosti KNAV v roce 2002* [Report on the Activity of the Library of the Academy of Science for the year 2002], edited by Ivana Kadlecová and Jarmila Burgetová. http://www.lib.cas.cz/informace/Informace%202_2003.htm#10.

Stolarik, M. Mark, ed. *The Slovak Republic: A Decade of Independence.* Wauconda, Ill.: Bolchazy-Carducci, 2003.

Svitkova, Katarina. "The Evolution of the Third Sector in Slovakia." Research Paper, Center for Economic Research and Graduate Education, Charles University in Prague, January 16, 2004. http://home.cerge-ei.cz/svitkova/npos/Slovak.htm.

Szomolányi, Soňa. "Central European Transition Paths, Parallels and Differences: The Case of Slovakia." *Slovak Sociological Review* 27, nos. 7–8 (1995): 17–29.

———. *Kľukatá cesta Slovenska k demokracii* [Slovakia's Crooked Path to Democracy]. Bratislava, Slovakia: STIMUL, 1999.

———. "The National Elite and Democratic Deficit in Slovakia." In *The Rule of Law in Central Europe: Reconstruction of Legality, Constitutionalism, and Civil Society in the Post-Communist Countries*, edited by James Young and Jiři Přibáň, 118–38. London: Ashgate, 1999.

Szomolányi, Soňa, and John Gould, eds. *Slovakia: Problems of Democratic Consolidation and the Struggle for the Rules of the Game.* CIAO Books, Columbia International Affairs Online, 1997. http://www.ciaonet.org/book/gould/index.html.

Toma, Peter A., and Dušan Kováč. *Slovakia: From Samo to Dzurinda.* Stanford, Calif.: Hoover Institution Press, 2001.

Učeň, Peter. "Slovakia." *European Journal of Political Research* 45, nos. 7–8 (December 2006): 1254–59.

U.S. Department of State. *SEED Act Implementation Report, Fiscal Year 1992.* Washington, D.C.: U.S. Department of State, January 1993.

———. *Slovak Country Report on Human Rights Practices for 1998.* http://www.state.gov/www/global/human_rights/1998_hrp_report/slovakre.html.

———. *Slovak Country Report on Human Rights Practices for 2006.* http://www.state.gov/g/drl/rls/hrrpt/2006/78838.htm.

———. *U.S. Government Assistance to Eastern Europe under the Support for East European Democracy (SEED) Act II: Country Assessment: Slovakia.* http://www.state.gov/p/eur/rls/rpt/64016.htm.

Warhola, James W. "The 2004 Slovak Presidential Election: Ivan Gasparovic and the Western Alliance." *In the National Interest.* http://www.inthenationalinterest .com/Articles/Vol3Issue17/Vol3Issue17Warhola.html.

Williams, Kieran, ed., "Slovakia After Communism and Mečiarism." SSEES Occasional Papers No. 47. London: School of Slavonic and East European Studies, 2000.

———. "Slovakia Since 1993." In *Security Intelligence Services in New Democracies: The Czech Republic, Slovakia, and Romania,* edited by Kieran Williams and Dennis Deletant, 123–58. Studies in Russian and Eastern European History. New York: Palgrave, 2001.

Williams, Kieran, and Dennis Deletant. *Security Intelligence Services in New Democracies: The Czech Republic, Slovakia, and Romania.* Studies in Russian and Eastern European History. New York: Palgrave, 2001

Wolff, Stefan. "'Bilateral' Ethnopolitics after the Cold War: The Hungarian Minority in Slovakia, 1989–99." *Perspectives on European Politics and Society* 2, no. 2 (2001): 159–95.

ONLINE AND PERIODICAL RESOURCES

Central and East European Online Library. http://www.ceeol.de.

Contemporary European Studies Faculty of Arts, Olomouc University, Czech Republic. http://www.ces.upol.cz.

International Issues and Slovak Foreign Policy Affairs. Research Center of the Slovak Foreign Policy Association. http://sfpa.sk/sk/publikacie/international-issues.

Slovenská Politologická Revue (Slovak Political Science Review). Katedra politológie, Filozofická fakulta, Univerzita sv. Cyrila a Metoda v Trnave (Department of Political Science, Philosophical Faculty, Cyril and Methodius University, Trnava). http://www.ucm.sk/revue. A second publication with the same name in English but using the title *Slovenský politologický časopis* in Slovak is published by the Slovak Political Science Association of the Slovak Academy of Science in Bratislava. http://www.szpv.sk.

Sociológia—Slovak Sociological Review (Sociologický ústav—Slovenská akadémia vied. Institute of Sociology—Slovak Academy of Sciences. http://www.sav.sk/index .php?lang=sk&charset=&doc=publish-journal&journal_no=36.

Středoevropské politické studie (Central European Political Studies, in Czech). A peer-reviewed online journal edited by the International Institute of Political Science of Masaryk University, Brno. http://www.cepsr.com/clanek.php?ID=324.

Studia Politica Slovenská (Slovak Political Studies), Ústav Politických Vied Slovenskej Akadémie Vied (Institute of Political Science, Slovak Academy of Sciences). http://www.upv.sav.sk/index.php?id=132.

Zahraničná politika (Foreign Policy) Research Center of the Slovak Foreign Policy Association. http://sfpa.sk/sk/publikacie/zahranicna-politika.

INDEX

www.ingramcontent.com/pod-product-compliance
Lightning Source LLC
Chambersburg PA
CBHW021859020426
42334CB00013B/400